MARYLAND/DELAWARE
TRAVEL ✦ SMART®

ALSO INCLUDES WASHINGTON, D.C.

D0109108

Sailboats on Chesapeake Bay

MARYLAND DELAWARE

TRAVEL ★ SMART®

ALSO INCLUDES WASHINGTON, D.C.

Sheila Kinkade

John Muir Publications
Santa Fe, New Mexico

Avalon Travel Publishing
5855 Beaudry Street, Emeryville, CA 94608

Formerly published by John Muir Publications

Printed in the United States of America.
First edition. Second printing February 2001

ISSN 1522-1520
ISBN 1-56261-424-X

Editors: Sarah Baldwin, Elizabeth Wolf
Graphics Editor: Heather Pool
Production: Marie J.T. Vigil
Cover design: Janine Lehmann
Design: Janine Lehmann & Linda Braun
Typesetting: Diane Rigoli
Map style development: Bruce Daniel—American Custom Maps,
   Jemez Springs, NM, USA
Map illustration: Scott Lockheed, Carta Graphics
Printer: Publishers Press
Front cover photos: *small*—© V. E. Horne/Unicorn Stock Photos (United States
                  Capitol)
          large—© Cindy Tunstall (Tilghman Island)
Back cover photo: © Jean Higgins/New England Stock (State House in Annapolis, MD)

Distributed to the book trade by
Publishers Group West
Berkeley, California

HOW TO USE THIS BOOK

T his *Maryland/Delaware Travel•Smart* guidebook is organized in 14
destination chapters, each covering the best sights and activities,
restaurants, and lodging available in that specific destination. Thanks
to thorough research and experience, the author is able to bring you
only the best options, saving you time and money in your travels. The
chapters are presented in logical sequence so you can follow an easy
route from one place to the next. If you were to visit each destination
in chapter order, you'd enjoy a complete tour of the best of Maryland,
Delaware, and the capital region.

Each chapter contains:

- User-friendly maps of the area, showing all recommended sights,
  restaurants, and accommodations.
- "A Perfect Day" description—how the author would spend her time
  if she had just one day in that destination.
- Sightseeing highlights, each rated by degree of importance:
  ★★★ Don't miss; ★★ Try hard to see; ★ See if you have time; and
  No stars—Worth knowing about.
- Selected restaurant, lodging, and camping recommendations to suit
  a variety of budgets.
- Helpful hints, fitness and recreation ideas, insights, and random
  tidbits of information to enhance your trip.

The Importance of Planning. Developing an itinerary is the best way
to get the most satisfaction from your travels, and this guidebook makes
it easy. First, read through the book and choose the places you'd most
like to visit. Then, study the color map on the inside cover flap and the
mileage chart (appendix) to determine which you can realistically see in
the time you have available and at the travel pace you prefer. Using the
Planning Map (pages 10–11), map out your route. Finally, use the lodging recommendations to determine your accommodations.

Some Suggested Itineraries. To get you started, six itineraries of
varying lengths and based on specific interests follow. Mix and match
according to your interests and time constraints, or follow a given itinerary from start to finish. The possibilities are endless. *Happy travels!*

SUGGESTED ITINERARIES

With the *Maryland/Delaware Travel•Smart* guidebook, you can plan a trip of any length—a one-day excursion, a getaway weekend, or a three-week vacation—around any special interest. To get you started, the following pages contain six suggested itineraries geared toward a variety of interests. For more information, refer to the chapters listed—chapter names are bolded and chapter numbers appear inside black bullets. You can follow a suggested itinerary in its entirety, or shorten, lengthen, or combine parts of each, depending on your starting and ending points.

Discuss alternative routes and schedules with your travel companions—it's a great way to have fun, even before you leave home. And remember: Don't hesitate to change your itinerary once you're on the road. Careful study and planning ahead will help you make informed decisions as you go, but spontaneity is the extra ingredient that will make your trip memorable.

© Leo de Wys, Inc./Jon Hicks

The Lincoln Memorial in Washington, D.C.

Best of the Region Tour

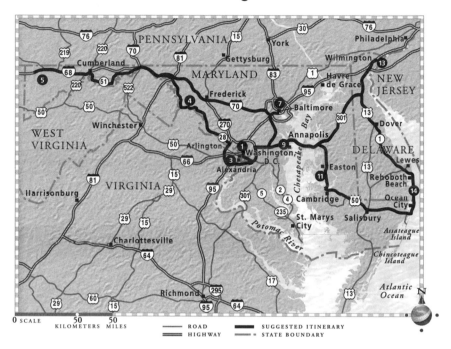

Take the following tour if you want to sample the area's world-class museums, major historical sites, quaint towns, and natural attractions.

- ❶ **Washington, D.C.** (U.S. Capitol, White House, National Gallery)
- ❸ **Arlington and Alexandria** (Arlington National Cemetery, Old Town)
- ❹ **Chesapeake and Ohio Canal** (Great Falls Tavern, Harpers Ferry, Cumberland)
- ❺ **Western Maryland** (Deep Creek Lake, state parks)
- ❼ **Baltimore** (National Aquarium, Baltimore Museum of Art, Walters Art Gallery, Port Discovery, Harborplace)
- ❾ **Annapolis** (State House, historic houses, U.S. Naval Academy)
- ⓫ **Maryland's Eastern Shore** (Assateague Island, Easton, St. Michaels)
- ⓮ **Delaware Coast** (Cape Henlopen State Park, Lewes, Rehoboth)
- ⓭ **Wilmington and the Brandywine Valley** (Winterthur Museum and Gardens, Grand Opera House, Longwood Gardens)

Time needed: 2 weeks

History Lover's Tour

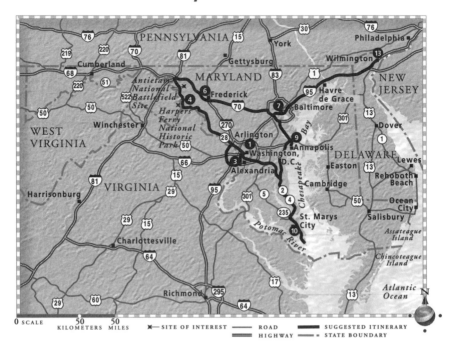

The area is steeped in colonial, pre-Revolutionary, and Civil War history, with a wealth of sights that paint a vivid portrait of American history.

- ⓭ **Wilmington and the Brandywine Valley** (Hagley Museum, Nemours Mansion and Gardens, Winterthur Museum and Gardens)
- ❼ **Baltimore** (Fort McHenry, Baltimore and Ohio Railroad Museum, Maryland Historic Society, Mount Vernon)
- ❻ **Frederick County** (Frederick historic district, Civil War–related sites)
- ❹ **Chesapeake and Ohio Canal** (Antietam National Battlefield, Harpers Ferry, Cumberland)
- ❶ **Washington, D.C.** (U.S. Capitol, White House, monuments and memorials, Portrait Gallery, Archives, Holocaust Memorial Museum)
- ❸ **Arlington and Alexandria** (Arlington National Cemetery, Old Town)
- ❿ **Southern Maryland** (Jefferson Patterson Park, St. Marys City)
- ❾ **Annapolis** (William Paca House and Garden, other historic houses)

Time needed: 12 days

Nature Lover's Tour

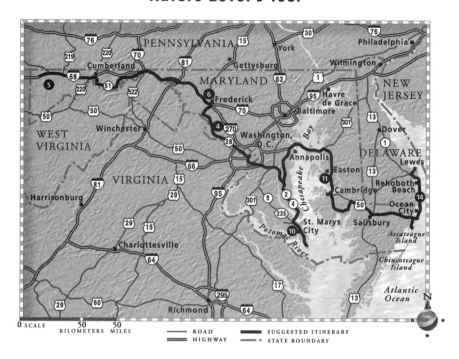

The mid-Atlantic region has much to offer nature lovers, from the mountains of Western Maryland to the waters of the Chesapeake Bay and the Atlantic coastal areas of Delaware and Maryland. The region's many national and state parks afford visitors miles of hiking trails.

⑤ Western Maryland (Deep Creek Lake, state parks)

⑥ Frederick County (Cunningham Falls State Park, Catoctin Mountain State Park, Sugarloaf Mountain)

❾ Chesapeake and Ohio Canal (184-mile towpath, Great Falls Tavern)

⑩ Southern Maryland (Battle Creek Cypress Swamp, Calvert Cliffs, Calvert Maritime Museum, Flag Ponds Nature Park, Point Lookout)

⑪ Maryland's Eastern Shore (Assateague Island, Blackwater Wildlife Refuge)

⑭ Delaware Coast (Cape Henlopen State Park, Bombay Hook National Wildlife Refuge, Prime Hook National Wildlife Refuge)

Time needed: 2 weeks

Arts and Culture Tour

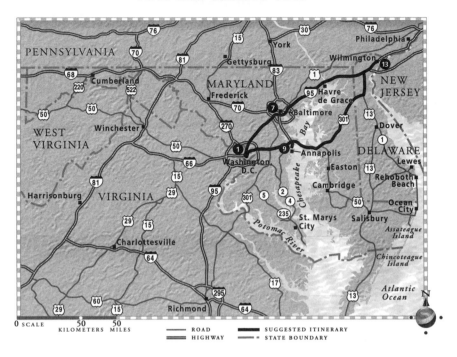

0 SCALE 50 50
KILOMETERS MILES

ROAD   SUGGESTED ITINERARY
HIGHWAY   STATE BOUNDARY

D.C. alone has enough museums, theater, and music to keep arts lovers busy for two weeks or more. But Baltimore also boasts several fine museums, concert halls, and theater venues; Annapolis has gorgeously furnished historic homes; and Wilmington offers spectacular estates and gardens just north of the city.

- **Washington, D.C.** (Smithsonian Museums, National Gallery, Phillips Collection, Corcoran Gallery, Folger Shakespeare Library, Kennedy Center, National Theater)
- **Baltimore** (Baltimore Museum of Art, Walters Art Gallery, American Visionary Art Museum, Edgar Allen Poe House, theater, music)
- **Wilmington and the Brandywine Valley** (Hagley Museum, Nemours Mansion and Gardens, Winterthur Museum and Gardens, Delaware Museum of Art, Rockwood Museum, Grand Opera House)
- **Annapolis** (William Paca House and Garden, other historic houses)

Time needed: 1–2 weeks

Family Fun Tour

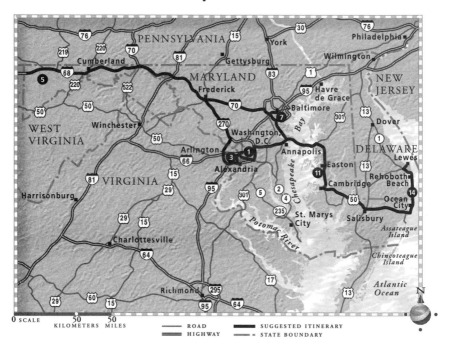

Families traveling with children will find plenty of kid-friendly options on this tour—from a variety of child-oriented museums in Baltimore and Washington to outdoor recreation opportunities, including biking, hiking, rafting, skiing, swimming, and more.

❶ **Washington, D.C.** (Air and Space Museum, National Zoological Park, Goddard Space Flight Center, Capital Children's Museum)

❸ **Arlington and Alexandria** (Newseum)

❺ **Western Maryland** (Deep Creek Lake, state parks)

❼ **Baltimore** (National Aquarium, Port Discovery, Baltimore Zoo, Baltimore and Ohio Railroad Museum)

⓫ **Maryland's Eastern Shore** (beaches)

⓮ **Delaware Coast** (beaches)

Time needed: 2 weeks

Outdoor Adventure Tour

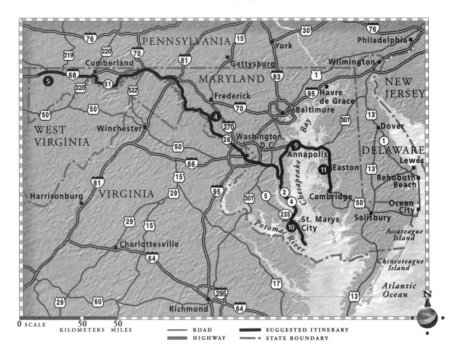

Much of this tour depends upon your favored form of outdoor adventure. The C&O Canal is great for casual hiking and mountain biking. Western Maryland offers camping and hiking, along with white-water rivers, lakes, and ski slopes. Annapolis, a sailing capital, can be reached from outside Baltimore via a 13-mile bike trail. The Eastern Shore is great for biking, boating, windsurfing, fishing, hunting, and canoeing. Southern Maryland affords ample biking, hiking, boating, and sport fishing.

- ❺ **Western Maryland** (hiking, camping, white-water rafting, skiing)
- ❹ **Chesapeake and Ohio Canal** (hiking, mountain biking)
- ❿ **Southern Maryland** (hiking, biking, boating, fishing)
- ❾ **Annapolis** (sailing, biking)
- ⓫ **Maryland's Eastern Shore** (biking, boating, canoeing, windsurfing, fishing, hunting)

Time needed: 12 days

USING THE PLANNING MAP

A major aspect of itinerary planning is determining your mode of transportation and the route you will follow as you travel from destination to destination. The Planning Map on the following pages will allow you to do just that.

First, read through the destination chapters carefully and note the sights that intrigue you. Then, photocopy the Planning Map so you can try out several different routes that will take you to these destinations. (The mileage chart in the appendix will help you to calculate your travel distances.) Decide where you will be starting your tour of Maryland, Delaware, and the capital region. Will you fly into Washington or Baltimore, or will you start from somewhere else? Will you be driving from place to place or flying into major transportation hubs and renting a car for day trips? The answers to these questions will form the basis for your route design.

Once you have a firm idea of where your travels will take you, copy your route onto the additional Planning Map in the appendix. You won't have to worry about where your map is, and the information you need on each destination will always be close at hand.

Maryland blue crab

Maryland Office of Tourism Development

Planning Map: Maryland/Delaware

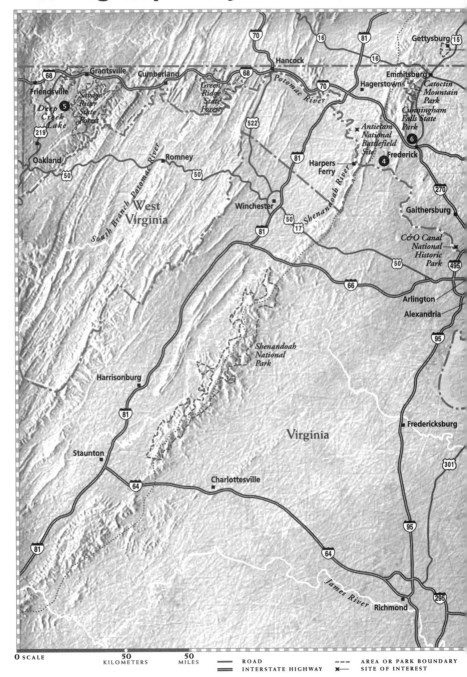

O SCALE
50 KILOMETERS
50 MILES

—— ROAD
═══ INTERSTATE HIGHWAY

- - - AREA OR PARK BOUNDARY
×—— SITE OF INTEREST

.... APPALACHIAN TRAIL
▬ ▪ STATE BOUNDARY

WHY VISIT MARYLAND, DELAWARE, AND THE CAPITAL REGION?

Anyone truly curious about the United States—its history, culture, and ideals—will want to visit Maryland, Delaware, and the capital region at least once in his or her life. Inscribed on the area's architectural monuments are the words of the nation's founding fathers—words that still inspire pride and patriotism. Here you can walk across battlefields where thousands of soldiers lost their lives during the Civil War and visit memorials to those who lived and died in pursuit of the ideals upon which the United States was founded. These ideals often stand in sharp contrast to unfolding political and social dramas, and yet they remain central to our national identity.

Here lie myriad opportunities to learn—firsthand—about America's history, politics, and judicial system, as well as its achievements in science and the arts. Where else can you revisit colonial, Revolutionary, and Civil War history, touch a moon rock, see the paintings of Sargent and Whistler, and tour the home of the president of the United States—all within a two-hour drive? But for all the monuments, battlefields, and museums devoted to U.S. history and culture, the area is also home to many institutions that look well beyond our own backyard. The Smithsonian, for example, pays tribute to nearly every cultural group and major accomplishment on the planet. Internationally known museums, such as the National Gallery, house works by the likes of Vermeer, da Vinci, and van Gogh, while other institutions, such as the United States Holocaust Memorial Museum, remind us of our shared global history and the lessons of humankind.

In addition to a plethora of museums and historic homes, the area's cities boast colorful neighborhood cafés and well-kept gardens. Outside major urban centers, you can comb miles of coastline and explore national parks and forests. Birdwatchers and anglers pursue their pastimes on the 180-mile path running beside the Chesapeake and Ohio Canal, from Washington to Cumberland, while white-water enthusiasts battle the Youghiogheny River's turbulent waters. The key to planning a good trip is to pace yourself. Take your time and pause to reflect along the way—this is a rich journey.

LAY OF THE LAND

The combined area of Maryland, Delaware, and the District of Columbia covers less than 12,000 square miles. Even so, this relatively small region contains diverse geographic features—sandy beaches, coastal cliffs, biologically rich marshland, swamps, gently rolling hills, fertile farmland, gorges, waterfalls, and mountainous terrain. The area is loosely divided into three primary land regions: the Atlantic Coastal Plain, the Piedmont plateau, and the Appalachian region. The Atlantic Coastal Plain stretches along much of the East Coast of the United States from New Jersey to the tip of Florida. Coastal plain areas are generally flat, seldom rising more than 80 feet above sea level. All but the northern tip of Delaware, and most of Maryland east of the Chesapeake, is considered coastal plain.

Extending from New Jersey to Alabama, the Piedmont plateau consists largely of rolling hills and rich farmland. The Appalachian region begins in western Maryland where the eastern Continental Divide crosses through the state, resulting in more mountainous terrain. At 3,360 feet Backbone Mountain is the highest in the state. In the western portion of Maryland, the man-made Deep Creek Lake is the state's largest freshwater lake.

By far the region's most distinguishing feature is the Chesapeake Bay, the largest estuary in the country, running 180 miles in length and between 5 and 30 miles wide. The total length of its shoreline, including its tributaries, measures roughly 4,000 miles. An estuary is formed when freshwater streams and rivers meet and mix with salty ocean water. Estuaries, fragile ecosystems, are extremely productive habitats. Chesapeake is an Algonquin Indian name that translates loosely as "great river with an abundance of fish with hard shells." The Chesapeake Bay serves as a spawning ground for shellfish and saltwater fish. Its salt marshes provide shelter and food for birds and waterfowl, and resting places for migratory birds such as ducks and geese. Located within the bay are a number of islands, including Deal, Kent, Smith, South Marsh, Taylors, and Tilghman.

Miles of beaches make up the coasts of Maryland and Delaware. At the southernmost point of the Maryland coast is Assateague Island, where wild ponies roam free amidst windswept sand dunes and sea grass. In sharp contrast to the more developed coastal areas just to the north, this preserved national treasure and other protected areas in the region are places to experience the simple pleasures and rejuvenating effects of nature.

FLORA AND FAUNA

With more than 30 state parks, seven state forests, and four national parks, the region offers myriad opportunities for exploring the great outdoors and local plant and animal life. In the spring and summer, walking trails are lined with an assortment of wildflowers—including black-eyed Susans, tiger lillies, wild roses, honeysuckle, daisies, and mountain laurel. Roughly a third of the region remains forested. The most common trees to be found are oak, maple, beech, poplar, yellow locust, and white ash, with oaks being the most prevalent. In fact, Maryland is distinguished as having the country's largest white oak tree, measuring 107 feet high and 35 feet around. Magnolia, dogwood, and crepe myrtle are also prevalent. Southern Delaware's swamplands provide fertile ground for bald cypress and red cedar. The wooded areas of Maryland and Delaware are home to raccoons, deer, and foxes; the more remote mountain areas sometimes offer a glimpse at a black bear.

Birdwatching is a popular pastime that can be enjoyed in coastal areas, along the Chesapeake and Ohio Canal path, or in the mountains to the west. The Chesapeake Bay provides a natural habitat for Canada geese, swans, ospreys, and the occasional bald eagle. More than 40 varieties of duck have been identified in shoreline areas, including canvasback, red-breasted, black, and wood ducks. Just north of Dover, Delaware, is the Bombay Hook National Wildlife Refuge, where more than 250 species of migratory birds make their nests between November and June in the park's 23 square miles of salt marsh. On Maryland's eastern shore good birdwatching locations include the Blackwater National Wildlife Refuge and the Assateague Island National Seashore. Within the state's coastal plain areas, birdwatchers are apt to see mockingbirds, fish hawks, and crows. The Piedmont is home to cardinals and wrens, while ravens, orioles, bluebirds, warblers, and thrushes make their homes elsewhere in the state. Not surprisingly, the Maryland state bird is the black-and-yellow Baltimore oriole.

Freshwater fishing enthusiasts will find bass, carp, trout, and white perch in the region's lakes and streams. The Chesapeake Bay, while grappling with a host of environmental concerns, offers the richest fishing opportunities, with perch, bluefish, striped bass, and more than 200 other fish varieties inhabiting its waters. Oysters, clams, blue crab, and other shellfish are also abundant, although they continue to be threatened by pollution and the bay's increasing human population.

HISTORY

B ecause of the strategic location of Maryland and Delaware along
the mid-Atlantic coast, the region has long been a hub of commerce and politics. History has strongly molded the culture of the
region, as have national politics. Key events during the colonial era,
Revolutionary War, and Civil War all took place here.

Prior to the arrival of the first European explorers in the early
1600s, the area was largely inhabited by the Algonquins and other
Native American tribes. By the mid-1700s, white settlers had forced
most of the Indians out. Henry Hudson first arrived in Delaware in
1609, but it wasn't until 1638 that a permanent settlement was established by Sweden. Maryland's first colonists arrived aboard two ships,
the *Arc* and the *Dove*, in 1634. The passengers set out to establish a
safe haven for Catholics, who were being persecuted in England. Lord
Baltimore, whose family owned the colony, granted them land. These
early settlers founded St. Mary's City in what is now southern
Maryland. Here they prospered, establishing farms and trading posts
on the shores of the Chesapeake Bay. Their colony soon became
known as Maryland. Fifteen years after their arrival, a group of
Puritans arrived, establishing a colony at Annapolis that grew to
become a thriving commercial hub and, in 1783, the colonial capital.

In the 1760s a border dispute between Maryland and Pennsylvania (Delaware at that time was part of Pennsylvania) resulted in the
hiring of two surveyors, Charles Mason and Jeremiah Dixon, to determine the official border. Later, during the Civil War, the Mason-Dixon
Line served as the dividing line between slave and free states.

While Maryland largely avoided involvement in the Revolutionary War, it ended up playing a pivotal role in the War of 1812, when
the British laid siege on Baltimore. While British gunships bombarded
Baltimore's Fort McHenry, a young lawyer named Francis Scott Key
watched from the decks of a nearby truce ship. He documented what
he saw in a song that would eventually be recognized as the nation's
anthem, "The Star Spangled Banner."

Maryland and Delaware were both slave states at the outbreak of
the Civil War but had ties to both sides. Federal troops occupied
Maryland during the war to safeguard its loyalty. Maryland saw no
major action during the war until September 17, 1862, when, at the
Battle of Antietam, more than 23,000 troops were killed or wounded.
It would go down in history as the single bloodiest day of the war.

During the late nineteenth and early twentieth centuries, commercial activity grew in the region. Baltimore and Wilmington continued to develop into important shipping ports. Immigrant populations arrived in both cities, contributing to the region's vitality and diversity. One of those immigrants, a Frenchman by the name of Eleuthère Irenée du Pont de Nemours, started a gunpowder factory on the banks of the Brandywine River in Delaware. His swift-rising fortune paralleled the rise of industrialism.

Today the mid-Atlantic region enjoys economic growth and continues to see an increase in the number of businesses choosing to operate here. Yet major cities like Baltimore and Washington face a host of urban ills, including poverty, unemployment, rising school dropout rates, violence, drug use, and crime. The region is grappling with ways to ensure that more of those currently living on the fringes of society can participate in and benefit from its growth.

CULTURES

The major urban areas within the region collectively represent a veritable melting pot of different cultures. Baltimore and Washington both have large African American populations. Both cities have also attracted significant immigrant populations from Asia, Latin America, and Europe, as reflected in neighborhoods such as Washington's Chinatown and Baltimore's Little Italy. Small pockets of Maryland are also home to Quakers, who, amidst the region's rapid growth and development, adhere to a traditional lifestyle. Located in the Chesapeake Bay, Smith Island retains an Old World character, with many of its inhabitants continuing to speak with the accent of their ancestors. Life on the island remains somewhat removed from that of the mainland; many islanders rely heavily on the bay for their livelihoods. With the Mason-Dixon Line dividing Maryland and Delaware, the former is theoretically part of the South, while the latter marks the beginning of the northern states. Still, there is an intermingling of northern and southern cultures in both states.

THE ARTS

Maryland, Delaware, and Washington have rich repositories of some of the world's most notable art works. Washington is home to many museums, including the National Gallery of Art, the National Portrait Gallery, the Corcoran Gallery of Art, and the Smithsonian's various museums showcasing outstanding collections of Asian, African, and modern art. Just north, in Baltimore, the Baltimore Museum of Art houses an impressive collection of old master paintings, along with an extensive Impressionist collection. The nearby Walters Art Gallery, modeled after an Italian Renaissance palace, features more than 30,000 works of art spanning 5,000 years. Collectors of contemporary art will enjoy exploring the art galleries of Dupont Circle in Washington and the more limited opportunities in Baltimore. Be sure to pick up a copy of the *City Paper*, the local alternative newspapers (coincidentally sharing the same name) in both Washington and Baltimore, for up-to-date information on current exhibits and shows. Outside these two cities, the Delaware Museum of Art has an impressive collection of pre-Raphaelite paintings, and the small towns dotting the coast have galleries that specialize in works by local artists.

The region's many well-preserved homes represent a variety of architectural styles ranging from early colonial to Federal to Victorian. Admirers of colonial furnishings will marvel at the 180-room former du Pont family home in Wilmington, housing the finest collection of early American antiques in the world. Annapolis boasts more than 1,500 eighteenth-century houses, churches, and public buildings. Antiquing is a popular pastime in a number of Maryland towns, among them Frederick and Ellicott City, just outside of Baltimore.

Theater arts also thrive in the capital region, drawing both national and international performances. Washington boasts the John F. Kennedy Center for the Performing Arts, the National Theater, the Folger Shakespeare Theatre, and Arena Stage, where a number of prominent actors got their start. Baltimore also attracts big-name performers to its Lyric Opera House and Morris Mechanic Theater.

Musical offerings range from live music at Georgetown nightspots to the Baltimore and Washington symphony orchestras. For a special summer evening, consider packing a picnic and listening to the Baltimore Symphony Orchestra play beneath the stars at Oregon Ridge State Park just north of the city. Great Washington escapes include classical musical concerts held at the Phillips Museum on Sunday afternoons and brunch at the Corcoran Gallery of Art, where diners are entertained by either gospel singers or jazz bands.

In Delaware, Wilmington's Grand Opera House hosts the Delaware Symphony, Opera Delaware, and a variety of well-known classical, jazz, and pop artists.

CUISINE

The cuisine of Maryland can be summed up in one word: crab. Steamed or boiled, hard- or soft-shelled, with or without hearty spices, crabs are the centerpiece of local cuisine. If you're new to the area, you'll want to try cracking your own crabs (and maybe even attempting to catch one) at least once. A number of crab houses in Baltimore and other coastal towns serve steamed crabs as they've been served for decades: spread out on a table on top of brown paper so the ensuing mess can be easily disposed of. Armed with a wooden mallet and pick (and usually garbed in a plastic or paper bib), you hammer and crack these hard crustaceans until you're either full or too tired to continue. It's great fun and a true Maryland tradition. If you're not in the mood for a full hands-on experience, try a crab cake or sauteed soft-shell crab in season.

While crabs take center stage at Maryland eateries, the region delivers a range of seafood options due to its proximity to the Chesapeake Bay and Atlantic Ocean. Whether you're in the mood for shellfish—scallops, oysters, clams, and the like—or just plain fish, there are plenty of great restaurants to tempt your palate. Many of these are located in small towns along the Chesapeake Bay and Maryland and Delaware coasts, offering soothing views of the water. If seafood isn't your thing, in this ethnic melting pot you'll find a wide variety of cuisines to suit your tastes. Superb ethnic restaurants in Washington and Baltimore offer Afghan, Cuban, Chinese, Japanese, Thai, Moroccan, Brazilian, and Lebanese foods—the list goes on.

Each chapter of this book includes a range of dining options—both in price and in menu options. Restaurant listings begin with less expensive options, followed by medium and high-priced cuisine. Also included are a number of cafés, where you can linger with the locals while reading the paper and sipping cappuccino. During spring, summer, and fall, you'll also want to check out farmers markets, farm stands, orchards, and roadside carts where you can purchase fresh produce and locally prepared jams, jellies, breads, and pies.

OUTDOOR ACTIVITIES

Opportunities to enjoy Maryland and Delaware's diverse natural habitats abound, whether you're after pine-scented mountain air or ocean breezes. In the nation's capital, outdoor activities range from rowing and sailing on the Potomac to biking and hiking the trails of Rock Creek Park or Roosevelt Island.

Maryland and Delaware possess hundreds of miles of trails for walking, hiking, biking, and horseback riding. The longest is the 184.5-mile Chesapeake & Ohio Canal towpath running along the Potomac River from Washington to Cumberland, Maryland. At the gateway to western Maryland, the 40-mile section of the Appalachian Trail that runs along the crest of South Mountain offers nice views and joins the C&O Canal towpath at the Potomac River. Venture to Cunningham Falls State Park (just north of Frederick) and follow short or long trails that lead to a 78-foot waterfall.

Biking is a popular pastime in the region, with plenty of places to rent equipment if you can't bring your own. One well-traveled route is the 13.3-mile Baltimore and Annapolis Trail leading from Glen Burnie, Maryland, to Annapolis. The trail follows the track bed of the no-longer-functioning Baltimore & Annapolis Railroad, passing by wooded areas, backyards, and suburban shopping malls. The 21-mile trip along the Northern Central Railroad Trail and Bike Trail takes cyclists from Ashland, Maryland, north to the Pennsylvania line, following the very same route taken by Abraham Lincoln to deliver the Gettysburg Address. Additional routes exist throughout the western portion of the state, southern Maryland, and the Eastern Shore. In fact, a number of bed-and-breakfasts on the lower Eastern Shore have banded together to offer cyclists luggage transfer to their next night's lodging. Diehard bike enthusiasts may wish to join the annual "Cycle Across Maryland," typically held in late July and lasting four to five days.

The region's many rivers, streams, and lakes offer a number of worthwhile canoeing opportunities. On the eastern shore of Maryland, paddlers head to the Choptank River and Marshyhope and Tuckahoe Creeks. In the western portion of the state, the Savage and Youghiogheny Rivers are popular with kayakers and white-water rafters. Boating and fishing opportunities are plentiful in the Chesapeake Bay area and along the Delaware and Maryland shoreline. Windsurfers, sea kayaks, and sailboats of all sizes can be rented in most major towns along the bay and Atlantic coast. Fishing charters are also available. Maryland's eastern shore has long been hailed for its hunting opportunities.

In the winter, downhill skiing is an option in western Maryland, where the Wisp Ski Resort offers 14 miles of downhill slopes. Elsewhere in the state, cross-country ski and snowmobile trails allow for outdoor adventure in cold-weather months.

PLANNING YOUR TRIP

HOW MUCH WILL IT COST?

The cost of travelling in and around the mid-Atlantic region of Maryland and Delaware obviously depends on individual tastes and length of stay. The attractions, lodging, and dining options included in this guide are designed to accommodate a range of budgets. If you and a partner are looking to spend a week in the region, stay at moderately priced hotels, and eat reasonably well, expect to spend roughly $700 to $800 a piece. Note that during the summer, the high season, most of the more popular places hike up their rates and are booked well in advance. You can generally expect to find low-cost accommodations (under $60 per night) outside the major cities if you plan ahead. Within the major metropolitan areas, you can expect to pay a minimum of $75 to $100 per night, not including often hefty taxes. Many of the bed-and-breakfasts listed are competitively priced, with rooms starting just under $100 and going as high as $250 per night. Both the Baltimore and Washington chapters identify B&B reservation services that can guide you to smaller homes in the area offering lodging at lower rates. If you're looking for budget accommodations in a major city like Washington, your best bet is a hostel. They typically cost no more than $20 per night, but be prepared to sleep in a bunk bed in a shared room.

Likewise, it's easy to save money by buying food and preparing it yourself. Generally, it makes more sense to eat a big breakfast or lunch and save money on more costly dinners. Included throughout this guide are the names of popular cafés that provide affordable meals as well as great people-watching and, occasionally, live music. While you can eat relatively inexpensively if you plan ahead, you might also want to splurge every once in a while at one of the region's many fine restaurants, so those options are included as well.

Visitors to Washington may take advantage of the fact that admission to the majority of area sights is free, thanks to the generosity of taxpayers. This includes the Smithsonian museums, the White House, the U.S. Capitol, and a number of other popular attractions. This is not true in Baltimore, where you can pay as much as $14 for entry into an attraction such as the National Aquarium (however, this is one of the finest aquariums in the country and expensive to maintain). It makes good sense to call ahead to the departments of tourism for Washington, Maryland, and Delaware for basic travel information and available coupons. The phone numbers for each are listed in the appendix under "Resources."

WHEN TO GO

Spring and fall are optimal seasons to explore the capital region and surrounding areas, while winter is the perfect time to revel in the area's many cultural opportunities. Summer is prime beach season on the Maryland and Delaware coasts.

Spring arrives early in the region. Washington's famed cherry trees, a gift from the Japanese government in 1912, are apt to be in bloom in early April, and temperatures in the 60s are not uncommon in early May, making the area a prime destination for the winter-weary. By early May colorful azaleas and rhododendrons blanket formal gardens and the exteriors of public buildings. Just north of Baltimore, the Harvey Smith Ladew Topiary Gardens, featuring nearly 20 acres of sculpted gardens, is awash with color in early spring. Outside of Wilmington, the 980-acre grounds of the Winterthur Museum are in full bloom in the spring and feature a variety of native and exotic plants. Nearby, the Nemours Mansion boasts one of the finest examples of formal French-style gardens in America; it is ablaze with color in the spring and summer months.

By the beginning of July, humidity makes walking the streets of the region's major cities a bit sticky. Still, this is a popular time for families with children and foreign visitors to explore the area. The land on which our nation's capital sits was once a swamp, and while landfill made it possible to build one of the world's finest cities, humidity levels in mid- and late summer are high. Summer is a busy season along the Chesapeake Bay and Delaware and Maryland coasts, with a variety of outdoor sporting activities and natural parks to explore. Western Maryland is a great place to head in the summer because of its slightly cooler mountain temperatures and soothing rivers and lakes.

Autumn is an excellent time to travel the entire region, with warm days, cool nights, and fall foliage providing a colorful backdrop. The winter months are perfect for exploring the region's indoor cultural riches. Or, if winter sports are your passion, western Maryland offers downhill skiing, and the region's many parks often accommodate cross country skiers and snowmobile enthusiasts.

TRANSPORTATION

The capital region is served by several major airports, including the Baltimore-Washington International Airport (BWI), Ronald Reagan Washington National Airport, and Washington Dulles International Airport, located 40 minutes west of Washington. Amtrak has eight rail stations in the Maryland area that connect directly to Maryland's Area Rail Commuter (MARC) system, including Washington's Union Station, Baltimore's Penn Station, and West Virginia's historic Harper's Ferry.

Running Monday through Friday, with 75 trains on three lines, MARC service operates in the Baltimore-Washington corridor, eight Maryland counties, and northeastern West Virginia. The Brunswick Line, with café-car service and first-class compartments, runs between Martinsburg, West Virginia, and Washington, D.C., with 15 stops in between. The Camden Line connects Baltimore's Inner Harbor (at Camden Yards) with Washington, D.C., with nine stops along the way. MARC's Penn Line links Perryville to midtown Baltimore and Washington, with 10 other stops en route.

Both Baltimore and Washington have subway systems serving the downtown and surrounding communities. The Washington Metro features five lines that travel from downtown Washington to stops in Maryland and Virginia. Baltimore Metro trains operate between the city and the northwestern suburb of Owings Mills. The metro also links with the above-ground light rail system, which runs between northern Anne Arundel County and Timonium in Baltimore County.

Bus service connects a number of areas within Maryland and Delaware. D.C. Greyhound bus lines serve the following locations in Maryland: Baltimore, Cambridge, Easton, Salisbury, and Ocean City. Washington is also a major terminal for Greyhound with stations in nearby Silver Spring and Laurel, Maryland. Greyhound also provides regular service between Baltimore and Wilmington and several of Delaware's coastal towns.

CAMPING, LODGING, AND DINING

If you're looking to experience the region while camping, Maryland and Delaware offer a variety of options. Regrettably, the District of Columbia does not, although camping facilities do exist in nearby Greenbelt, Maryland. Twelve miles northeast of Washington,

Greenbelt Park consists of 1,176 acres of forests and nature trails surrounded by development. The campground is open year-round for RV and tent camping.

Wherever camping options do exist, information is included in this guide. During busy summer and early fall months, it's best to make reservations at state parks, national parks, and national forests, all of which have different reservation systems. Delaware state parks generally do not accept reservations for family campsites, but operate on a first-come, first-served basis. Roughly three-quarters of state parks in Maryland take reservations at the park office for a small fee. Reservations for cabins in Maryland can be made a year in advance but require a week's stay from Memorial Day through Labor Day.

Maryland has 20 state parks, four state forests, and four national parks. Camping facilities are available at all state parks and forests. Cabins can be rented at six state parks: Cunningham Falls, Elk Neck, Herrington Manor, New Germany, James Island, and Martinak. The 40 miles of Appalachian Trail running through western Maryland also make for a great three- to four-day camping trip.

Delaware has 12 state parks and three state forests. Five of the state parks have public camping facilities; two of these are near the ocean and three are further inland. Camping season is generally April through October. A daily fee is charged at all state parks, although you may purchase annual permits for unlimited entrance into 10 of these parks during the fee season.

Depending on your price range and tastes, the capital region offers a range of accommodations. Included in the lodging section within each chapter of this guide are a variety of lodging choices, from inexpensive motels to quaint bed-and-breakfasts to five-star hotels. Although price ranges are noted, remember that they vary significantly from season to season and according to occupancy rates. It's best to call ahead and inquire whether your hotel of choice is offering any special discounts. Summer is the busiest season while the weeks following the winter holiday season are the least expensive time to travel. Don't simply show up during the spring, summer, or fall months without a reservation or you may find yourself spending most of your holiday looking for rooms. Also, be forewarned that many of the larger hotel chains in Baltimore, Washington, and Wilmington often cater to convention crowds and can be somewhat on the impersonal side.

In the dining section of each chapter, a wide variety of restaurants are included. Some are well known while a few are frequented primarily by locals. Price ranges tend to change often, so these have been omitted. In the major cities, a number of hotels have standard suites with basic kitchen amenities; others include breakfast in the room rate, so be sure to ask. Some museums have excellent cafés, allowing for minimal interruption to your cultural immersion. Picnicking is also an option in urban and rural areas, with plenty of small grocers, farm stands, and well-maintained parks and open spaces.

RECOMMENDED READING

Given the rich history of the mid-Atlantic region and wealth of cultural and outdoor opportunities, it's no surprise the recommended reading list is long. If you're planning on exploring the Chesapeake Bay or going anywhere near Maryland's eastern shore, James Michener's *Chesapeake*, while fictional, offers a detailed yet fast-moving account of the region's history, wildlife, and culture. The story begins with the area's early Native American inhabitants and traces the arrival of the first English settlers, as well as the first slaves. In deftly weaving his tale, Michener describes the decline of the region's wildlife and water quality. The 800-plus-page book grew out of the author's experiences living in a historic fishing village on the shores of the Chesapeake in 1975. Also recommended is John Bowen's *Adventuring in Chesapeake Bay Country*, a comprehensive guide to the region, including maps and information on boating and fishing, sports, history, and conservation efforts. For a look at one traditional culture on the bay that has remained relatively unchanged over the last 300 years, pick up a copy of *An Island Out of Time: A Memoir of Smith Island in the Chesapeake* by Tom Horton. The author, who spent three years on the island, takes a close look at a tight-knit community with strong ties to the natural world surrounding them.

To gain an understanding of the complex social issues affecting not only Baltimore but a host of other American cities, read *The Corner: A Year in the Life of an Inner City Neighborhood* by David Simons and Edward Burns. The authors, whose early work inspired the Emmy-award-winning television program *Homicide*, chronicle goings-on on a Baltimore street corner over a one-year period. The book questions the effectiveness of law enforcement policies and the welfare system in improving inner city life. For a more upbeat look at Baltimore culture and who's who in the city, try *Baltimore: If You Lived Here, You're Home* by Michael Olesker. The book is a compilation of moving and at times humorous newspaper columns written by Olesker over the last 20 years for the *Baltimore Sun* and *News American*. "Baltimore is a city of tribal rituals," writes Olesker, "of neighbors sharing steamed crabs in their backyard and downtown waitresses who call their customers 'Hon' without worrying about the sociological implications."

Dozens, perhaps hundreds, of books have been written on Washington insider politics and on the men and women who have dominated the capital scene throughout history. Two authors provide equally cynical portraits of the power games that dominate our nation's capital. Pulitzer Prize–winning author Hedrick Smith offers an in-depth view of life inside the beltway in *The Power Game: How Washington Works*. Smith, former Washington Bureau Chief of the *New York Times*, paints a portrait of the culture of the federal government, peppering his prose with illustrative anecdotes. Charles Peters' *How Washington Really Works* likewise takes a close look at insider politics. Peters, editor-in-chief of the *Washington Monthly*, includes in this fast-moving and witty book chapters on the press, lobbyists, federal bureaucracy, foreign service, the military, the court system, Congress, and the White House.

To fully enjoy the hiking and other outdoor activities recommended in this book, consider purchasing the National Audubon Society's *Nature Guide to Eastern Forests* and/or the Society's *Field Guide to North American Birds—Eastern Region*. These durable, easily-packed guides contain color photographs that aid identification of the region's diverse trees, wildflowers, mammals, birds, and insects.

For exploring the Chesapeake Bay and the Maryland and Delaware coasts, you may wish to carry along a guide to the region's marine life. Again, the National Audubon Society Nature Guide series includes a *Guide to the Atlantic and Gulf Coast* for identifying and learning more about the region's birds, plants, fish, whales, and seashore creatures.

If traveling with children, pick up a copy of *Kidding Around Washington, D.C.*, from John Muir Publications. This guide, specially written for children ages 6 to 10, highlights entertainment, food, and sightseeing options aimed at young tastes and interests. In addition to factual information on the history and people who have made the capital what it is today, the book incorporates crossword puzzles, word searches, coloring pages, and mazes that will keep your child busy while hanging around the hotel or enduring lengthy car rides.

1
WASHINGTON, D.C.

M odeled after Europe's most celebrated capitals, Washington
exudes a majesty found nowhere else in America. From the halls
of Congress to the Smithsonian to the Holocaust Memorial Museum
to the National Gallery, both curious child and intellectual adult will
find plenty to satisfy. In fact, your greatest challenge may be summon-
ing the stamina to do and see all that interests you.

In 1791 President George Washington selected the site that
would become the nation's capital and hired French military engineer
Pierre Charles L'Enfant to design it. L'Enfant produced a grand
scheme for the city, with wide avenues radiating from scenic squares
and circles decorated with ornate fountains and sculptures. Despite the
genius of his design, L'Enfant ended up alienating the powers that be
and was fired in 1792. Still, much of his original plan was eventually
realized. Today Washington is a beautiful city with reflecting pools,
grassy malls, dignified public buildings, and a cultural wealth to be
shared and enjoyed by all.

Despite its physical charms and the ideals upon which it was built,
Washington is a place where strong egos and power politics tend to
overshadow everyday life. Woodrow Wilson once said of it, "The real
voice of the great people of America sometimes sounds faint and dis-
tant in that strange city." The peculiar political climate of Washington
fuels what is commonly referred to as an "inside the beltway" mental-
ity. If you can put cynicism aside, your stay in Washington will be rich
indeed.

A PERFECT DAY IN D.C.

How you go about defining the perfect day in Washington depends largely on where your interests lie and whether or not you have children. Nevertheless, there are a number of "must dos." Begin your day with a tour of the White House. Not only is it an extraordinary building, but how often do you get a chance to visit the home of a head of state? (See the section on the White House under "Sightseeing Highlights" for tips on avoiding lengthy delays and ensuring that you do indeed get in.) Next, head to the Mall and the Washington Monument. From the monument, you can take in the view of the Capitol to the east and the reflecting pool and Lincoln Memorial to the west. Continue heading east along the Mall until you arrive at the Smithsonian Institution's information center, known as "the Castle," where you can obtain information about each of the Smithsonian's museums. If you have time to visit only one Smithsonian museum, make it the nearby Air and Space Museum. From there, walk to the Capitol, if only to step inside and marvel at the height of the dome and inner fresco.

Next, visit the East Wing of the National Gallery of Art, with its collection of twentieth-century art and changing exhibits. There you may also take tea and enjoy a well-earned rest at one of the museum's cafés. By now, you should be sufficiently exhausted, but weather and light permitting, try to complete your Mall walk by heading west past the Washington Monument to the Vietnam Veteran's Memorial and Lincoln Memorial (considered even more spectacular at night). For dinner, try one of the many restaurants in Dupont Circle—perhaps a lively outdoor café if it's warm. If you still have energy, browse a late-night bookstore before heading back to your hotel.

GETTING AROUND THE CITY

D.C. is shaped like a diamond with its corners pointing north, east, south, and west. Near the center of the diamond is the U.S. Capitol, from which point the city is divided into quadrants as follows: Northwest (NW), Northeast (NE), Southwest (SW), and Southeast (SE). North Capitol Street runs north from the Capitol building, South Capitol Street runs south, and East Capitol Street runs east (the Mall is to the west). Numbered streets run north-south, starting with First Street on both sides of North Capitol and South Capitol Streets; while lettered streets run east-west, starting with A Street on both sides of East Capitol Street and with C Street on both sides of the Mall. Because many street names are repeated in each zone (e.g., there's an intersection of Sixth and E Streets in every quadrant), the zone designation in any address is especially important. Thrown into the mix are avenues, named after states, that cut across the grid and usually intersect at traffic circles. This layout makes the city relatively easy to navigate, though it's helpful to keep a map on hand because there are exceptions to the city's otherwise logical layout.

The Mall, where a great many of the city's major sights are clustered, extends west from Capitol Hill and ends at the Lincoln Memorial and the Potomac River. It is bounded on the north by Constitution Avenue and on the south by Independence Avenue. Beyond Capitol Hill and the Mall, most of the city's hotels, restaurants, and attractions are in Northwest D.C., which includes downtown, Dupont Circle, Adams Morgan, and Georgetown (see the next chapter for Georgetown listings).

Given the hassle and expense of parking, it's best to acquaint yourself with the city's subway system. The Washington Metro, considered one of the best subway systems in the country, is clean and efficient. Taxis are a bit problematic because the city operates on a "zone" system, as opposed to metered fares. While this can be advantageous if you're traveling between points in the same zone, crossing three or four zones can be quite expensive. Be sure to confirm your fare ahead of time so you won't be taken by surprise.

The following sightseeing highlights are divided into subject categories: Federal government–related sights, monuments and memorials, Smithsonian museums, other art museums, and a general category for sights that don't fit into the above categories. While a majority of the sights are clustered around the Mall, some fall in northwest D.C. or outside the city limits. In order to locate any of these sights, refer to the map page indicated at the end of each listing.

FEDERAL GOVERNMENT SIGHTSEEING HIGHLIGHTS

★★★ **United States Capitol**—Set on 68 acres overlooking the Mall, the Capitol was constructed with the highest ideals in mind—despite what may actually occur there. The central rotunda and dome dominate the building. The dome is 180 feet high, measures 95 feet across, and weighs 9 million pounds. The 19-foot bronze statue on top of the dome is called *Freedom*. Tours of the Capitol begin in the rotunda,

THE MALL

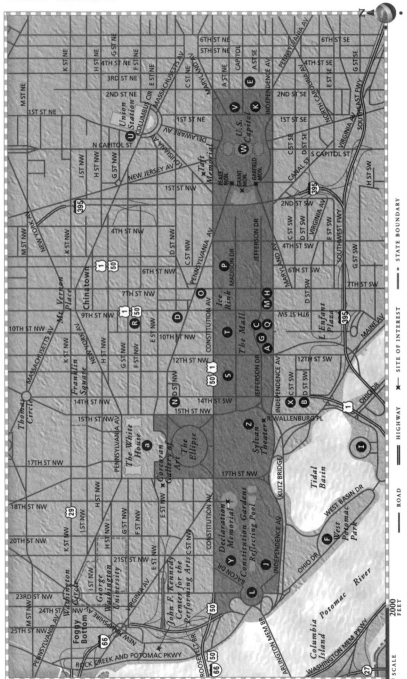

Sights

Ⓐ Arthur M. Sackler Gallery

Ⓑ Bureau of Engraving and Printing

Ⓒ Enid Haupt Garden

Ⓓ Federal Bureau of Investigation

Ⓔ Folger Shakespeare Library

Ⓕ Franklin Delano Roosevelt Memorial

Ⓖ Freer Gallery of Art

Ⓗ Hirshhorn Museum and Sculpture Garden

Ⓘ Jefferson Memorial

Ⓙ Korean War Memorial

Ⓚ Library of Congress

Ⓛ Lincoln Memorial

Ⓜ National Air and Space Museum

Ⓝ National Aquarium

Ⓞ National Archives

Ⓟ National Gallery of Art

Ⓠ National Museum of African Art

Ⓡ National Museum of American Art

Ⓢ National Museum of American History

Ⓣ National Museum of Natural History

Ⓤ National Postal Museum

Ⓥ Supreme Court

Ⓦ United States Capitol

Ⓧ United States Holocaust Memorial Museum

Ⓨ Vietnam Veteran's Memorial

Ⓩ Washington Monument

ⓐ The White House

although tickets must be obtained outside the main gates. In peak summer months, be prepared to wait as long as two to three hours for entrance. Highlights include the fresco in the center of the dome, *The Apotheosis of George Washington*, painted by Constantino Brumidi, and large oil paintings chronicling major events in American history. The north and south wings of the building were added in the 1850s to accommodate government growth following the addition of new states to the Union. To see Congress in action in the House and Senate chambers, you'll have to obtain a gallery pass from the office of your representative or senator. To locate the appropriate office, call 202/224-3121. Contrary to what one might think, the Democrats sit to the right and Republicans to the left. If at the Capitol around midday, lunch at the Capitol restaurant and perhaps see a legislator or two.

Details: *Entrance on E. Capitol and 1st Sts NW; 202/225-6827. Open Memorial Day–Labor Day daily 9–8, rest of the year daily 9–4:30.*

Free guided tours depart every 15 minutes 9–3:45 and last about 30 minutes. Restaurant, on first floor, open Mon–Fri 7:30–3:30 when Senate is in session, 11–3:30 otherwise. See map on page 30. (1 hour)

★★★ **The White House**—Formerly known as the Executive Mansion, Congress officially proclaimed the president's home the White House in 1902. The first president to actually sleep here was the nation's second president, John Adams, who moved in on November 1, 1800, well before it was finished. Successive occupants of the 132-room mansion have each placed their personal stamp on this famous home. Most recently, George Bush had a horseshoe pit installed and Bill Clinton a jogging track. Highlights of the White House tour include the white and gold **East Room**, where presidential news conferences take place. Teddy Roosevelt is said to have allowed his children to ride their pet pony here. The **Blue Room**, an oval reception room, is decorated in the Empire style and features famous portraits of John Adams, Thomas Jefferson, and Andrew Jackson. Also featuring Empire-style furnishings is the **Red Room**, which is used for state receptions. The **Green Room** is decorated as a Federal-style parlor. Paintings of Benjamin Franklin, John Quincy Adams, and Abigail Adams adorn the walls. The West Wing houses the president's **Oval Office**.

Details: 1600 Pennsylvania Ave. NW; 202/456-7041. Open Tue–Sat 10–12. Free. March through September tickets are dispensed at the visitors center, 1450 Pennsylvania Ave. NW, in the Commerce Department's Baldridge Hall on a first-come, first-served basis; they are often gone by 9 a.m. In other months, go directly to the Southeast Gate before 10 a.m. or to the East Gate after 10 a.m. (both on East Executive Ave., between the White House and the Treasury Building). For advance tickets, you can write your representative's or senator's office 8 to 10 weeks in advance to request special VIP passes for tours between 8 and 10 a.m., but these tickets are hard to get. On select weekends in April and October, the White House is open for garden tours. See map on page 30. (2 hours)

★★ **Bureau of Engraving and Printing**—Ever wonder how money is made or what steps the government takes to prevent counterfeiting? At the Bureau of Engraving and Printing visitors can watch as more than $22.5 million a day in bills is produced. A 25-minute self-guided tour allows visitors to watch money being made. Exhibits include counterfeit money and an enlarged photo of a $100,000 bill designed for official transactions. The largest bill printed for general use since 1969 has been $100. At the visitors center you can play money-related electronic games and view $1 million on display. The Bureau is also responsible for designing and printing Federal Reserve notes, most U.S. postage stamps, Treasury securities, identification cards, naturalization certificates, and other special security documents.

Details: 14th and C Sts. SW; 202/874-3188. Open Mon–Fri 9–2. In summer get tickets early in the day because tours fill up quickly. Free. See map on page 30. (1 hour)

★★ **Federal Bureau of Investigation**—In what could be considered a commendable PR effort, the Federal Bureau of Investigation opens its doors to the public for weekday tours. In fact, the FBI headquarters is one of the capital's biggest draws; expect long lines during summer months. The tour begins with a brief video describing the agency's work today. Other stops on the tour include a gallery of the FBI's "Greatest Hits", including cardboard cutouts of old-time gangsters such as John Dillinger; a wall of the nation's Ten Most Wanted; a display of modern organized crime groups; the DNA Analysis Lab; and the Firearms Evidence Collection featuring more than 5,000 pistols, machine guns, and other weapons.

Details: 10th St. and Pennsylvania Ave. NW; 202/324-3447. One-hour tours Mon–Fri 8:45–4:15. Free. See map on page 30. (1½ hours)

★ **Library of Congress**—Established in 1800 for the use of Congress, the Library of Congress is the world's largest library, containing some 113 million items, only a fourth of which are books. Growing every day, the library's materials occupy more than 575 miles of shelves. The library is made up of the Thomas Jefferson Building, with the adjoining Adams Building, and the James Madison Building. If your time is limited, stop into the Jefferson Building's Great Hall with its soaring arches, columns, mosaics, and murals. The view of the main reading room from the viewing gallery is spectacular. Researchers need not worry about getting lost in the stacks; librarians retrieve book requests and only members of Congress are allowed to check them out. Classic films are shown free of charge in the library's Mary Pickford Theater.

Details: Madison Building, 101 Independence Ave. SE; 202/707-8000; open Mon–Sat 8:30 a.m.–5 p.m. Jefferson Building, 1st St. and Independence Ave; open Mon–Sat 10–5:30. Admission to all buildings is free. See map on page 30. (1 hour)

✮ **Supreme Court**—While touring the Capitol area, it's worth walking by the Supreme Court building, if not stepping inside. The building, completed in 1935 and designed by architect Cass Gilbert of St. Paul, Minnesota, is fashioned after a Greek temple with a portico of Corinthian columns and pediment representing the themes of Liberty, Authority, Order, Council, and Research. The interior features two beautiful rooms: the Great Hall, lined with busts of all former chief justices, and the Courtroom.

The court is in session from October through late April on Monday, Tuesday, and Wednesday from 10 a.m. to 3 p.m. Visitors may attend oral arguments, but seating is limited. From mid-May through early July, the public can attend brief sessions (about 15 minutes) of the Supreme Court at 10 a.m. on Monday, during which time the justices release orders and opinions. About 150 gallery seats are set aside for the general public, so arrive at least an hour early. When court is not in session, free lectures are given in the courtroom on court procedure and the building's architecture. Lectures are given 9:30 a.m. to 3:30 p.m. every hour on the half-hour. Visitors are also encouraged to view a 20-minute film on the workings of the court. The court building features a cafeteria, a gift shop, and changing exhibits. *Details: 1 1st St. NE; 202/479-3000. Open Mon–Fri 9–4:30. Free. See map on page 30. (1 hour)*

MONUMENT AND MEMORIAL SIGHTSEEING HIGHLIGHTS

✮✮✮ **Lincoln Memorial**—Dedicated in 1922, the Lincoln Memorial attracts more than 6 million visitors a year. Ironically, the opening day ceremony was segregated; black audience members, including Booker T. Washington, who gave a speech, were asked to view the proceedings from a separate area. The memorial, fashioned after a Greek temple, is surrounded by 36 columns representing the states of the Union at the time of Lincoln's death. Bronze plaques on the north and south walls are inscribed with the Gettysburg Address and Lincoln's Second Inaugural Address. The 19-foot statue of a seated Lincoln looking down is by Daniel Chester French. Above the inscriptions are two 60-foot murals, *Emancipation* and *Reunion* by Jules Guerin. The most dramatic view of the memorial occurs at night.

Details: 23rd St. NW between Constitution and Independence Aves.; 202/426-6895. Open daily 24 hours, staffed daily 8 a.m.–midnight. Free. See map on page 30. (30 minutes)

★★★ **Vietnam Veteran's Memorial**—The names of the 58,156 Americans who were killed or deemed missing in action in the Vietnam War are inscribed on the face of the Vietnam Memorial. The names are listed in chronological order from 1959 to 1975. The polished black granite of the memorial forms a broad V-shape with the wall rising in height at the midpoint, symbolizing the height of the conflict. Directories posted at the entrance and exit to the wall list the names in alphabetical order. Completed in 1982, the wall is one of the most visited sites in Washington. Visitors often leave flowers, letters, photographs, and uniforms in memory of a loved one. These are collected by the National Park Service and stored in a warehouse in Lanham, Maryland. The memorial was designed by Maya Ying Lin, a 21-year-old Yale architecture student who was selected in a 1981 competition. In 1984 a life-size sculpture, *The Three Servicemen*, by Frederick Hart, and an American flag flying from a 60-foot staff were added to the memorial. On Veteran's Day in 1993, the **Vietnam Women's Memorial** was unveiled nearby.

Details: Constitution Gardens, Constitution Ave. and 23rd St. NW; 202/634-1568. Open daily 24 hours, staffed daily 8 a.m.–midnight. Free. See map on page 30. (30 minutes)

★★ **Jefferson Memorial**—Dedicated in 1943, the Jefferson Memorial houses a 19-foot bronze statue of the third president of the United States and author of the Declaration of Independence. Its walls are inscribed with excerpts from his writings. The rotunda, based on the Pantheon in Rome, was designed by architect John Russell Pope. Jefferson's fondness for the dome-shaped Pantheon is echoed in the rotundas he designed for the University of Virginia and his home at Monticello.

Details: Tidal Basin, south bank; 202/426-6821. Open daily 24 hours, staffed daily 8 a.m.–midnight. Free. See map on page 30. (30 minutes)

★★ **Washington Monument**—For a panoramic view of the city, take the elevator to the top of the Washington Monument. The marble obelisk stands 555 feet high and has 898 steps leading to the top (which you can also take up or down). The monument was officially opened to the public in 1888. Guided tours are given, subject to staff availability, on weekends at 10 a.m. and 2 p.m.

Details: Constitution Ave. and 15th St. NW; 202/426-6839. Open Apr–Labor Day 8 a.m.–midnight; reduced hours off-season. Tickets available at the 15th St. kiosk. Free. See map on page 30. (30 minutes)

✯ **Franklin Delano Roosevelt Memorial**—Opened to the public in May 1997, the FDR Memorial commemorates the achievements of the 32nd president of the United States during his 12 years in office, from 1933 to 1945. Highlighting historical milestones such as the Depression, World War II, and the passage of the New Deal, the expansive memorial is divided into four distinct areas, each representing one of FDR's terms in office. "The only thing we have to fear is fear itself" is just one of the many quotes from the president inscribed on the red granite walls. The memorial's cascading waterfalls, views of the tidal basin, and park-like atmosphere make it a soothing place to reflect on one man's achievements and one of the most turbulent periods in American history.

Details: West Potomac Park between the Tidal Basin and the Potomac River. Open daily 8 a.m.–midnight. Free. See map on page 30. (30 minutes)

✯ **Korean War Memorial**—The Korean War Memorial was dedicated in 1995 on the 42nd anniversary of the war's end. The memorial consists of a column of soldiers marching toward an American flag, along with a reflecting pool and a granite wall etched with war scenes.

Details: Between Independence Ave. SW and the Lincoln Memorial. See map on page 30. (30 minutes)

SMITHSONIAN SIGHTSEEING HIGHLIGHTS

*The Smithsonian was born of the desire of James Smithson, a British scientist, to create in Washington "an establishment for the increase and diffusion of knowledge among men." Upon his death in 1829, Smithson maintained that should his nephew Henry James Hungerford die without an heir, Smithson's fortune should go to the United States to establish the museum. Today, the Institution that bears Smithson's name consists of 14 museums; nine of its buildings are located within a short distance along the Mall. Your visit to the Smithsonian should begin with the **Castle** (1000 Jefferson Dr. SW, 202/357-2700), the first official Smithsonian museum, established in 1855. It's open from 10 a.m. to 5 p.m. Here you can pick up a map and brochures, learn of current exhibits, and plan your day. The Castle building serves as the Institution's administrative offices and houses the Smithsonian Information Center. At the center, visitors may view a 20-minute video providing an overview of the various Smithsonian museums. Located just behind the Castle is the **Enid Haupt Garden** offering a quiet, colorful resting place to either catch your breath or plan your attack. Tasteful benches line the flowerbeds.*

★★★ **National Air and Space Museum**—If attendance records are any indication, the jewel in the crown of the Smithsonian's many offerings is the National Air and Space Museum. Opened in 1976, the Air and Space is the most visited museum in the world, attracting more than 10 million visitors each year. The museum's 23 galleries tell the story of aviation from the earliest attempts at human flight to the space race. Interactive exhibits demonstrate how flight is possible. On display in the museum's Milestones of Flight gallery are the Wright Brothers' 1903 *Flyer 1*, the world's first successful aircraft; Charles Lindbergh's *Spirit of St. Louis*, the first airplane to complete a nonstop solo transatlantic flight; Amelia Earhart's Lockheed *58 Vega*; the *Apollo 11* command module used on the first manned lunar landing mission; and a sample moon rock that visitors may touch. Also on display is the controversial Boeing B-29 *Enola Gay*, which dropped the first atomic bomb on Hiroshima, Japan. Be sure to check out what's being shown on the five-story IMAX screen at the Samuel P. Langley Theater. The theater features many regular IMAX films such as *Blue Planet*, *To Fly!*, *The Dream Is Alive*, and *Destiny in Space*. Special IMAX presentations are also shown at night.
Details: Independence Ave. and 7th St. SW; 202/357-2700; open daily 10–5:30. Free. See map on page 30. (2 hours)

★★★ **National Zoological Park**—While better known for his plan for New York City's Central Park, Frederick Law Olmsted planned the original design for the National Zoological Park. Covering 163 acres, the zoological park is considered among the foremost zoos in the world. Today the zoo's most famous occupant is Hsing Hsing, a giant Chinese panda who can be seen during feeding times chomping on bamboo. Less well publicized are the zoo's Komodo dragons, the only ones in the country. Highlights at the zoo are the Great Ape House; the Great Flight Cage, home to more than 30 species of bird; Amazonia, a re-creation of Amazon rain-forest habitat and its inhabitants; and the Cheetah Conservation Area, a grassy compound that provides running space for these super-fast cats.
Details: 3001 Connecticut Ave. NW; 202/673-4717. Grounds open daily at 6 a.m., buildings open 9–6. Free. See map on page 46. (1–2 hours)

★★ **Arthur M. Sackler Gallery**—A wealthy medical researcher and publisher, Arthur M. Sackler began collecting Asian art as a student in the 1940s. Opened in 1987, the gallery that bears his name is dedicated to showcasing Asian art. Exhibition areas are entirely underground.

The permanent collection includes works from China, the Indian subcontinent, Persia, Thailand, Indonesia, Japan, and Korea. *Details: 1050 Independence Ave. SW; 202/357-2700. Open daily 10–5:30. Free. See map on page 30. (1–2 hours)*

★★ **Freer Gallery of Art**—Considered among the best collections of Asian art in the world, the Freer Gallery first opened in 1923. Museum benefactor Charles L. Freer was a wealthy Detroit industrialist who spent much of his later years collecting art. The gallery's permanent collection includes more than 26,000 works of art from the Far and Near East dating from Neolithic times to the early twentieth century. The collection is so large that only 2 to 3 percent of its holdings are on display at any one time. Regularly on display are folding Japanese screens, Chinese jades and bronzes, Korean ceramics, examples of Islamic art, and the works of American artists who were influenced by the Orient. *Details: 12th St. and Jefferson Dr. SW; 202/357-2700. Open daily 10–5:30. Free. See map on page 30. (1–2 hours)*

★★ **Hirshhorn Museum and Sculpture Garden**—In 1966 Joseph H. Hirshhorn, a Latvian immigrant who made his fortune in this country running uranium mines, donated his extensive collection of nineteenth- and twentieth-century art to the Smithsonian. Opened in 1974, the Hirshhorn Museum manages a collection that includes 4,000 paintings and drawings and 2,000 sculptures. Included in the collection are American artists such as Eakins, Pollock, Rothko, and Stella. European and Latin masters include Francis Bacon, Fernanado Botero, Magritte, Miro, and Victor Vasarely. The **Hirshhorn Sculpture Garden** displays 58 sculptures by Henry Moore, as well as works by Honore Daumier, Max Ernst, Alberto Giacometti, Auguste Rodin, Pablo Picasso, and Man Ray. *Details: Independence Ave. and 7th St. SW; 202/357-2700. Open daily 10–5:30; sculpture garden open daily 7:30 a.m. to dusk. Free. See map on page 30. (1 hour)*

★★ **National Museum of African Art**—Founded in 1964, the National Museum of African Art is the only national art museum dedicated to the collection, exhibition, and study of African art. The permanent collection consists of more than 7,000 objects including masks, carvings, textiles, jewelry, and personal utensils. Highlights include a display of Royal Benin art from Nigeria, and the Eliot Elisofon Photo-

graphic Archives, with more than 300,000 photographic prints and transparencies on African arts and culture. The museum offers special events, children's programs, films, lectures, storytelling, and guided tours.
  Details: *950 Independence Ave. SW; 202/357-4600. Open daily 10–5:30. Free. See map on page 30. (1 hour)*

★★ **National Museum of American Art**—Devoted to showcasing American artistic achievements, this museum occupies half of the old patent office building, one of the finest examples of Greek Revival architecture in the country. (The other half houses the National Portrait Gallery.) The museum's holdings include more than 37,400 works of American art, from the colonial period through the present. Works include paintings, drawings, graphic arts, sculpture, photography, and folk art. Among the more popular exhibits are George Catlin's portraits of Indian life, as well as the large-scale landscapes by Thomas Moran, Frederick Church, and Albert Bierstadt. Also featured are works by Winslow Homer, John Singer Sargent, John Henry Twachtman, Edward Hopper, Jasper Johns, and Robert Rauschenberg. Note: The museum is expected to close in early 2000 for major building renovations, scheduled to take two years.
  Details: *8th and G Sts., NW; 202/357-2700. Open daily 10–5:30. Free. See map on page 30. (1 hour)*

★★ **National Museum of American History**—No matter what your interests, the National Museum of American History has something to pique your curiosity—from medical and medieval instruments to military uniforms, Tiffany glass to Disney cartoon drawings. The museum houses more than 16 million artifacts, including Judy Garland's ruby slippers from *The Wizard of Oz*, a collection of inaugural ball gowns worn by the nation's first ladies, and the original Star-Spangled Banner, the flag that inspired Francis Scott Key to write what would become the national anthem. Assuming a prominent place in the museum is a Foucault pendulum consisting of a 240-pound brass bob suspended by a 54-foot steel cable. In addition to Dorothy's shoes, the History of American Entertainment Collection features costumes from *Superman*, the chairs used by Archie and Edith Bunker in *All in the Family*, and Henry Winkler's jacket from *Happy Days*.
  Details: *Constitution Ave. and 14th St. NW; 202/357-2700. Open daily 10–5:30. Free. See map on page 30. (2 hours)*

★★ **National Museum of Natural History**—While the most popular item on display at the Museum of Natural History is the Hope Diamond, the museum's 120 million other artifacts and specimens afford other points of interest. Standing just below the museum's rotunda is a 13-foot-high African elephant, reputedly the largest ever killed. Running second to the popularity of the Hall of Gems, the Dinosaur Hall displays fossilized skeletons such as a 90-foot long diplodocus, a 28,000-year-old bison found frozen in Alaska, a saber-toothed cat, a mastodon, and a mammoth. In the Museum's Discovery Room, visitors may handle objects such as elephant tusks, seashells, rocks, feathers, and petrified wood. While Orkin is more often associated with products to kill pests, the O. Orkin Insect Zoo, funding for which was provided by the pest control magnate, features more than 60 species of live insects, from termites to tarantulas. Also displayed are artifacts from indigenous cultures in Asia, Africa, the Pacific, and the Americas.

Details: *Constitution Ave. and 12th St. NW; 202/357-2700. Open daily 10–5:30. Free. See map on page 30. (2 hours)*

★★ **National Portrait Gallery**—The faces of many of the most prominent figures in American history are displayed at the National Portrait Gallery. The collection includes more than 7,000 images, including those of all U.S. presidents and notable figures who were important in the lives of Americans (although images other than those of a president cannot be made part of the permanent collection until at least 10 years after the subject's death). Note: As is the case with the neighboring National Museum of American Art (above), the Portrait Gallery will be closed in early 2000 for renovation, expected to take two years.

Details: *8th and F Sts. NW; 202/357-2700. Open daily 10–5:30. Free. See map on page 42. (1–2 hours)*

★ **National Postal Museum**—Stamp collectors and enthusiasts won't want to miss the National Postal Museum, which houses the National Philatelic Collection (the largest in the world), with more than 55,000 U.S. and foreign stamps. Exhibits trace the history of mail service from colonial times to the present, including the days of the Pony Express. Visitors learn how today's mail makes its way to its final destination.

Details: *2 Massachusetts Ave. NE; 202/357-2700. Open daily 10–5:30. Free. See map on page 30. (1 hour)*

OTHER ART MUSEUM SIGHTSEEING HIGHLIGHTS

★★★ **National Gallery of Art**—Home to one of the world's foremost collections of Western painting, sculpture, and graphic arts from the Middle Ages through the twentieth century, the National Gallery comprises two buildings. To view the museum's holdings in chronological order, it's best to start with the West Building. Opened in 1941 as a result of a gift to the nation by financier Andrew Mellon, the West Building is dominated by the Great Rotunda, a dome surrounded by 24 marble columns. The building's more than 100 separate galleries showcase paintings by Italian, Spanish, German, French, Dutch, Flemish, French, British, and American artists. Great European masters represented include Botticelli, Leonard da Vinci, Raphael, Titian, El Greco, Vermeer, Rubens, and Rembrandt. Also on display are an impressive array of nineteenth-century works by Manet, Monet, Renoir, van Gogh, and others. The American collection includes paintings by Homer, Sargent, Copley, Cole, and Whistler. The East Building was added in 1978 in response to the gallery's changing needs. Designed by architect I. M. Pei, the East Building has a far more contemporary feel that befits the twentieth-century art and changing exhibitions generally displayed here. On display are sculpture and paintings by Picasso, Matisse, Moore, Calder, Rothko, Pollock, and others.
*Details: Constitution Ave. between 3rd and 4th Sts. NW; 202/737-4215. Open Mon–Sat 10–5, Sun 11–6. Free. See map on page 30.
(2–3 hours)*

★★★ **Phillips Collection**—Just blocks from Dupont Circle, the Phillips Collection is distinguished as the first museum of modern art in the country; it now houses over 2,500 works of nineteenth- and twentieth-century European and American painting and sculpture. On display are works by Braque, Cézanne, Klee, O'Keeffe, Matisse, and Bonnard. Among the collection's most famous paintings are Renoir's *Luncheon of the Boating Party*, Degas' *Dancers at the Bar*, van Gogh's *Entrance to the Public Garden at Arles*, and Cézanne's self-portrait.
Details: 1600 21st St. at Q St. NW; 202/387-2151. Open Tue–Sat 10–5, Thu to 8:30, Sun 12–5. Tours offered Wed and Sat at 2 p.m. $6.50 adults. See map on page 42. (1–2 hours)

★★ **Corcoran Gallery**—Founded in 1859 and located just blocks from the White House, the Corcoran Gallery is one of the oldest museums in

NORTHWEST WASHINGTON, D.C.

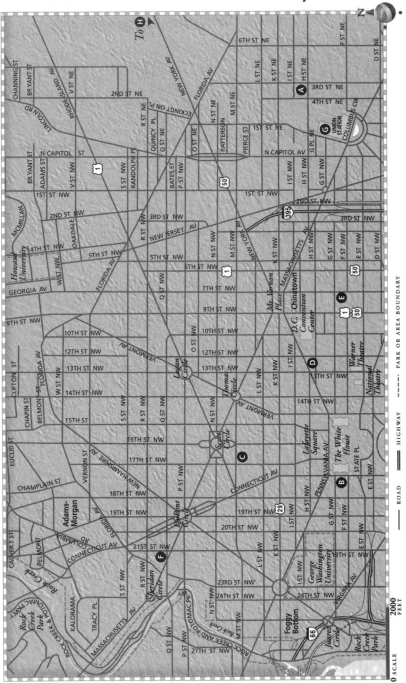

Sights

Ⓐ Capital Children's Museum

Ⓑ Corcoran Gallery

Ⓒ National Geographic Society's Explorer's Hall

Ⓓ National Museum of Women in the Arts

Ⓔ National Portrait Gallery

Ⓕ Phillips Collection

Ⓖ Union Station

Ⓗ United States National Arboretum

the country and houses one of the finest collections of American art from colonial times to the present. The gallery's permanent collection numbers more than 11,000 works, focusing chiefly on American art, from colonial portraiture to Hudson River landscape paintings to twentieth-century modernism. The Corcoran also includes paintings by great American portraitists such as John Copley, Gilbert Stuart, Rembrandt Peale, John Singer Sargent, Thomans Eakins, and Mary Cassatt. The Walker Collection displays European art works from the late nineteenth and early twentieth centuries including works by Courbet, Monet, Pissarro, and Renoir. One of the museum's most talked about works is Hiram Powers' *Greek Slave*, a statue of a nude woman with her wrists chained that so shocked Victorian audiences that separate viewing hours were established for men and women. The museum's **Café des Artistes** serves continental breakfasts, light lunches, an English tea, and dinner on Thursday when the museum is open late. Sunday brunch is also popular with live performances by gospel singers and a jazz band.

Details: 500 17th St. NW; 202/639-1700. Open Wed–Mon 10–5, Thu to 9. $3 adults, $5 families suggested donation. Free guided tours daily Mon–Fri at noon, Sat and Sun at 10:30, noon, and 3. See map on page 42. (1–2 hours)

✿ **National Museum of Women in the Arts**—Works by such prominent female artists as Georgia O'Keeffe, Mary Cassatt, Frieda Kahlo, Barbara Hepworth, and Judy Chicago are all part of the permanent collection of the National Museum of Women in the Arts. The museum houses more than 2,000 works by 500 women artists spanning the sixteenth through the twentieth centuries. *Details: 1250 New York Ave. at 13th St. NW; 202/783-5000. Open Mon–Sat 10–5, Sun 12–5. Suggested donation $3. See map on page 42. (1 hour)*

OTHER SIGHTSEEING HIGHLIGHTS

★★★ **United States Holocaust Memorial Museum**—Completed in 1993, the Holocaust Memorial is a masterpiece of contemporary museum architecture. While its subject matter is not for the faint-hearted, the museum draws nearly 5,000 visitors each day and offers a profound educational experience. Visitors are urged to purchase tickets for the permanent exhibition well in advance, although a number of rooms are open to the public without prior ticketing. Young visitors to the permanent exhibition are advised to be at least 11 years of age.

Highlights of the permanent exhibition include a railroad car once used to transport Jews from the Warsaw ghetto to the gas chambers of Treblinka, a vast collection of shoes worn by concentration camp victims, and memorabilia from an entire town whose Jewish inhabitants were killed. Also included are exhibits on the Nazis' use of propaganda and the American and world response to the early years of the Third Reich. The exhibit concludes with accounts of the resistance, liberation, and survivors' efforts to rebuild their lives. With its exposed brick walls and arches based on the design of the Auschwitz prison camp, the Hall of Remembrance evokes feelings of fear and loneliness. *Details: 100 Raoul Wallenburg Pl. at 15th St. SW; 202/488-0400. Open daily 10–5:30. Tickets, required for permanent exhibition, may be ordered in advance ($1.75 handling fee) by calling 800/400-9371; same-day tickets available free from museum box office, open daily at 9 a.m. in summer and at 10 a.m. rest of the year. See map on page 30. (2 hours)*

★★ **National Archives**—Even if you can't stay for long, it's worth visiting the National Archives to view some of the nation's most important historical documents. Here the Declaration of Independence, United States Constitution, and Bill of Rights are sealed within bronze and glass cases. Other notable artifacts include the Emancipation Proclamation, the Japanese surrender papers from World War I, and some of the Watergate tapes, along with Richard Nixon's letter of resignation.

Details: Constitution Ave. between 7th and 9th Sts. NW; 202/501-5000. Open 10–5:30, later in summer. Free. See map on page 30. (1 hour)

★★ **National Geographic Society's Explorers Hall**—Ever touched a tornado? Explored the solar system? Looked at Earth from 23,000 miles away? These are a sample of the interactive activities available at the National Geographic Society's Explorer's Hall, located at the Society's headquarters. Here advanced technology takes you around the planet. Visitors may begin their tour with a seven-minute video showcasing the Society's work, which began in 1888. Geographica, an interactive science center, demonstrates how caves are formed and showcases the study of humankind's origins. Short-term exhibitions focus on topics as diverse as dinosaurs in Africa and a frozen Inca mummy in the Andes. Other artifacts on display include a 3.9 billion-year-old moon rock, equipment from Admiral Robert E. Perry's 1909 expedition to the North Pole, and a model of the diving saucer in which Jacques Cousteau dropped 25,000 feet beneath the surface of the ocean. Don't miss the opportunity to take your seat in Earth Station One, a 72-seat amphitheater that takes visitors on a journey around the world.

Details: 1145 17th St. at M St. NW; 202/857-7588. Open Mon–Sat 9–5, Sun 10–5. Free. See map on page 42. (2 hours)

★★ **Washington National Cathedral**—Completed in 1990, the Washington National Cathedral is the sixth largest in the world. At 676 feet above sea level, the top of its central tower is the highest point in Washington. It was in 1907 that the cathedral's foundation stone was laid, with President Theodore Roosevelt speaking at the ceremony. The cathedral is in the fourteenth-century Gothic style with nave, flying buttresses, transepts, ribbed vaulting, and gargoyles. While administered by the Episcopal Church, it serves as a house of prayer for all people. Helen Keller and President Woodrow Wilson are among those interred here. While visiting the cathedral, be sure to stop at **Bishop's Garden**, a traditional English-style garden located on the grounds with boxwoods, ivy, tea roses, yew trees, and an assortment of stonework from European ruins.

Details: Massachusetts and Wisconsin Aves.; 202/537-6200. Open Mon–Sat 10–4:30 (extended in summer), Sun 12:30–4:30. Gardens open daily until dusk. Guided tours available Mon–Sat 10–11:30 and 12:45–3:15, Sun 12:30–2:45. Donations requested. See map on page 46. (1 hour)

SURROUNDING AREA

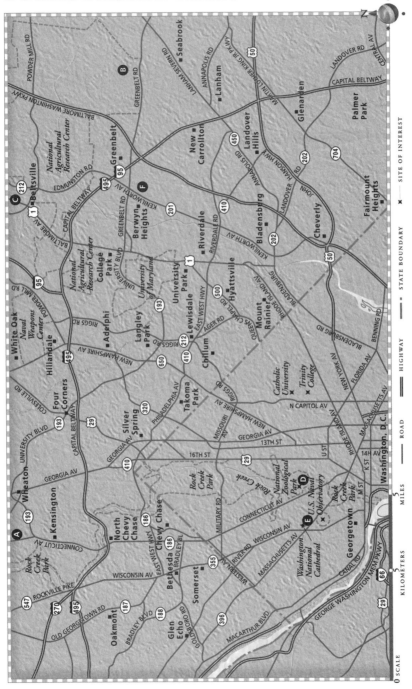

Sights

Ⓐ Brookside Gardens

Ⓑ Goddard Space Flight Center

Ⓒ National Cryptologic Museum

Ⓓ National Zoological Park

Ⓔ Washington National Cathedral

Camping

Ⓕ Greenbelt Park

✩ **Folger Shakespeare Library**—The world's largest collection of the Bard's printed works is housed at the Folger Shakespeare Library, a gift to the American people from Henry Clay Folger and his wife Emily Jordan Folger. Today the collection consists of more than 280,000 books and manuscripts; 27,000 paintings, drawings, engravings, and prints; and a variety of musical instruments, costumes, and films. However, most of these holdings are accessible only to scholars and researchers. Other visitors may view changing exhibits in the Great Hall, tour the Elizabethan Theatre, or stroll through the Elizabethan Garden. The library also regularly schedules concerts, plays, lectures, and readings.
    Details: 201 E. Capitol St. SE; 202/544-4600 or 202/544-7077 (box office). Open Mon–Sat 10–4. Tours given Mon–Fri at 11 a.m., Sat at 11 a.m. and 1 p.m. Free. See map on page 30. (30 minutes)

✩ **National Aquarium**—Established in 1932, the National Aquarium is the oldest public aquarium in the country, although it can hardly compete with some of the newer, larger aquariums in Baltimore, Boston, and New York. Housed in the basement of the Department of Commerce Building, the aquarium is home to some 1,700 creatures representing more than 200 varieties of fish, amphibians, and reptiles. An open tank allows visitors to touch and/or inspect sea urchins, starfish, and snails. Look for the shark feedings each Monday, Wednesday, and Saturday at 2 p.m.; and piranha feedings on Tuesday, Thursday, and Sunday at 2 p.m.
    Details: Pennsylvania Ave. and 14th St. NW; 202/482-2825. Open daily 9–5. $2 adults. See map on page 30. (1–2 hours)

☆ **Union Station**—When it opened with great fanfare in 1907, Union Station was the largest train station in the world. By the early 1980s, as a result of steady decline in train travel, the station had fallen into disrepair and rain seeped through its roof. In 1988, following a major renovation, the station unveiled a second time and is once again a thriving train station with three levels of shops, restaurants, and entertainment. Its elegant 96-foot-high ceiling makes the building one of the city's great public spaces and a fitting venue for inaugural balls and other events.

Details: 50 Massachusetts Ave. between 1st and 2nd Sts. NE; 202/371-9441. Shops open Mon–Sat 10–9, Sun 12–6. See map on page 42. (1–2 hours)

☆ **United States National Arboretum**—The National Arboretum stands out as an oasis in one of Washington's grittier neighborhoods. Situated on 444 acres, the arboretum's 9.5 miles of roads take visitors through rhododendrons, azaleas, magnolias, holly trees, peonies, ferns, and other flora. Visitors are urged to stop by the National Herb Garden and National Bonsai Collection, a gift from Japan, featuring more than 50 miniature trees, some of which are more than 300 years old. Tours, lectures, and workshops are offered on a regular basis.

Details: 3501 New York Ave. NE; 202/245-2726. Open daily 8–5. Free. See map on page 42. (1–2 hours)

Brookside Gardens—Covering 50 acres, Brookside Gardens encompasses a variety of themed gardens, including winter, formal, rose, fragrance, and azalea gardens. In addition, two conservatories showcase seasonal flower displays and permanent tropical plants. Guided tours are available, along with a horticultural library and educational programs.

Details: 1500 Glenallan Ave., Wheaton, Maryland; 301/949-8230. Open daily 9 a.m.–dusk. Free. See map on page 46. (1 hour)

Capital Children's Museum—Upon first sight, the Capital Children's Museum appears to lack some of the contemporary dazzle of other, better-kept offerings in the capital area. Some paint has peeled and carpets have torn. But how many of the best family playrooms suffer the same fate as a result of years of carefree play? The museum, which has a welcome international scope, is designed to be highly interactive. Kids may drive a Metrobus, slide down a firehouse pole, or make Mexican hot chocolate. They can also learn how cartoon animations are made, wander through a maze, or fill a room with gigantic soap bubbles. *Details: 800 3rd St. at H St. NW; 202/675-4125. Open Tue–Sun 10–5. $6 adults and children over 2, $4 seniors. See map on page 42. (2 hours)*

Goddard Space Flight Center—The center is named for Dr. Robert Goddard, who launched the world's first successful rocket on March 16, 1926. While the liquid-fuel rocket stayed in the air for only two and a half seconds, it made history. In 1959 NASA established the Goddard Space Flight Center as the first major scientific laboratory operating solely for the exploration of space. At the center visitors can sit inside a mock-up of the Gemini Space Capsule, tour space-related exhibits, view brief movies on the subject, and tour the grounds' collection of rockets. Reservations can be made for special presentations. *Details: Soil Conservation and Greenbelt Rds., Greenbelt, Maryland; 301/286-8981; open daily 9–4; tours Mon–Sat at 11:30 and 2:30. Free. See map on page 46. (1 hour)*

National Cryptologic Museum—Here you can learn about how the government breaks secret codes and gathers intelligence from radio signals, messages, and radar. The museum chronicles the history of intelligence from 1526 to today. On display are cryptographic books from the sixteenth century, World War II cipher machines, and a contemporary supercomputer built to break codes. *Details: Colony Seven Rd., near Fort Meade, Maryland; 301/688-5849. Open Mon–Fri 9–3, Sat 10–2. Free. See map on page 46. (1½ hours)*

PROFESSIONAL SPORTS

Washington has much to offer pro-sports fans. The **Redskins** football team plays at Jack Kent Cooke Stadium, 301/276-6050, in Raljon, Maryland. For basketball, the **Washington Wizards** play at the 20,600 seat MCI Center, 601 F Street NW, 202/624-9732. Hockey fans can witness the **Washington Capitals**, also at the MCI Center. For tickets to MCI Center events, call Ticketmaster, 202/432-SEAT. For baseball you'll need to go to where the rest of Washington goes to view the sport: Baltimore (see chapter 7). For details on the **Orioles** schedule, call Oriole Park at Camden Yards, 410/685-9800.

FITNESS AND RECREATION

No doubt walking to and from, in and around Washington's many cultural attractions will provide even diehard fitness fans with more than enough exercise in the course of day. Still, if you become totally saturated with museums and cerebral exercises, you'll find several options for unwinding. For nearby biking and boating opportunities, see the chapters on **Georgetown** and the **C&O Canal**. Runners enjoy the 4.5-mile loop encircling the **Mall**, which passes the Capitol, the Smithsonian museums, the reflecting pool, and the Lincoln Memorial. Washington is also extremely fortunate to have **Rock Creek Park**, a 1,750-acre greenbelt, within its boundaries. In addition to 15 miles of trails that take you into unspoiled woods, the park has a bicycle path, a bridle path, playgrounds, and picnic areas. The Rock Creek Park Horse Center at the corner of Military and Glover Roads NW, 202/362-0117, offers year-round lessons and trail rides. Those seeking to navigate the waters of the Potomac should inquire at the **Thompson Boat Center**, 2900 Virginia Ave. NW, 202/333-9543. The center rents canoes, rowing shells, and kayaks from April through October from 6 a.m. to 8 p.m. Lessons are also available.

FOOD

While Washington would have trouble claiming a cuisine all its own, local restaurateurs have done a great job inventing their own tastes and borrowing from afar. Because the city has long drawn people from around the world, it has developed both an international flavor and cosmopolitan tastes. Those restaurants highlighted below are grouped according to four of the city's major geographic areas: Adams Morgan, Dupont Circle, Capitol Hill, and downtown. Be sure to consult the chapter on Georgetown for other great dining options.

By far the greatest concentration of international cuisine in Washington is found in Adams Morgan. Along its two major streets, Columbia Road and 18th Street, you'll find food from around the world, often at reasonable prices. **Meskerem**, 2434 18th St. NW, 202/462-4100, serves authentic Ethiopian fare. You have the option of dining Ethiopian-style if you wish, on leather cushions on the floor. Dishes are served with *injera*, a type of flatbread used to scoop up mouthfuls of this flavorful food. Named after the Broadway hit, **Miss Saigon**, 1847 Columbia Rd. NW, 202/667-1900, serves artfully presented Vietnamese food including spring rolls, grilled meats, and clay-pot dishes. For Brazilian, try the **Grill from Ipanema**, 1858 Columbia Rd. NW, 202/986-0757, known for serving *feijoada*, a traditional stew, on certain days of the week.

For a lively atmosphere and great people watching, **Perry's**, 1811 Columbia Rd. NW, 202/234-6218, is the place. In the summertime its roof deck is a local hot spot. In addition to sushi dishes, other menu items include fresh seafood dishes, "Perry's bouillabaisse," and designer pizzas. A few doors down is **Cashion's Eat Place**, 1819 Columbia Rd. NW, 202/797-1819. Cashion's features a changing modern-American menu with plenty of seafood options, garlic mashed potatoes, and great desserts. Also popular is **Cities**, 2424 18th St. NW, 202/328-7194. Cities is best known for frequently changing its decor and its menu to reflect tastes from different regions of the world.

Dupont Circle boasts a variety of great restaurants, a number of which offer outdoor dining. Most can be found while strolling on Connecticut Avenue north of the circle itself. For more than 30 years **Kramerbooks & Afterwords Café**, 1517 Connecticut Ave. NW, 202/387-1462, has dominated as one of the most popular neighborhood hangouts. Open 24 hours a day, it's a coffeehouse, full-service restaurant, and bookstore all in one. As if to rally the two neighborhood Starbucks, tea drinkers now have a rival outpost: **Teaism**. Located at 2009 R St. NW, 202/667-3827, it's a teahouse in the Asian tradition, serving a vast variety of teas, curried dishes, tandoori kabobs, noodle salads, chutneys, and Asian box meals. Diners order at the counter and pick up their meal when their number's called. This is great food at a reasonable price. Another Asian option is **Raku**, 1900 Q St. NW, 202/265-RAKU. From skewered chicken and shrimp to a variety of noodle dishes, Raku offers a melange of tastes from China, Japan, Thailand, Indonesia, and elsewhere in Asia.

Another local favorite is **City Lights of China**, 1731 Connecticut Ave. NW, 202/265-6688. Occupying a space below street level, City Lights offers both traditional and unusual Chinese dishes and gets high ratings for consistently good food. For Italian, try **La Tomate**, 1701 Connecticut Ave. NW, 202/667-5505. Its white tablecloths, windows overlooking Connecticut Avenue, pasta dishes, and rich desserts all contribute to a satisfying meal. Across the street is the **Odean Café**, 1714 Connecticut Ave. NW, 202/328-6228, offering a livelier, decidedly louder, Italian experience.

One of the most popular, healthy, and romantic restaurants in the

NORTHWEST WASHINGTON, D.C.

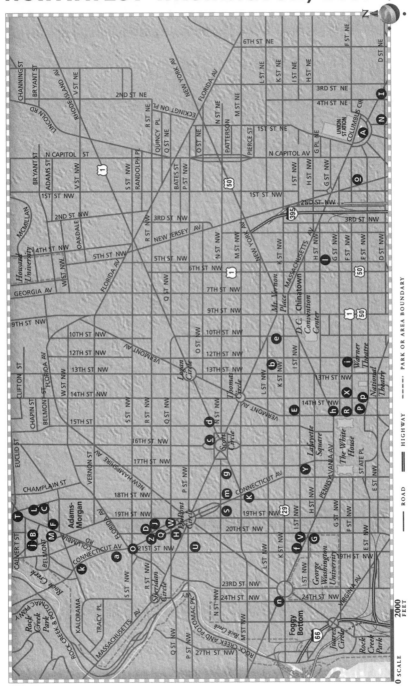

Food

- Ⓐ America
- Ⓑ Cashion's Eat Place
- Ⓐ Center Cafe
- Ⓒ Cities
- Ⓓ City Lights of China
- Ⓔ Georgia Brown's
- Ⓕ Grill from Ipanema
- Ⓖ Kinkead's
- Ⓗ Kramerbooks and Afterwords Café
- Ⓘ La Brasserie
- Ⓙ La Tomate
- Ⓚ Le Lion D'or
- Ⓛ Meskerem
- Ⓜ Miss Saigon
- Ⓝ The Monocle
- Ⓞ Nora's
- Ⓟ Occidential Grill
- Ⓠ Odean Café
- Ⓡ Old Ebbitt Grill
- Ⓢ Palm Restaurant
- Ⓣ Perry's
- Ⓤ Pesce
- Ⓥ Primi Piatti
- Ⓦ Raku
- Ⓧ Red Sage Café and Chili Bar
- Ⓨ Taberna del Alabardera
- Ⓩ Teaism

Lodging

- ⓐ Courtyard Marriott
- ⓑ Days Inn Premier
- ⓒ Doubletree Park Terrace
- ⓓ Holiday Inn Central
- ⓔ Hostelling International
- ⓕ Hotel Lombardy
- ⓖ Hotel Tabard Inn
- ⓗ Hotel Washington
- ⓘ J. W. Marriott Hotel
- ⓙ Kalorama Guest House
- ⓚ Normandy Inn
- ⓛ Red Roof Inn
- ⓜ Renaissance Mayflower Hotel
- ⓝ St. James
- ⓞ Washington Court Hotel
- ⓟ Willard Inter-Continental Hotel

Note: Items with the same letter are located in the same town or area.

area is **Nora's**, 2132 Florida Ave. NW, 202/462-5143. Located in a renovated brick townhouse, Nora's serves fresh, delicious organic cuisine in a soothing atmosphere. Reservations are recommended at this upscale spot. For great seafood, try **Pesce**, 2016 P St. NW, 202/466-FISH. Pesce offers a casual atmosphere with colorful hand-painted wooden fish hanging from exposed brick walls. The menu changes daily, reflecting the freshest catches.

On Capitol Hill the best place to try to spot the occasional congressperson is **The Monocle**, 107 D St. NE, 202/546-1002, though the food is rather average. For a wide variety of quick foods, try the Food Court at Union Station, 50 Massachusetts Ave. NE. The station houses several restaurants including **America**, 202/682-9555; and the **Center Café**, 202/682-0143, a two-level, oval restaurant situated in the center of the main hall. Housed in two adjoining townhouses, **La Brasserie**, 239 Massachusetts Ave. NE, 202/546-9154, offers traditional French food and outdoor dining in warm-weather months.

Downtown D.C. features a range of excellent restaurants to suit a variety of budgets. It's worth a visit to the city's oldest saloon, the **Old Ebbit Grill**, 675 15th St. NW, 202/347-4801, where you can often see prominent D.C. movers and shakers. The menu includes everything from burgers to oysters to roast leg of lamb. A more costly spot to people-watch is the venerable **Palm Restaurant**, 1225 19th St. NW, 202/293-9091. Featuring American/Italian food, the walls feature caricatures of politicians and media personalities who have dined here.

Southwestern food connoisseurs will love the **Red Sage Café and Chili Bar**, 605 14th St. NW, 202/638-4444. The restaurant has an upscale dining area downstairs and the more casual Chili Bar upstairs for the cost-conscious. The decor exudes the Wild West with buffalo-hide upholstery, a Western landscape mural, and a painted sky with clouds and lightning. For a taste of the New South, try **Georgia Brown's**, 950 15th St. NW, 202/393-4499, for everything from fried green tomatoes to beef tenderloin with a bourbon-pecan sauce.

Kinkead's, 2000 Pennsylvania Ave. NW, 202/296-7700, features new American cuisine in an elegant, contemporary setting. Downstairs, you can dine for less on tapas and raw bar fare; while more expensive, impeccably flavored seafood entrées are available upstairs. Across the street, **Primi Piatti**, 2013 I St. NW, 202/223-3600, offers Italian cuisine at moderate prices.

If you have the money to spend on true "haute cuisine," Washington has a number of options. **Coeur de Lion**, 926 Massachusetts

Ave. NW, 202/414-0500, serves continental cuisine, exquisitely prepared. Reservations are essential, as are a jacket and tie. Located within
the Willard Hotel, the **Occidental Grill**, 1475 Pennsylvania Ave. NW,
202/783-1475, features innovative "new American" dishes in elegant
surroundings. For the best of Spanish cuisine, try **Taberna del
Alabardera**, 1776 I St. NW, 202/429-2200. It offers sophisticated dining and unsurpassed tapas.

LODGING

Washington offers a wide variety of places to stay depending on your
price range and preferred location. While a number of the less-
expensive chains have hotels located near the Mall and its myriad cultural offerings, smaller, more quaint accommodations are a quick metro
ride away. As the number of area visitors fluctuates throughout the year,
be sure to ask for discounts and special rates. If a hotel is undersold during any given weekend, chances are you'll get a better deal. For additional lodging suggestions, see the chapter on Georgetown.

For information on and reservations at area bed-and-breakfasts,
try the **Bed and Breakfast League/Sweet Dreams and Toast**, P.O.
Box 9490, Washington, D.C. 20016, 202/363-7767. A similar service is
Bed & Breakfast Accommodations Ltd., P.O. Box 12011, Washington, D.C. 20005, 202/328-3510.

Undoubtedly the cheapest place to stay in Washington is
Hostelling International, located near the capital's major attractions
at 1009 11th St. NW, 202/737-2333. A popular destination among foreign travelers, its facilities include a communal kitchen, laundry, lock-
ers, game room, and small store where basic sundries and food can be
purchased. The cost is $18 for members and $21 for nonmembers.

A favorite resting place in Washington, whether for a relaxed meal
or overnight stay, is the **Hotel Tabard Inn**, 1739 N St. NW, 202/785-
1277. Tucked away on a quiet side street just two blocks from Dupont
Circle, the inn—named after the famous hostelry in Chaucer's *Canterbury
Tales*—is the oldest continuously operated hotel in Washington. Its 40
guest rooms are furnished with antiques and, while some pieces are a bit
more frayed than others, the hotel retains an Old World charm. Before
or after a night out, guests may sink into the couches in the main drawing room, complete with cozy fireplace, wood paneling, and a low ceiling. The dining room serves breakfast, lunch, and dinner, with a
courtyard for warm-weather dining. Single rooms with a private bath run

$99 to $150, rooms with a shared bath $59 to $90. Each additional person pays $15. Room rates include a complimentary breakfast.

Located on a quiet, tree-lined street just blocks from Adams Morgan and a short distance from Dupont Circle is the **Kalorama Guest House**, 1854 Mintwood Pl. NW, 202/667-6369. Comprising four Victorian townhouses and a total of 31 rooms, the guest house offers a warm and congenial atmosphere. Rooms, many of which have decorative fireplaces, are furnished with a mixture of antiques and reproduction furniture. Rates run from $40 to $65 for a single room with shared bath ($45 to $75 for two people) and $55 to $85 for a single room with a private bath ($60 to $95 for two people). Two-room suites are also available for $80 to $115.

Within a reasonable price range are the Washington metro area's four Holiday Inns. Located six blocks from the White House and within walking distance to the Mall is the **Holiday Inn Central**, Rhode Island at 15th Street NW, 202/483-2000 or 800/248-0016. If you can endure the Musac in the front lobby, you'll enjoy the cheerful environment, variety of room options, underground parking, rooftop swimming pool, and fitness room. Rates run from $69 to $179 depending upon availability. Also reasonably priced but a little more worn in appearance is the **Days Inn Premier**, located near the Convention Center at 1201 K Street NW, 202/842-1020 or 800/562-3350. Rooms run from $69 to $105.

Located close to China Town restaurants and within walking distance of many attractions, including the Smithsonian museums, is the **Red Roof Inn**, 500 H St. NW, 800/234-6423 or 202/289-5959. Amenities include an exercise room, sauna, gift shop, and coffee shop. Rooms start at $75 (in the off-season), $115 during busier months.

Just north of Dupont Circle is the **Normandy Inn**, 2118 Wyoming Ave. (at Connecticut) NW, 202/483-1350. The inn was a student dormitory and later a bed-and-breakfast before being fully renovated in the mid-1990s. The atmosphere is fresh, cheerful, and relaxing. Its 75 rooms, while on the smallish side, are handsomely decorated in antique reproduction furniture and are equipped with a minifridge, small safe, ironing board, and coffeemaker. Rates run from $79 to $155 depending on the season.

Also recently renovated, the **Courtyard Marriott**, 1900 Connecticut Ave. NW, 202/332-9300, offers rooms ranging from $115 to $160. The hotel has an outside pool, a health facility, and valet parking for $10.

Located just off Washington Circle, mere blocks from George-town and the Kennedy Center, is the **St. James**, 950 24th St. NW, 202/457-0050 or 800/852-8512. Suites are very nicely decorated with stocked kitchens, sofa beds, and marble baths. The hotel offers an out-door pool, exercise facility, and underground parking for an additional fee. Rates run from $115 to $135 for a studio, $145 to $195 for a one-bedroom suite, and $225 to $275 for a two-bedroom suite. Be sure to call ahead and inquire about any weekend specials.

Well situated within view of the Washington Monument and just six blocks north of the White House is the **DoubleTree Park Terrace**, 1515 Rhode Island Ave. NW, 202/232-7000 or 800/222-TREE. Its 220 rooms are furnished with antique reproductions and offer voicemail and a minibar. Suites with kitchenettes are also avail-able. Prices range from $99 to $179.

Close to the National Theater and the Mall is the **J.W. Marriott Hotel**, 1331 Pennsylvania Ave. NW, 202/393-2000. While the hotel, with 772 rooms, caters mostly to convention crowds, it is conveniently located and has all the amenities, including an indoor pool, sauna, two restaurants, and two lounges. Rooms start at $89 (during the slow sea-son) and climb to $224 in the peak summer months. Within walking distance of Union Station and the Capitol is the **Washington Court Hotel**, 525 New Jersey Ave. NW, 202/628-2100 or 800/321-3010. The hotel has 250 rooms, an atrium lobby, health club, and piano bar. Rooms run from $115 to $189.

If you can afford to pay more to stay in a hotel with impeccable furnishings and a great location, try the **Hotel Lombardy**, 2019 Pennsylvania Ave. NW, 202/828-2600 or 800/424-5486. Formerly a residential building, the hotel consists of 125 spacious "apartments," each beautifully decorated using German and Italian fabrics, oriental woolens, original local art, and hand-painted, imported silk renderings. Rooms go from $120 to $150 for a single, and from $140 to $179 for a double. Master suites are also available for $150 to $180 (single) and $170 to $200 (double). The newly opened Venetian Room with its fire-place, mahogany cabinets, and spot lighting provides a dignified yet cozy refuge for drinks or a meal. Featuring fine northern Italian cuisine at reasonable prices, the Café Lombardy overlooking Pennsylvania Avenue is popular among locals as well.

Just two blocks from the White House and within walking dis-tance to the Mall is the **Willard Inter-Continental Hotel**, 1401 Pennsylvania Ave. NW, 202/628-9100. For 150 years the Willard has been a part of Washington high society and site of countless balls and special events. Indeed, the hotel has hosted heads of state from around the world and every president from Franklin Pierce in 1853 to Bill Clinton in the 1990s. Other notable guests include Mark Twain, Mae West, and the Duke of Windsor. The main lobby with its chandeliers, columns, and elaborately carved ceilings exhibits the grandeur of a bygone era. Naturally, such elegance does not come without a price. Single rooms begin at $350 and doubles at $380. One- and two-bedroom suites are available starting at $800.

Adjacent to the Willard, slightly less grand, and more affordable is the **Hotel Washington** at 15th Street and Pennsylvania Avenue NW, 202/638-5000 or 800/424-9540. Completed in 1918, the hotel is now a National Landmark planned by the same architects who designed the New York Public Library. Its outdoor rooftop bar, open from May to October, is a popular favorite among locals owing to its panoramic views of the city. Single rooms run $166 to $218, depending upon the size and view. Double rooms run $181 to $232. Suites are also available from $426 to $650.

Also holding its place in Washington history is the **Renaissance Mayflower Hotel**, 1127 Connecticut Ave. NW, 202/347-3000. The hotel was opened in 1925 for Calvin Coolidge's inauguration. Listed on the National Register of Historic Places, it's worth a look even if you're not planning to stay there. The hotel's first-floor promenade features huge crystal chandeliers, gilded ceilings, and Italian marble floors. For more than 60 years presidential inaugural balls have been held here. The hotel has 660 rooms, covering almost an entire city block. Rooms run from $135 (in the off-season) to $295.

CAMPING

Campsites are available just 12 miles northeast of downtown Washington at **Greenbelt Park**, 301/344-3948. Obviously you shouldn't expect to be surrounded by wilderness, since the area is well developed. The 1,176-acre park, open year-round, has 174 RV and tent campsites. Sites are available on a first-come, first-served basis.

NIGHTLIFE

Washington has long been famous as a cultural center, attracting some of the world's best performers and touring shows. To find out what's

playing where, consult Washington's free alternative newspaper, the
City Paper, Friday's *Washington Post* "Weekend" section, or *Where
Washington*, a complimentary magazine detailing special events, available in many hotel lobbies. Tickets to most local shows can be purchased through TicketMaster, 202/432-7382 or 800/551-7328. Same-day-of-performance, half-price tickets are available through Ticket-Place, Lisner Auditorium, 730 21st St. NW, 202/842-5387.

Each year the **Arena Stage**, Washington's most respected resident company, hosts a variety of productions presented in three theaters—the Fischandler, a theater in the round; the fan-shaped Kreeger, and the cabaret-style Old Vat Room. The Arena is located at Sixth Street and Maine Avenue SW; call 202/488-3300 for schedule information.

With an opera house, a concert hall, two stage theaters, and a film theater, the **John F. Kennedy Center for the Performing Arts**, on New Hampshire Avenue at Rock Creek Parkway, 202/467-4600 or 800/444-1324, promises a variety of cultural fare. Fifty-minute tours of the facility are given between 10 a.m. and 1 p.m. daily. Of interest is the Hall of Nations, where visitors can view flags of all nations recognized by the U.S. and gifts from more than 40 countries, including the 18 one-ton crystal chandeliers from Sweden that light the Grand Foyer. The JFK Center is open daily from 10 a.m. to 9 p.m.

For Broadway shows, check out what's playing at the **National Theater**, 1321 Pennsylvania Ave. NW, which presents pre- or post-Broadway shows throughout the year. Call 202/528-6161 or 800/447-7400 for schedule information. The **Warner Theater**, 1299 Pennsylvania Ave. NW, 202/783-4000, boasts a lavish interior and presents Broadway and Off-Broadway shows, dance, and popular music artists. The **Lincoln Theater**, 1215 U St. NW, 202/328-6000, offers gospel, jazz, R&B, and comedy acts. Tickets may be obtained through the box office or by calling 800/551-SEAT or 202/432-SEAT.

Shakespeare buffs will want to check out the **Shakespeare Theatre**, 450 7th St. NW, 202/393-2700, where four plays are staged each year by the Shakespeare Theatre troupe. In June the company performs free plays under the stars at Carter Barron Amphitheater.

In addition to theater, Washington offers a variety of nightlife options, from comedy clubs to discos to dimly lit bars featuring soothing jazz. Be sure to check the Georgetown chapter for the area's hottest venues.

Some of the best jokes in town can be heard at the **Improv**, 1140 Connecticut Ave. NW, 202/296-7008, which has welcomed top

Saturday Night Live performers as well as the likes of Jerry Seinfeld, Rosie O'Donnell, and Ellen Degeneres. Shows begin at 8:30 p.m. Sunday through Thursday and at 8:30 and 10:30 p.m. on Friday and Saturday. You can also dine there.

For dancing, there's **The Edge**, 56 L St. SE, 202/488-1200, a gigantic dance club with four dance floors and changing themes. With its high-tech, multilevel setting, **Club Zei**, 1415 Zei Alley NW (14th between H and I Streets NW), 202/842-2445, is reminiscent of some of the more popular New York dance clubs and features a wall of television sets. One of the most popular night spots in town, the **9:30 Club**, 815 V St. NW, 202/265-0930, hosts the best alternative rock bands to come through the area. For Brazilian ambiance, music, and dancing, try **Coco Loco**, 810 7th St. NW, 202/289-2626. On Fridays there's an 11 p.m. floor show featuring Brazilian exhibition dancers. If you're not up to dancing yourself, it's a great place to simply sit back and watch.

For an elegant evening of jazz, snuggle into **The Nest** at the Willard Inter-Continental Hotel, 1401 Pennsylvania Ave. NW, 202/637-7440. This cozy cocktail lounge features live jazz performances on Friday and Saturday nights by both local and nationally recognized performers. The cover charge ranges from $7.50 to $20.

2

GEORGETOWN

While officially part of Washington, Georgetown has a character all its own. Brick row houses, many of which are painted white or pastel shades, line the streets. The Potomac River forms the southern boundary of Georgetown, lending picturesque views from the walking paths, restaurants, and outdoor cafés along its banks. Long home to Washington's well-to-do, Georgetown has a number of prominent and influential residents, many of whom rue the fact that its main commercial center is now overrun most weekend nights with fun-loving twenty-somethings. Georgetown is a great place to walk, browse in book and antique stores, enjoy a variety of foods, and be entertained. Trendy shops, restaurants, and taverns are plentiful, but beware the lack of accessible parking.

Settled in the 1700s by Scottish immigrants, Georgetown is a century older than Washington proper. Originally named George after George II, it later became George Towne and finally Georgetown. Its location on the Potomac contributed to its growing role as a commercial center and tobacco port. With the completion of the C&O Canal in 1850, coal from Cumberland, Maryland, was exported through Georgetown. Oceangoing vessels loaded with coal sailed up and down the eastern seaboard unloading their cargo at major cities.

Today Georgetown isn't just about shopping and eating. Walking up and down its streets, you can admire the Georgian, Federal, and Victorian architectural styles. Dumbarton Oaks, near Georgetown's northern boundary, earned its place in history as the setting for the

GEORGETOWN

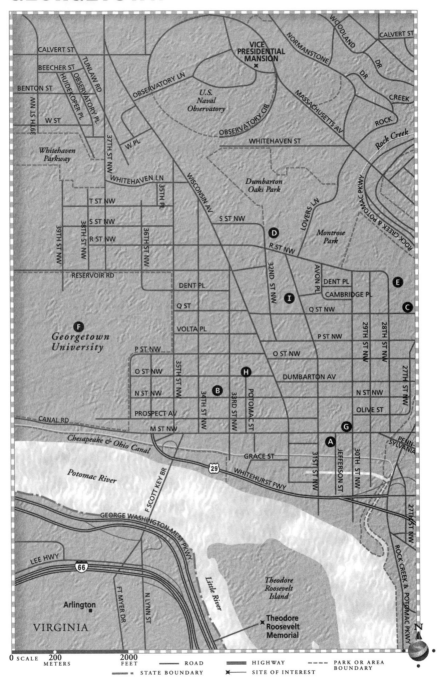

CALVERT ST
BEECHER ST
BENTON ST
TUNLAW RD
OBSERVATORY RD
HUIDEKOPER PL
OBSERVATORY PL
39TH ST NW
W ST
37TH ST NW
W PL
Whitehaven Parkway
WHITEHAVEN LN
35TH PL
T ST NW
39TH ST NW
38TH ST NW
S ST NW
R ST NW
36TH ST NW
RESERVOIR RD

OBSERVATORY LN
VICE PRESIDENTIAL MANSION ✕
U.S. Naval Observatory
OBSERVATORY CIR
WHITEHAVEN ST
WISCONSIN AV
Dumbarton Oaks Park
S ST NW
R ST NW

WOODLAND
NORMANSTONE
CALVERT ST
DR
DR
MASSACHUSETTS AV
CREEK
ROCK
Rock Creek
LOVERS LN
Montrose Park
POTOMAC PKWY
ROCK CREEK & POTOMAC

Ⓓ
DENT PL
Ⓕ
Georgetown University
Q ST
VOLTA PL
P ST NW
O ST NW
35TH ST NW
N ST NW
34TH ST NW
PROSPECT AV
M ST NW
32ND ST NW
Ⓘ
R ST NW
AVON PL
DENT PL
CAMBRIDGE PL
Ⓔ
Ⓒ
Q ST NW
P ST NW
29TH ST NW
28TH ST NW
O ST NW
Ⓗ
DUMBARTON AV
27TH ST NW
Ⓑ
33RD ST NW
POTOMAC ST
N ST NW
OLIVE ST

CANAL RD
Chesapeake & Ohio Canal
Potomac River
F SCOTT KEY BR
29
GRACE ST
WHITEHURST FWY
31ST ST NW
JEFFERSON ST
30TH ST NW
Ⓐ
Ⓖ
PENN-SYLVANIA
27TH ST NW
ROCK CREEK & POTOMAC PKWY
GEORGE WASHINGTON MEM PKWY
LEE HWY
66
FT MYER DR
N LYNN ST
Arlington
VIRGINIA
Little River
Theodore Roosevelt Island
Theodore Roosevelt Memorial ✕

N

0 SCALE 200 METERS
2000 FEET
—— ROAD
═══ HIGHWAY
---- PARK OR AREA BOUNDARY
▪▪▪ STATE BOUNDARY
✕ SITE OF INTEREST

Sights

Ⓐ Chesapeake & Ohio Canal

Ⓑ Cox's Row

Ⓒ Dumbarton House

Ⓓ Dumbarton Oaks

Ⓔ Evermay

Ⓕ Georgetown University

Ⓖ Old Stone House

Ⓗ St. John's Church

Ⓘ Tudor Place

first discussions leading to the formation of the United Nations. Its impeccable gardens are well worth a visit. Georgetown University, the first Catholic university in the nation, is a leading educational institution with renowned programs in medicine, law, foreign service, business, and the liberal arts. Schedule plenty of time for your visit and wear good walking shoes.

A PERFECT DAY IN GEORGETOWN

To experience the real historic and architectural wonders of Georgetown, you'll want to stray from the commercial hub of M Street and Wisconsin Avenue. Begin your day on the northern border of Georgetown at Dumbarton House. From there, meander past the front gates of Evermay, a Georgian manor house. Walk down 28th Street to M Street (it's all downhill) to the Old Stone House. From there head to the National Park Service office at the C&O Canal, where you can learn about the canal and, from April to October, enjoy mule-drawn boat rides. After exploring the canal, visit the nearby Washington Harbour complex and have lunch. Then walk up to the 3300 block of N Street to Cox's Row. From there you can continue walking west to Georgetown University or turn around and walk past the exterior of St. John's Church. Nearby Wisconsin Avenue is lined with trendy boutiques, shops, galleries, and antique stores. From there walk up to Dumbarton Oaks. Afterward, meander back down the hill on Wisconsin Avenue or 31st Street to find the perfect spot for dinner.

SIGHTSEEING HIGHLIGHTS

★★★ **Chesapeake and Ohio Canal**—The beginnings of the C&O Canal, which first opened in 1850, are a must-see during your visit to Georgetown. The canal, stretching for 184.5 miles from Georgetown to Cumberland, Maryland, is open to the public for walking, running, mountain biking, and birdwatching. For further information on the canal, see the chapter on the C&O Canal. In Georgetown, the National Park Service operates a visitors center where you can learn more about the canal and sign up for a 45-minute mule-drawn boat trip during warm-weather months.
   Details: 1057 Thomas Jefferson St. NW; 202/653-5190. Open daily Apr–Oct 8:30–4:30, weekends during the rest of the year depending upon staff availability. Boat rides $5.50 adults, $4.50 seniors, $3.50 children. (30 minutes–1 hour)

★★ **Dumbarton House**—Located not far from Dumbarton Oaks (see below), this classic example of Federal-style architecture emphasizes balance and light. The two-story brick mansion was built in roughly 1805. Today it serves as the headquarters of the National Society of the Colonial Dames of America, which purchased the house in 1928 and restored it to elegance. Eight of the rooms are decorated with period antiques. The collection includes Federal-style furniture, Chinese export porcelain, and a portrait painted by Wilson Peal in Georgetown in 1789.
   Details: 2715 Q St. NW; 202/337-2288. Open Tue–Sat 10–12:15. Closed Aug and Dec 25–Jan 1. $3 suggested donation. (1 hour)

★★ **Dumbarton Oaks**—Located just north of Georgetown proper, Dumbarton Oaks features a beautiful museum and exquisitely landscaped gardens. Its name is derived from the original great oaks that dominated the property and the name Dumbarton, after the Rock of Dumbarton in Scotland. The museum houses renowned collections of Byzantine and pre-Columbian art in a two-story brick mansion. The house was completed in 1801 with substantial additions made later in that century. The house is best known as the setting of the Dumbarton Oaks Conferences in 1944. Here allied powers gathered to discuss the formation of the United Nations. Surrounding the house is a 10-acre formal garden designed in the 1920s with elements from the Arts and Crafts movement, including teak chairs and benches, iron gates, and stone statuary.
   Details: 1703 32nd St. NW; 202/342-3200. Gardens open Apr–Oct

daily 2–6, $3 adults, $2 children and seniors; Nov–Mar daily 2–5, free. Museum open Tue–Sun 2–5, $1 suggested donation. (1½ hours)

★★ Old Stone House—Distinguished as Washington's oldest building, the Old Stone House was built in 1764 by a cabinetmaker named Christopher Layman who moved to Georgetown from Pennsylvania to take advantage of the area's increasing commercial activity. The walls of the house are made of fieldstone and six rooms have been fully restored—the kitchen, workshop, back parlor, front parlor, and two bedrooms. Each room is sparsely decorated the way it would have appeared in pre-Revolutionary times. The downstairs consists of what would have been Layman's shop and the family's kitchen; bedrooms are upstairs. The National Park Service maintains the house and the English garden in the rear, where dogwood and crabapple trees, roses, and lilies grow.
 Details: 3051 M St. NW; 202/426-6851. Open Memorial Day–Labor Day daily 9–5, rest of year Wed–Sun 9–5. Free. (30 minutes)

★★ Tudor Place—This former home of Martha Washington's granddaughter, Martha Custis Peters, stands as a fine example of neoclassical architecture. Completed in 1816, the yellow stucco house features a dramatic two-story domed portico on the south side. Inside visitors may view chairs that belonged to George Washington, Francis Scott Key's desk, and other historic items brought from Mount Vernon. The house is surrounded by extensive gardens.
 Details: 1644 31st St. NW; 202/965-0400. Tours given Tue–Fri at 10, 11:30, 1, and 2:30; Sat on the hour 10–4. Reservations strongly suggested. $6 suggested donation. (1 hour)

★ Cox's Row—The five Federal houses that make up Cox's Row (from 3327 to 3339 N Street NW) are named after John Cox, a former mayor of Georgetown, who built them in 1817. Nearby, at 3307 N Street, is the former home of John F. Kennedy and his family. Unfortunately, the houses can be viewed only from the outside, but the surrounding area makes for a lovely walk.
 Details: 3327–3339 N St. NW. (15 minutes)

★ Georgetown University—The nation's first Roman Catholic University, Georgetown was founded in 1789 by John Carroll, the first Catholic bishop in America, a statue of whom sits inside the main entrance on 37th

Street. Despite its Catholic orientation, Georgetown University has always embraced students of all religious faiths. Today's student body, numbering over 12,000, hails from more than 100 countries. The well-landscaped campus offers pleasant surroundings for a walk.

Details: 37th and O Sts. NW; 202/687-5055. (30 minutes)

✸ **St. John's Church**—Built in 1809, St. John's Church was designed by Dr. William Thornton, architect of the U.S. Capitol. Located just west of Wisconsin Avenue, the church, known for its impressive stained-glass windows, has welcomed many a president and other notable public figures.

Details: 3240 O St. NW; 202/338-1796. Mon–Fri 9 a.m.–noon and 1–3 p.m. Sunday services held at 9 and 11 a.m. (15 minutes)

Evermay—Though you may catch a glimpse of Evermay only from outside its front gate, this Georgian manor is a sight to behold. Built in the early 1800s by Samuel Davidson, the mansion is now privately owned.

Details: 1623 28th St. NW. (10 minutes)

FITNESS AND RECREATION

While walking the streets of Georgetown can in itself be considered good exercise, several areas access walking, jogging, and biking trails. With its views of the Potomac, the **C&O Canal** towpath provides a picturesque walking or jogging route. The Georgetown portion of the towpath can get congested with visitors, but the further west you go, the less foot traffic you'll encounter. **Rock Creek Park** offers a clearly marked path, also accessible from M Street near the Four Seasons Hotel. If stairs are your thing, try climbing or running the 75 **"Excorcist Steps,"** so called because of their appearance in the film by that name. The foot of the stairs can be accessed at M and 36th Streets. Several outfits in town rent biking equipment as well as sculls, kayaks, and canoes for navigating the Potomac.

FOOD

What Georgetown lacks in accessible parking it more than makes up for in abundant dining options. From wood-paneled pubs that have served area residents for more than 50 years to ethnic eateries, trendy hot spots, and quiet, romantic hideaways, you'll find a restaurant that satisfies.

For inexpensive French fare in a casual atmosphere, try **Café La Ruche**, 1039 31st St. NW, 202/965-2591. Tucked away on a quiet side street, the café serves soups, salads, quiches, sandwiches, and mouthwatering pastries in an authentic setting complete with Parisian street signs. In the summer months, patrons can dine beneath the stars in the café's garden courtyard. Also serving reasonably priced French food is **La Madeleine**, 3000 M St. NW, 202/337-6975, a combination café and cafeteria. Diners select their food with tray in hand. La Madeleine serves fresh-baked croissants, sandwiches on baguettes, salads, pizzas, pasta, and dinner entrées including lamb *navarin* and seafood cocotte. The cafeteria approach allows diners to see what they're getting and save on tipping while the exposed brick walls and wooden beams create a warm, Old World atmosphere.

If you're in the mood for a neighborhood pub atmosphere, there are plenty to choose from. Opened in 1933, **Martin's Tavern**, 1254 Wisconsin Ave. NW, 202/333-7370, is extremely popular among the Washington glitterati, including journalists, congresspeople, and the occasional cabinet member. Past regulars include John F. Kennedy, Richard Nixon, and Lyndon Johnson. Martin's features intimate booths, dark wood paneling, white tablecloths, and walls decorated with classic hunting prints. In addition to great weekend brunches, the tavern serves lunches and dinners with an assortment of beef, seafood, and pasta dishes. Strategically located at the corner of Wisconsin and M Streets, **Nathan's**, 3150 M St. NW, 202/338-2000, has long been an area hot spot. A clubby bar, Nathan's also serves surprisingly good food. Also popular, though far more predictable, is **Houston's**, 1065 Wisconsin Ave. NW, 202/338-7760. Serving chicken, steak, ribs, burgers, and salads, Houston's draws big crowds. Open 24 hours a day, **Au Pied de Cochon**, 1335 Wisconsin Ave. NW, 202/333-5440, is a popular place to meet for a drink or enjoy hearty French food, including quiches, crêpes, ratatouille, and coq au vin. The walls are decorated with black-and-white photographs of its more prominent patrons.

If touring the Georgetown campus or simply trying to get a feel for campus life, stop into **The Tombs**, 1226 36th St. NW, 202/337-6668, a favorite among local residents, and faculty and students at the university. Occupying a nineteenth-century Federal-style home, The Tombs has low ceilings and exposed brick walls, creating a cozy, and at times rowdy, atmosphere. Menu items range from burgers, salads, and sandwiches to reasonably priced specials like broiled salmon. Arrive during off-hours to avoid waiting for a table.

GEORGETOWN

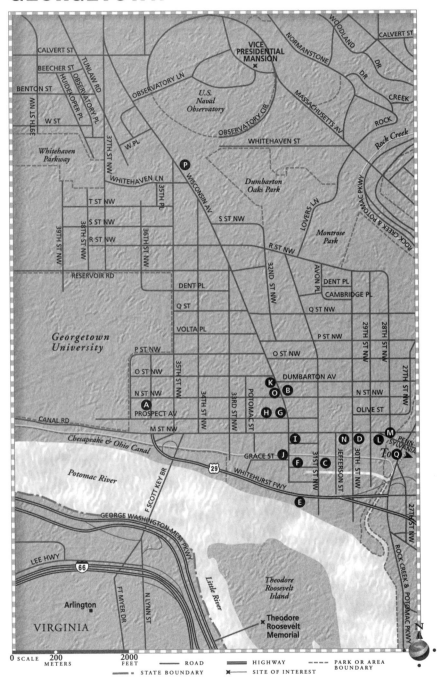

Food

- **A** 1789
- **B** Au Pied de Cochon
- **C** Café La Ruche
- **D** Citronelle
- **E** Hisago
- **F** Houston's
- **D** La Madeleine
- **G** Martin's Tavern
- **H** Morton's of Chicago
- **I** Nathan's
- **J** Pappa Razzi
- **K** Sarinah Satay House
- **E** Sequoia
- **A** The Tombs
- **L** Vietnam Georgetown

Lodging

- **M** Four Seasons Hotel
- **N** Georgetown Dutch Inn
- **O** Georgetown Inn
- **P** Holiday Inn Georgetown
- **D** Latham Hotel
- **Q** Wyndham Bristol Hotel

Note: Items with the same letter are located in the same town or area.

Georgetown is home to a number of trendy restaurants with lively decor and creative cuisine. For one of the best restaurant views—if not *the* best—in the city, try **Sequoia**, 3000 K St. NW, 202/944-4200, in the Washington Harbour complex. Sequoia has high ceilings and gigantic windows looking out over the Potomac. In the summer, its terrace with umbrella-shaded tables is particularly popular. Diners may choose from salads and pasta to more expensive seafood, poultry, and meat dishes such as charcoal-grilled venison loin and grilled pork tenderloin with garlic smashed potatoes. Reservations are recommended. Also popular is **Papa Razzi**, 1066 Wisconsin Ave. NW, 202/298-8000, for its lively atmosphere and unique setting in a former firehouse. The menu features classic Italian cuisine, including salads, pizzas from its wood-burning oven, pasta, and meat dishes. As befits a restaurant of this name, celebrity photographs deck the walls.

Diverse flavors from around the world are to be enjoyed at a host of ethnic restaurants in Georgetown. **Vietnam Georgetown**, 2934 M St. NW, 202/337-4536, serves authentic Vietnamese cuisine in an upscale setting. Dishes include delicately seasoned soups, curried soft-shell crab, charcoal-grilled shrimp with thin noodles, and cinnamon beef with orange. In warm-weather months, seating is available in the restaurant's outdoor garden, festooned with little white lights.

Although on the pricey side, **Hisago**, 3050 K St. NW, 202/944-4181, serves traditional Japanese fare including sushi, sashimi, and tempura dishes in an authentic environment. The restaurant is located in the Washington Harbour complex on the shores of the Potomac. To take advantage of a rare opportunity to sample Indonesian cuisine, try the **Sarinah Satay House**, 1338 Wisconsin Ave. NW, 202/337-2955. In addition to a succulent array of chicken, shrimp, and beef satays, the restaurant serves a variety of curry and noodle dishes.

If money is no object, you'll find many fine dining establishments in Georgetown. **Citronelle**, 3000 M St. NW, 202/625-2150, located in the Lantham Hotel, is one of the finest restaurants in the Washington area. Famous for his particular brand of California French cuisine, Chef Michel Richard is known to inject a bit of whimsy into his creations. The restaurant recently underwent a costly renovation making it all the more spectacular. If you feel like a great meal and don't want to shell out for dinner, try lunch, which is available on weekdays. Reservations are recommended. If meat is what you're after, there's no place quite like **Morton's of Chicago**, 3251 Prospect St. NW, 202/342-6258, where a cart of exquisite cuts of beef is literally wheeled up to your table so you can make a truly informed decision. Seafood lovers, rest assured, Morton's also caters to your tastes.

To immerse yourself in the historic architecture of the city while dining, try **1789**, 1226 36th St. NW, 202/965-1789. Occupying an eighteenth-century house near the Georgetown University campus, the restaurant is decorated with early American furnishings and etchings for a quiet, elegant atmosphere. The food, while pricey, is superb. Reservations are highly recommended.

LODGING

Georgetown offers a number of lodging options ranging from practical accommodations with in-room cooking facilities to elegant, high-priced hotels. For additional lodging options nearby, see the chapters on Washington and on Arlington and Alexandria.

For a reasonably priced stay in Georgetown, try the **Holiday Inn Georgetown**, 2101 Wisconsin Ave. NW, 202/338-4600 or 800/HOLIDAY. Located roughly a half-mile north of busy M Street, the inn is convenient to the action of Georgetown without being in the middle of it. Its 296 rooms were recently renovated and run $79 in the off-season winter months and $149 in the peak months of May through November. Also moderately priced is the **Wyndham Bristol Hotel**, 2430 Pennsylvania Ave. NW, 202/955-6400 or 800/WYNDHAM. The Wyndham is located on the edge of Georgetown, close to downtown attractions, the John F. Kennedy Center for the Performing Arts, and the Foggy Bottom metro stop. Its guest rooms and suites all have kitchen areas and minibars. Rooms begin at $104 in the off-season and rise to $145 in busy months. Be sure to inquire about any weekend specials or discounts. Located in the heart of Georgetown is the **Georgetown Dutch Inn**, 1075 Thomas Jefferson St. NW, 202/337-0900 or 800/388-2410. The all-suite inn is housed in a brick building and offers a complimentary breakfast and free parking (a real benefit in light of the area's congested streets). Suites consist of a living room, one or two bedrooms, and kitchen area with a refrigerator, stove, and sink. Prices range from $115 to $175 depending on the season and occupancy rates.

On the more expensive side is the **Georgetown Inn**, 1310 Wisconsin Ave. NW, 202/333-8900. The hotel bills itself as a "traditional American inn with fine European style and Colonial warmth." Housed in an understated brick building, the inn has 95 rooms and suites, along with an exercise room, restaurant, and lounge. Single rooms run from $145 to $195, double rooms from $165 to $205, and suites from $199 to $255. Valet parking is available for an additional $15. Also occupying an elegant brick building is the **Latham Hotel**, 3000 M St. NW, 202/726-5000 or 800/368-5922. Located just a short distance from the C&O Canal, the hotel is beautifully decorated and has an outdoor swimming pool. It is also home to one of the finest restaurants in the city, Citronelle. Rooms range from $189 to $350 depending on the season, with a $20 fee for additional persons.

By far the finest luxury accommodations in Georgetown are to be had at the **Four Seasons Hotel**, 2800 Pennsylvania Ave. NW, 202/342-0444 or 800/332-3442. The hotel, conveniently located within a short walk of the area's best eating and shopping opportunities, is a popular meeting place for native Washingtonians seeking elegant surroundings. Guests may take advantage of the Fitness Club, featuring the latest equipment, as well as a sauna, Jacuzzi, and indoor lap pool. For an additional fee you can partake in aerobics classes or enjoy a massage. Single rooms start at $325, doubles start at $355, and prices can run as high as $2,500 for the Presidential Suite. Weekend and holiday rates are available upon request.

NIGHTLIFE

Georgetown is frequently abuzz weekends until the wee hours of the morning. In addition to a plethora of popular bars, Georgetown offers a variety of live music options and comedy shows. Jazz enthusiasts will want to check out **Blues Alley**, 1073 Wisconsin Ave. NW, 202/337-4141, where performers such as Wynton Marsalis, Lou Rawls, and Maynard Ferguson have been known to play. New Orleans–style cuisine is also available; diners should reserve a table in advance. Shows take place Monday through Thursday and Sunday at 8 and 10 p.m. On Fridays and Saturdays an additional performance is offered at midnight. The box office is open daily from noon to 10:30 p.m. For dancing, check out **Chelsea's**, 1055 Thomas Jefferson St. NW, 202/298-8222. Chelsea's features live Latin, African, Arab, and Persian music, along with weekend performances by the Capitol Steps, a popular local comedy troupe that parodies the Washington political scene. To reserve tickets, call or stop by the box office.

3

ARLINGTON AND ALEXANDRIA

A lthough they neighbor one another, Arlington and Alexandria have distinct characteristics, and each town offers visitors something different. Covering 25.7 square miles, Arlington sprawls along the southwest bank of the Potomac, a mixture of close-knit office buildings and open spaces. There are three sights well worth seeing here: Arlington National Cemetery for the honor and patriotism it represents, the Pentagon for its sheer scale, and the Newseum for amusement as well as edification.

For out-of-towners, Alexandria is far easier to grasp because most of its major attractions are concentrated in one area. First settled in the 1670s, Alexandria became a thriving tobacco port in the early eighteenth century. In 1748 George Washington, then a surveyor, helped map out the city's streets. Robert E. Lee grew up here. The historic character of the city is preserved in the well-known area of Old Town, home to more than 2,000 eighteenth- and nineteenth-century buildings. Here you can tour any number of historic homes and sights, enjoy delicious food, and shop for antiques and arts and crafts.

A PERFECT DAY IN ARLINGTON AND ALEXANDRIA

Start your day with a visit to Arlington National Cemetery. From here make your way to the Newseum, equally popular among older children and adults. Then head to Alexandria to enjoy lunch and a leisurely stroll around Old Town. A recommended first stop is the visitors cen-

ARLINGTON

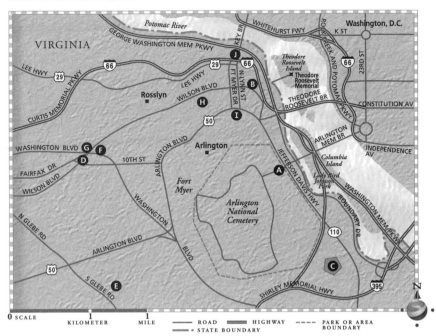

Sights

Ⓐ Arlington National Cemetery

Ⓑ Newseum

Ⓒ The Pentagon

Food

Ⓓ Café Dalat

Ⓔ Carlyle Grand Cafe

Ⓕ Little Viet Garden

Ⓖ Queen Bee Restaurant

Ⓗ Red, Hot & Blue

Lodging

Ⓘ Days Inn Arlington

Ⓙ Key Bridge Marriott Hotel

ter at Ramsay House, where you can pick up maps and information on guided walking tours of the city. You can step back in time with a visit to the boyhood home of Robert E. Lee and/or the Carlyle House, or view contemporary arts and crafts at the Torpedo Factory Arts Center.

ARLINGTON SIGHTSEEING HIGHLIGHTS

The Arlington Visitors Center is located at 735 S. 18th St., 703/358-5720 or 800/677-6267.

★★★ **Newseum**—Ever wondered how you'd look as a television news reporter in front of the White House? Ever dreamed of seeing your face on the cover of *Sports Illustrated?* Curious about what was going on in the world the day you were born? You can find out at the Newseum, a unique institution filled with interactive exhibits and demonstrations that bring alive the world of newsgathering. Included is a visual history of newsgathering from the spoken stories of ancient times to today's information superhighway. On display is the greatest collection of historic newspapers, magazines, and news broadcasts ever assembled. At the Ethics Center you can learn about the difficult choices faced by journalists every day. Freedom Park memorializes those journalists who lost their lives reporting the news. In the Interactive Newsroom you can try your hand at being a reporter or editor, create your own television broadcast, or see how you'd look as a weather person. A Birthday Banner interactive touch screen allows you to pull up the headlines from the day you were born. While entry to the museum is free, a fee is charged for taking home your own video broadcasts, magazine covers, or Birthday Banners.
   Details: 1101 Wilson Blvd.; 703/284-3544 or 888-NEWSEUM. Open Wed–Sun 10–5. Free. (1–2 hours)

★★ **Arlington National Cemetery**—Directly across the Potomac River from Washington is Arlington National Cemetery, established as the nation's cemetery in 1864. Row after row of simple white headstones mark the graves of more than 250,000 American war dead. Among those buried here are William Howard Taft, Oliver Wendell Holmes Jr., Rear Admiral Robert Peary, William Jennings Bryan, Justice Earl Warren, and General Omar Bradley. To the west of the visitors center are the Kennedy graves, where President John F. Kennedy,

Department of the Army

Members of the 3rd U.S. Infantry place flags in Arlington National Cemetery.

two of his children who died in infancy, and his wife, Jacqueline
Bouvier Kennedy Onassis, are buried. Nearby is the grave of Robert
Kennedy. JFK's grave is marked by an eternal flame and excerpts from
his inaugural address. At the **Tomb of the Unknown Soldier**, the
remains of unidentified soldiers from both world wars, Korea, and
Vietnam are buried. Lying in a sarcophagus beneath the tomb is the
body of an unknown soldier brought back from France after World
War I. Soldiers from the Army's Third U.S. Infantry keep watch over
the tomb 24 hours a day. The guard is changed every half-hour April
through September and every hour the rest of the year. The land on
which the cemetery lies was once the home of Robert E. Lee and his
wife, Mary Anna Randolph Custis, great-grandaughter of Martha
Washington. **Arlington House** stands as a stellar example of Greek
Revival architecture with commanding views of Washington. The
mansion has been restored to its 1861 appearance and is now administered by the National Park Service.

*Details: West end of Memorial Bridge; 703/607-8052. Open Apr–Sept
daily 8–7, rest of the year daily 8–5. Free. Tourmobiles from visitors center
provide only motorized transportation through the cemetery. A narrated tour
covers all major points of interest. The fare is $4.75 adults, $2.25 children.
Arlington House open Apr–Sept daily 9:30–6, rest of the year daily
9:30–4:30. Free. (2 hours)*

⭐⭐ **The Pentagon**—Covering 29 acres, the Pentagon is one of the
world's largest office buildings. Its corridors alone stretch 17.5 miles.
Completed in 1943, the five-sided building houses branches of the
Department of Defense. Guided tours leave every 30 minutes with a
limit of 30 people per tour. Tours last an hour and 15 minutes.

*Details: Off Route 395; 703/695-1776. Open Mon–Fri 9:30–3:30.
Photo ID required. Free. (2 hours)*

ALEXANDRIA SIGHTSEEING HIGHLIGHTS

*The Alexandria Visitors Center, 221 King St., 703/838-4200, is located at
Ramsay House, a modern reconstruction of an eighteenth-century house.*

⭐⭐ **Torpedo Factory Arts Center**—More than 160 artists—painters,
potters, jewelry makers, sculptors, and others—display their works,
most of which are for sale, at the Torpedo Factory Museum. The
building, used to manufacture torpedo casings during the First and

ALEXANDRIA

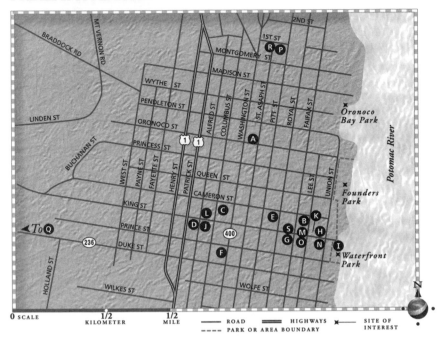

Sights

- Ⓐ Boyhood Home of Robert E. Lee
- Ⓑ Carlyle House
- Ⓒ Christ Church
- Ⓓ Friendship Firehouse Museum
- Ⓔ Gadsby's Tavern Museum
- Ⓕ The Lyceum
- Ⓖ Stabler Leadbeater Apothecary
- Ⓗ Torpedo Factory Arts Center

Food

- Ⓘ Chadwicks
- Ⓙ Elysium Dining Room

Food *(continued)*

- Ⓔ Gadsby's Tavern
- Ⓚ Landini Brothers
- Ⓛ South Austin Grill
- Ⓜ Two Nineteen
- Ⓝ Union Street Public House
- Ⓞ Warehouse Bar & Grill

Lodging

- Ⓟ Best Western Old Colony Inn
- Ⓠ Doubletree Guest Suites
- Ⓡ Holiday Inn Hotel and Suites
- Ⓢ Holiday Inn Select
- Ⓣ Morrison House

Note: Items with the same letter are located in the same town or area.

Second World Wars, is now divided into 83 studios and five galleries where visitors can watch artists and craftspeople at work. Also located in the building is the **Alexandria Archeology Museum and Laboratory,** where objects from recent excavations in Alexandria are displayed. Objects date back as far as 3,000 B.C. to the early twentieth century. *Details: 105 N. Union St.; 703/838-4565. Open daily 10–5. Archeology Museum (703/838-4399) open Tue–Fri 10–3, Sat 10–5, Sun 1–5. Free. (1 hour)*

✮ **Boyhood Home of Robert E. Lee**—For most of his early boyhood years, Confederate General Robert E. Lee lived in Alexandria. Today the stately Federal townhouse where he grew up has been restored and furnished with authentic period antiques.
Details: 607 Oronoco St.; 703/548-8454. Open Mon–Sat 10–4, Sun 1–4. $3 adults. (30 minutes)

✮ **Carlyle House**—When completed in 1753, Carlyle House was the grandest mansion in the new town of Alexandria. John Carlyle emigrated from Scotland in 1741 and became successful as a tobacco merchant. This elegant stone manor exemplifies Georgian architecture and is decorated with eighteenth-century furnishings.
Details: 121 N. Fairfax St.; 703/549-2997. Open Tue–Sat 10–4:30, Sun 12–4:30. Guided tours on the half-hour. $3 adults. (30 minutes)

✮ **Gadsby's Tavern Museum**—Built as a tavern in 1770 and added onto as a hotel in 1792, the building now housing Gadsby's Tavern Museum was once a center for Alexandria's social and political life. During his lifetime, George Washington celebrated his birthday here with a Birthnight Ball, today reenacted at the museum yearly.
Details: 134 N. Royal St.; 703/838-4242. Open Apr–Sept Tue–Sat 10–5, Sun 1–4; rest of the year Tue–Sat 11–4, Sun 1–4. $3 adults, $1 ages 11–17. (30 minutes)

✮ **The Lyceum**—Built in 1839 as the city's first cultural center, the Lyceum is now dedicated to collecting, preserving, and interpreting Alexandria's cultural and material history. Included in the permanent collection are prints, documents, photographs, furniture, and Civil War memorabilia. The museum sponsors changing exhibits, lectures, concerts, and educational programs throughout the year. Concerts are held at 4 p.m. most Sundays.

Details: 201 S. Washington St.; 703/838-4994. Open Mon–Sat 10–5, Sun 1–5. Free. (1 hour)

Christ Church—Built between 1767 and 1773, this charming church has a courtyard where 34 Confederate soldiers are buried and memorialized. Silver plaques mark the pews of George Washington and Robert E. Lee, both of whom worshiped here.
Details: 118 N. Washington St.; 703/549-1450. Open Mon–Sat 9–4, Sun 2–4. Free. (30 minutes)

Friendship Firehouse Museum—Hand-drawn fire engines and historic fire-fighting apparatus are on display at the Friendship Firehouse Museum. Established in 1774, the firehouse was the first volunteer fire company in Alexandria, with George Washington one of its founding members. The current firehouse was built in 1855 and restored in 1992. (30 minutes)
Details: 107 S. Alfred; 703/838-3891; open Fri and Sat 10–4, Sun 1–4. Free. (30 minutes)

Stabler-Leadbeater Apothecary Shop—The second-oldest apothecary shop in the country, the shop features a small museum of eighteenth-century apothecary items, including a sugar-coating machine. George Washington and members of the Robert E. Lee family were patrons of the shop.
Details: 105–107 S. Fairfax St.; 703/836-3713. Open Mon–Sat 10–4. $2 adults. (30 minutes)

FITNESS AND RECREATION

The **Mount Vernon Trail**, a 17-mile path extending from Mount Vernon through Alexandria to the Lincoln Memorial in Washington, parallels the Potomac River and is ideal for biking, jogging, and walking path. The Alexandria Visitor's Center offers a free map of sights to be seen along the trail as well as information on places to rent bikes. Another pleasant bike trip can be had on the **Old Dominion Railroad Regional Park**, a 45-mile paved linear path that connects with the Mount Vernon Trail on the Virginia side of the Potomac. For hiking and exploring close to the city, try **Theodore Roosevelt Island**, just 10 minutes from downtown D.C. The island, which has three miles of paths leading through woods and swampland and along rocky beaches, is located in the Potomac and can be reached from the Virginia side of the river. For additional information on outdoor activities near Washington, see the chapters on the C&O Canal, Frederick County, and D.C. itself, all of which list recreational activities within an hour of the city.

FOOD

The dining options listed below are grouped according to location, beginning with restaurants located in Arlington, and then by price range starting with the least expensive.

Arlington is known for its preponderance of great Vietnamese restaurants. **Little Viet Garden**, 3012 Wilson Blvd., 703/522-9686, opens its outdoor terrace during warm-weather months. Also winning consistently high ratings is the **Queen Bee Restaurant**, 3181 Wilson Blvd., 703/527-3444. **Café Dalat**, 3143 Wilson Blvd., 703/276-0935, though nothing fancy, is known for its efficient service and low-cost, high-quality food.

For an affordable, tasty meal in a lively bistro-like atmosphere, try the **Carlyle Grand Cafe**, 4000 S. 28th St., at the Village at Shirlington, 703/931-0777. The restaurant, open for lunch and dinner, specializes in new American and Californian cuisine with an emphasis on grilled foods. Its black-and-white tile floors, plants, and art deco flourishes give it a contemporary feel. Sidewalk dining is available when weather permits.

Specializing in Memphis-style barbeque, **Red, Hot & Blue**, 1600 Wilson Blvd., 703/276-7427, is known for its ribs and pulled-meat sandwiches. Photographs of famous politicians and blues musicians decorate the walls. Part of a local D.C. chain of restaurants, it's casual and affordable.

Alexandria boasts a wide variety of restaurants, from cajun to continental to colonial. One of the best pubs in town is the **Union Street Public House**, 121 S. Union St., 703/548-1785. Located just a block from the waterfront, Union Street has won many awards including *Washingtonian Magazine*'s "Best Bargain Award." The 200-year-old tavern has exposed brick walls, gas lights, pressed tin ceilings, and a quilt pattern tile floor. The menu includes a wide range of salads, sandwiches, steaks, pasta, and seafood dishes. For basic American food at a location close to the waterfront, try **Chadwicks**, 203 Strand St., 703/836-4442. The menu features a variety of salads, sandwiches, burgers, and wraps, along with seafood, chicken, and beef entrées. Multicolored booths and chili-pepper lights reinforce the Southwest theme at the **South Austin Grill**, 801 King St., 703/684-8969. A popular lunch or after-work spot, the restaurant serves a creative blend of salads, burritos, enchiladas, fajitas, and tacos.

Caricatures of local celebrities, past and present, decorate the walls of the **Warehouse Bar & Grill**, 214 King St., 703/683-6868. Specializing in New Orleans cuisine, the Warehouse is famous for its crab soup. Lunches include unique sandwiches and salads, and seafood, chicken, and beef entrées. Dinners range from pasta jambalaya to cajun veal Mardi Gras and spicy pecan-crusted chicken.

Specializing in classical Italian fare, **Landini Brothers**, 115 King St., 703/836-8404, is situated in a mid-nineteenth-century building with stone walls, slate floors, and exposed beams. The menu features traditional favorites such as melon with proscuitto, veal scaloppini, and chicken bolognese.

Strolling minstrels provide nightly entertainment for diners at **Gadsby's Tavern**, 138 N. Royal St., 703/548-1288. A true colonial dining experience is yours to be had at this eighteenth-century tavern where waiters dress in period costume. Menu items range from your basic chicken, steak, and seafood to colonial favorites like game pye, first watch stew, and English trifle. The restaurant is open for lunch, dinner, and Sunday brunch; dinner reservations are highly recommended.

For a truly elegant meal in the heart of Old Town, try **Two Nineteen**, 219 King St., 703/549-1141. Specializing in New Orleans–style creole cuisine, Two Nineteen is housed in a Victorian-era brick building with a front porch area for warm-weather dining. Lunch entrées range from Louisiana-style fried catfish to crawfish étouffée; dinner options include seafood gumbo, crabmeat imperial, shrimp *clemenceau*, and pasta jambalaya.

For a special night out, the Morrison House's **Elysium Dining Room**, 116 S. Alfred St., 703/838-8000, features creative continental fare in an elegant atmosphere. Recent menu items included veal saltimbocca and pepita-crusted salmon with sweet corn.

LODGING

The majority of hotels in Arlington are of the large chain variety. On the less expensive side is the **Days Inn Arlington**, 2201 Arlington

Blvd., 703/525-0300. Rooms run from $65 to $88. Within walking distance to Georgetown, the **Key Bridge Marriott Hotel**, 1401 Lee Hwy., 703/524-6400 or 800/327-9789, has 584 rooms, a fitness room, swimming pool, whirlpool, and beauty salon. Rooms in the front of the building overlook Washington while those in the rear have views of Georgetown and the Potomac River. Rooms run from $125 to $189 with an additional charge for parking.

In Alexandria the **Best Western Old Colony Inn**, 615 1st St., 703/739-2222 or 800/528-1234, was designed with care to reflect the historic charm of the area. The 151-room hotel has an exercise room, indoor and outdoor pools, a whirlpool, and a sauna. Rooms run from $69 to $89. Next door is the **Holiday Inn Hotel and Suites**, 625 First St., 703/548-6300 or 800/HOLIDAY. The 178-room hotel features a fitness center, garden gazebo, and complimentary parking. Rooms are $140 to $160.

The **DoubleTree Guest Suites**, 100 S. Reynolds, 703/370-9600 or 800/424-2900, features well-equipped studios and one- and two-bedroom suites, along with an outdoor pool and fitness room. All units have sleep sofas, full kitchens, and dining areas; some have terraces. Rates run from $109 to $125.

Located in the heart of Old Town, the **Holiday Inn Select**, 480 King St., 703/549-6080 or 800/368-5047, is within walking distance of most area sights. The inn, with 227 rooms, has an attractive brick courtyard and amenities including an indoor pool, sauna, workout room, enclosed parking, and free transportation to/from Reagan Airport and the Old Town metro. Rooms range from $139 to $189 during the high season from March through August. During the rest of the year guests can expect to pay $119 and up.

Without a doubt the finest hotel accommodations to be had in Alexandria are at the **Morrison House**, 116 S. Alfred St., Old Town, 703/367-0800 or 800/367-0800. The four-star hotel, designed after the grand manors of the Federal period (1790–1820), combines European and Early American features. Rooms are furnished with authentic Federal-period reproductions, including four-poster mahogany beds, brass chandeliers, and decorative fireplaces. The hotel is conveniently located within walking distance of most area sights and restaurants (although its Elysium Restaurant reputedly serves some of the best food in the city). Room rates begin at $150 and run as high as $295 for a suite. Access to a nearby health club is included. Be sure to inquire about special guest packages.

NIGHTLIFE

In Alexandria the **Alamo**, 100 King St., 703/739-0555, has live entertainment Wednesday through Sunday nights in the summer months and on weekends in the winter. Its upstairs dance floor is packed in the summer when the sounds emanating from the restaurant's open windows beckon passersby. Music ranges from R&B to rock to soul. The **Basin Street Lounge** at restaurant Two Nineteen, 219 King St., 703/549-1141, features live music ranging from swing to blues Tuesday through Saturday. A cover charge applies on weekends. For top names in folk and bluegrass music, try **The Birchmere**, 3701 Mount Vernon Ave., 703/549-5919.

4

CHESAPEAKE AND OHIO CANAL

At the time it was completed in 1850, the C&O Canal was considered an engineering marvel. Stretching 184.5 miles along the Potomac River from Washington, D.C., to Cumberland, Maryland, the canal provided a long-awaited means of transporting items such as coal, corn, wheat, flour, and lumber from inland mining and agricultural areas to the eastern seaboard. Not long after it was completed, the canal proved unable to compete with a more powerful form of transportation: the railroad. The canal was finally closed in 1924 following devastating floods, but it is now preserved as a National Historic Park for all to enjoy. On warm-weather days, walkers, joggers, cyclists, birdwatchers, fisherman, and boaters turn out to enjoy the canal's natural scenery and wildlife.

Ground was officially broken for the canal in 1828; President John Quincy Adams shoveled the first scoop of earth. The canal took 22 years to complete and cost roughly $22 million. It was divided by 74 lift locks that raised the canal bed from sea level at Georgetown to an elevation of 605 feet at Cumberland. Canal boats were generally 92 feet long and could carry cargo of up to 120 tons. The task of moving that cargo rested on the pulling power of two mules tied to the boat from a 100-foot-long rope. The mules would walk along the dirt towpath beside the canal. While the principle cargo was coal, lesser quantities of corn, wheat, flour, lumber, and limestone were shipped via the canal.

Since venturing from one end of the canal to the other is rare, this chapter focuses on the canal's most treasured spots, where you can

CHESAPEAKE AND OHIO CANAL

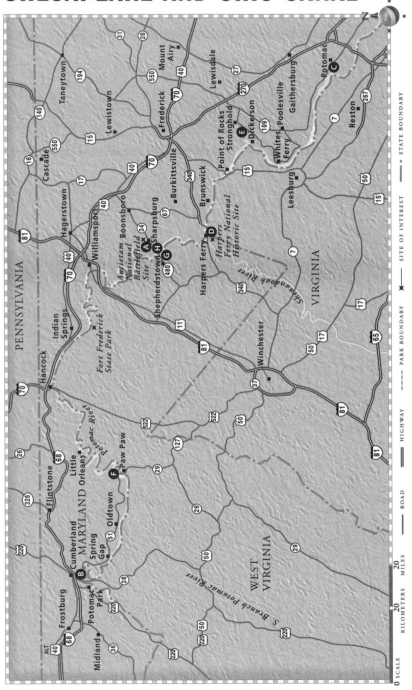

Sights

Ⓐ Antietam National Battlefield

Ⓑ Cumberland

Ⓒ Great Falls Tavern

Ⓓ Harper's Ferry, West Virginia

Ⓔ Monocacy Aqueduct

Ⓕ Paw Paw Tunnel

Ⓖ Shepherdstown, West Virginia

Food

Ⓓ The Anvil

Ⓖ Lost Dog Cafe

Ⓒ Old Anglers Inn

Ⓖ Old Pharmacy Café and Soda Fountain

Food (continued)

Ⓑ Oxford House

Ⓑ Uncle Tucker's Woodfired Pizza and Brewhaus

Ⓖ Yellow Brick Bank Restaurant

Lodging

Ⓓ Angler's Inn

Ⓖ Bavarian Inn

Ⓗ Ground Squirrel Holler

Ⓐ Inn at Antietam

Ⓑ Inn at Walnut Bottom

Note: Items with the same letter are located in the same town or area.

spend an afternoon, a day, or longer if you wish. Within a short distance of the canal are such historic sights as Antietam Battlefield and Harpers Ferry. Quaint nearby towns offer a variety of bed-and-breakfast accommodations. For information on the canal's starting point and nearby activities, see the chapter on Georgetown.

A PERFECT DAY ALONG THE CHESAPEAKE AND OHIO CANAL

The canal offers a variety of pleasant diversions—which ones you choose depends on how far you're willing to drive and on where you're starting from. If you're looking to experience nature and learn about the canal's history while staying close to Washington, consider renting a bike in Georgetown. If you start out early enough you can ride the 14 miles to the Great Falls Tavern Visitors Center, where you can enjoy great views of the rapids and, if you like, hop aboard a canal boat for a narrated ride. Pack a picnic lunch or stop by the Old Anglers Inn on the way back for a snack (albeit a costly one). Another great way to enjoy the canal is to base yourself at one of the quaint inns located near Antietam, Harpers Ferry, or Shepherdstown, West Virginia. From there you can spend the day walking parts of the canal and visiting historic sights such as Harpers Ferry and the Antietam National Battlefield. Afterward you can enjoy a pleasant afternoon strolling the streets of Shepherdstown or Harpers Ferry.

SIGHTSEEING HIGHLIGHTS

★★★ **Antietam National Battlefield**—More than 23,000 men were killed or wounded at the Battle of Antietam, where Union forces met and stopped the first Southern invasion of the North on September 17, 1862. Roughly 40,000 Southerners fought against the 87,000-man Federal Army under General George McClellan. Following the North's victory, Abraham Lincoln issued the Emancipation Proclamation on January 1, 1863, declaring free all slaves in the states in rebellion against the United States. From that point on, the war had the dual purpose of preserving the Union and ending slavery. At the battlefield's visitors center, you can view historical exhibits and a film shown on the hour. The battlefield is only four miles from Lock 38 near the bridge at Shepherdstown.

Details: Route 65, north of Sharpsburg, Maryland; 301/432-5124. Open daily June–Aug 8:30–6, Sept–May 8:30–5. $2 per person, $4 families. (1–2 hours)

★★★ **Great Falls Tavern**—Situated 14 miles upriver from Georgetown, the Great Falls Tavern played an important role throughout the canal's history. Today it provides an easy access point to the canal with stunning views of the churning white water and boulders that make up the falls. The tavern itself is now operated by the National Park Service as a visitors center and museum. Construction on the lockhouse that would eventually become the tavern began in 1828. In response to travelers' requests, the Canal Company built a three-story wing on the house to serve as a hotel. Opened in 1831, the Crommelin House soon became a center of activity and the nearby community grew to more than 100. In the 1870s, with more than 500 boats passing through the area each season, the tavern was a lively place. To demonstrate how boats passed through the lock system, canal rides are offered from mid-April through October Wednesday through Sunday. (Visitors are urged to call ahead for ticket and schedule information.) Visitors walking, biking, or fishing close to the falls are advised to exercise extreme caution; a number of accidental deaths have occurred over the years, mostly as a result of ignorance or carelessness.

Details: 11710 MacArthur Blvd., Potomac, Maryland; 301/299-3613; open daily 9–5. $4 per vehicle, $2 per person for visitors not arriving by car (tickets valid for seven days). (1–2 hours)

★★★ **Harpers Ferry, West Virginia**—Located at the confluence of the Potomac and Shenandoah Rivers separating Maryland, Virginia, and West Virginia, Harpers Ferry boasts a rich historical legacy. The town first reached prominence in the late eighteenth century because of its federal arsenal and armory, where many of the muskets and rifles used during the War of 1812 and Civil War were manufactured. Later, in 1859, abolitionist John Brown, accompanied by an 18-man army, raided the armory only to be captured by U.S. Marines under Colonel Robert E. Lee. Brown was later tried, convicted, and hung, although his actions galvanized the national debate over the issue of slavery.

Covering 2,300 acres, **Harpers Ferry National Historical Park** offers exhibits, hiking trails, and interpretive programs that explore the park's six major themes: Industry, John Brown, the Civil War, African American History, Environmental History, and Transportation. Each "Path Through History" addresses a specific set of events or circumstances that influenced the growth and development of Harpers Ferry. To make the most of your time, stop at the visitors center for information on park sites and activities including ranger-led tours and special programs.

Details: Intersection of U.S. 340 and Washington St.; 304/535-6298. Open daily 8–5. $5 per vehicle, $3 for individuals. (1–3 hours)

★★ **Cumberland**—The canal ends in Cumberland, Maryland, once a booming Victorian-era town that thrived at the crossroads of the C&O Canal and Baltimore and Ohio Railroad. Cumberland was the gateway to the frontier and an important railroad center. Begin your stay with a visit to the Allegany County Visitors Bureau in the basement of the Western Maryland train station for an orientation to area sights. Visitors can take in the city's architectural history with a walk through the **Washington Street Historic District**.

You should also try to catch a ride on the **Western Maryland**

Scenic Railroad. The railroad operates a steam locomotive, *Mountain Thunder*, which makes its way from Cumberland's Western Maryland Station Center to Frostburg's Old Depot. The 32-mile round-trip ride takes you through the Allegheny Mountains. Highlights along the trip include traveling through a mile-long gorge known as "The Narrows," over an iron truss bridge, and through a 914-foot-long Brush Mountain tunnel. For each round-trip journey, the steam engine consumes three tons of coal. The journey from Cumberland to Frostburg takes 45 minutes, with an hour-and-a-half layover in Frostburg to eat and shop.

Details: Train at 13 Canal St., 301/759-4400 or 800/872-4650. May–Sept train departs at 11:30 a.m. Tue–Sun; in Oct departures at 11 a.m. daily with an additional 4 p.m. ride Fri, Sat, and Sun; Nov– mid-Dec weekend-only departures at 11:30 a.m. $16 adults, $9.75 children May–Sept; $18 adults, $10.75 children Oct–Dec. Call ahead to inquire about special programs, including dinner and murder mystery train rides. (3 hours)

★★ **Paw Paw Tunnel**—At the time it was finished in 1850, the 3,118-foot Paw Paw Tunnel was one of the crowning achievements of the C&O Canal's construction. Named after the nearby town of Paw Paw, West Virginia (which itself was named after the pawpaw tree), the tunnel took nearly 14 years to build and was beset by labor unrest and financial problems. Initial cost estimates of $33,500 escalated to over $600,000 by the time the tunnel was completed. Crews worked for three shifts a day and often only advanced 10 to 12 feet per week. Gunpowder was used to blast out sections or rock that then had to be broken loose with a pick ax and hauled out by horse cart. For nearly 75 years, until the canal's closure in 1924, the tunnel enabled hundreds of boats carrying coal, farm products, and manufactured goods to pass through the mountain above. Today visitors walk the same path traveled by mules beside the canal, hearing the drip of water overhead. The nearby Tunnel Hill Trail takes you above the tunnel, providing views of the town of Paw Paw and Green Ridge State Forest, one of the largest forests in Maryland.

Details: Route 51, in Maryland, just across the state line from Paw Paw, West Virginia.

★★ **Shepherdstown, West Virginia**—Just five miles north of the Antietam National Battlefield is Shepherdstown, a charming college town well worth a day or weekend visit. Originally known as

Mecklenburg, this small town (population 1,800), the oldest in the state, has lots of character. West German Street is lined with quaint shops and restaurants, many of them housed in historic buildings. In addition to shopping and eating, try to visit the **Rumsey Steamboat Museum**, which houses a working replica of the first steamboat. It was designed by James Rumsey, inventor of the steam engine. Also of interest is the **Historic Shepherdstown Museum**, featuring artifacts and furnishings that trace the area's history. Across the Potomac from Shepherdstown is Ferry Hill Plantation at Lock 38. From there it's only three miles to the Antietam Creek Aqueduct.

Details: Steamboat Museum only open in summer Sat and Sun 10–5. To arrange a visit, go to O'Hurley's General Store, 205 E. Washington St. (Route 230 at the Railroad Crossing), 304/876-6907. Shepherdstown Museum at German and Princess Sts., 304/876-0910; open Apr–Oct Sat 11–5, Sun 1–4; free. (30 minutes)

☆ **Monocacy Aqueduct**—Nearly 150 yards long, the Monocacy Aqueduct is a monument, though somewhat beleaguered in its present state, to early-American civil engineering. The structure is one of 11 aqueducts along the canal that carried the canal waters and towpath over natural waterways. Completed in 1833, the aqueduct consists of six piers and seven arches. While it withstood efforts by Confederate troops to blow it up during the Civil War, nature is proving an admirable foe. The Park Service labored for nearly four years to stabilize the structure after heavy flooding in 1972, only to have raging floodwaters in 1996 further weaken this historic landmark. The aqueduct remains a popular spot among anglers and provides nice views of the confluence of the Monocacy and Potomac Rivers.

Details: Off Route 28, Dickerson. (30 minutes)

FITNESS AND RECREATION

One of the best ways to tour the canal is by bike. You can either take short day excursions or plan overnight trips, departing from one location, spending the night in a scenic area, and biking back the next day. Die-hard bikers have been known to travel the entire length of the canal in three days. Five days is considered a more reasonable time frame, allowing time for sightseeing along the way. The canal surface is rough; therefore mountain bikes or sturdy hybrids are recommended. Due to the lack of bike shops along the way, bikers are urged to bring along a basic repair kit. One of the easiest places to rent a bike for a brief trip is Georgetown. Other companies lead bike tours along the canal. Water sports are also popular along the canal. Kayaking and canoeing can be enjoyed in select spots, and a number of tour operators offer special packages.

Hiking is also an option, with plenty of places to enter the canal for a day or overnight stay. Campsites have been set up at convenient locations along the towpath, often no more than four to eight miles apart. For a truly memorable experience, try hiking the canal with a llama. The **Ground Squirrel Holler**, 6737 Sharpsburg Pike, Sharpsburg, offers two different hiking options in the late spring and early fall. The shorter, six-mile hike along the C&O Canal towpath takes roughly five hours and costs $50 per person. The longer, more strenuous 10-mile hike along the Paw Paw Tunnel Trail runs $60 per person and takes most of the day. All hikes include a gourmet box lunch.

Birdwatching is also a popular pastime along the canal. A variety of ducks, geese, woodpeckers, cardinals, herons, ospreys, hawks, and other birds frequent areas surrounding the canal. Some of the best birding to be had is within 20 miles of Georgetown. Anglers are also regular visitors to the canal. The Potomac is home to bass, shad, herring, and other fish species. Catfish, carp, and sunfish have been known to inhabit the canal itself.

FOOD

Located just 12 miles from Georgetown, the **Old Angler's Inn**, 10801 MacArthur Blvd., Potomac, Maryland, 301/365-2425, is a favorite among Washingtonians, who flock to this romantic (though some say over-rated) retreat to enjoy quality food in a rustic setting. Travelers to the canal can enjoy a walk along the towpath just across the street before stopping in for lunch, dinner, or a drink. In warm-weather months, an outdoor terrace allows for dining beneath the stars.

Built in 1860 to serve those traveling from the capital to the great estates of Maryland, the inn boasts a rich history. Today it operates solely as a restaurant serving excellent food, but for this be prepared to pay a price. Dinner menu items range from appetizers such as fresh lobster with Thai curry to entrées such as Norwegian salmon with shiitake mushroom and potato ragout to grilled veal chops. Reservations are highly recommended.

For casual dining in Harpers Ferry, try **The Anvil**, 1270 Washington St., 304/535-2582. Lunches include soups, sandwiches, salads, and quesadillas. Dinner entrées range from sauteed shrimp Frangelica and curried salmon, to filet mignon wrapped in bacon.

In Shepherdstown, West Virginia, a great place for designer coffee and biscotti is the **Lost Dog Café**, 134 E. German St., 304/876-0871. This extremely friendly, smallish café has a wonderful ambiance with folk art for sale and regularly scheduled live music. Just down the street is the **Old Pharmacy Café and Soda Fountain**, 138 E. German St., 304/876-2085, where you can get everything from an ice-cream soda to prime rib or fresh *mahi mahi*. Historic photographs of the pharmacy dating back as early as 1913 decorate the walls. Drugstore cabinets, storage containers, and an original soda fountain make for an authentic experience.

For slightly more upscale dining, try the **Yellow Brick Bank Restaurant**, 201 E. German St., 304/876-2208. While set in a bank building dating back to the 1780s, the dining areas have a decidedly contemporary feel with rose-colored walls and high ceilings. The scent of a wood-burning oven tempts your taste buds almost the minute you walk in the door. Lunchtime options range from soups and salads to original sandwiches and pasta dishes. Dinners include paella, grilled lamb chops, cornish game hen, and wild rockfish.

If you'd like to reward yourself with an excellent meal at the canal's terminus in Cumberland, try the **Oxford House**, 118 Greene St., 301/777-7101. Located in the Inn at Walnut Bottom, the Oxford House serves lunch and dinners in an intimate atmosphere. Lunches consist of a variety of sandwiches, soups, salads, and house specialties such as chicken *pomodora* over pasta and grilled salmon salad. Dinners are superb, rivaling some of the best restaurants in Washington, and although you'll pay less here, it'll still cost you. Appetizers include shrimp Pernod and mushrooms marsala. Dinner entrées range from apricot pork medallions to Wiener schnitzel.

For more casual fare in Cumberland, try **Uncle Tucker's Woodfired Pizza and Brewhaus**, 12901 Ali Ghan Rd., NE, 301/777-7232. Located in the basement of the Inn at Folck's Mill, Uncle Tucker's has a relaxed pub atmosphere with stone walls, exposed beams, red-and-white checkered tablecloths, and TV viewing for sports enthusiasts. Its creative pizzas are adorned with such delectable toppings as shrimp and calamari, fresh basil and artichoke hearts, and pancetta bacon and proscuitto ham.

LODGING

In highlighting places to stay along the canal, I've included lodging that is within walking distance, as well as excellent places to stay that are within a 15-minute drive. Some of these offer special canal packages that include fishing, canoeing, and raft trips; walks with llamas down the canal towpath; and complimentary mountain bikes for exploring the canal. You may wish to plan a weekend or more of moving from place to place along the canal, or situate yourself in one area where you can take in other local offerings as well. The following list presents lodging options in order from those closest to Washington to those nearer the terminus of the canal in Cumberland. For accommodations near the canal's starting point in Georgetown, see the lodging section in the chapter on Georgetown.

In Harpers Ferry, the **Angler's Inn**, 846 Washington St., 304/535-1239, is a bed-and-breakfast set in a 110-year-old Victorian home with a wraparound porch for relaxing on warm summer evenings. The inn is within walking distance of the Appalachian Trail and C&O Canal towpath and offers a range of fishing, canoing, and rafting packages. Room rates are $85 for two people and $70 for single occupancy, and include a full breakfast. Rooms have private baths and sitting rooms. The inn is approximately one mile from Lock 32 on the canal.

Located within the official boundary of the Antietam Battlefield and 3.5 miles from the canal at Shepherdstown, the **Inn at Antietam**, 220 E. Main St., Sharpsburg, Maryland, 301/432-6601, offers a soothing atmosphere and extremely congenial hosts. The inn, built in 1908, is set in a Victorian home on seven rolling acres. Its four suites each have a sitting room. Rooms run $95 during the week and $115 on weekends when a two-night stay is required.

Ever hiked with a llama? Your chance to do so could come with a night at the **Ground Squirrel Holler**, 6736 Sharpsburg Pike, Sharpsburg, Maryland, 301/432-8288. This country bed-and-breakfast is situated in a restored 1910 Victorian home on a five-acre farm where llamas graze. Rooms are tastefully decorated with oak furniture, have pressed-tin ceilings, and include down comforters. The scent of a wood-burning stove fills the air in cooler weather. Rates are $70 (single) and $80 (double) and include a hearty continental breakfast. Bathrooms are shared. Kids over 12 are welcome. Two different llama hikes are offered in April, May, October, and November. See "Fitness and Recreation," above, for details.

In Shepherdstown, West Virginia, the **Bavarian Inn**, Route 480, 304/876-2551, is a large luxury inn built in a Bavarian alpine style. Each of the 72 rooms has a balcony overlooking the Potomac River, and most have a fireplace, canopy bed, and sitting area. The inn has an exercise room, outdoor pool, and lighted tennis courts. Rooms range from $65 to $195 during the week and $80 to $250 on weekends.

If exploring the terminus of the canal in Cumberland or on your way to points further west, be sure to try the **Inn at Walnut Bottom**, 120 Greene St., Cumberland, 301/777-0003 or 800/286-9718, for its historic charm, proximity to the canal, and friendly staff, who go out of their way to make you feel at home. The inn consists of two adjoining townhouses, one built in 1820, the other in 1890. Its 12 guest rooms are decorated with antiques and period reproduction furniture. Complimentary bicycles are available for those wishing to spend the day exploring the canal. Afterward indulge yourself with a Danish bodywork treatment called "afspaending," offered by the inn for an additional fee. Hour-long sessions are given by innkeeper Kirsten Hansen, a native of Denmark who is certified in the technique. Rooms run from $79 to $120 and include a complimentary breakfast.

CAMPING

For general information on camping within the **C&O Canal National Historic Park**, contact the park's headquarters, P.O. Box 4, Sharpsburg, Maryland 21782, 301/739-4200. In addition, material can be obtained at four information centers operated by the National Park Service at Georgetown, Great Falls Tavern, Hancock, and Cumberland. There are three RV and tent campgrounds and one walk-in campground that operate on a first-come, first-served basis. They're open from May 1 to October 15 and stays are limited to 14 days. The park has a total of 30 hiker-biker campsites, each with a grill, trash can, portable toilet, picnic table, and hand-operated water pump. Stays are limited to one night at each location.

Scenic Route: Hancock to Cumberland

In making your way from points east to Cumberland, cross the West Virginia border at Hancock. Follow Route 522 to **Berkeley Springs**, a pleasant town whose waters have long been reputed to have curative powers. You might opt to break up your trip with a stay at the nearby **Coolfont Resort and Spa**, 304/258-4500 or 800/888-8768, where you can treat yourself to massages, facials, and herbal wraps. From here take Route 9 to Paw Paw. Here once again you'll cross the Potomac, this time to the Maryland side, where Route 9 becomes Route 51. Keep an eye out for signs to the **Paw Paw Tunnel** (see Sightseeing Highlights, page 90). Continue following Route 51 west as it meanders up and down hills, affording pleasant views of the river, wooded areas, and surrounding countryside. At various times you'll be passing through the southern reaches of the **Green Ridge State Forest**. At the **Spring Gap** recreation area, you'll find a pleasant spot to get out of the car and enjoy the quiet beauty of the Potomac. A few miles further down the road at **North Branch** is another drive-in recreation area. Nearby, at Lock 75 along the canal, a full-size replica of a canal boat, the *Cumberland*, is on display. From here it's only nine miles to the canal's terminus at Cumberland. ◼

HANCOCK TO CUMBERLAND

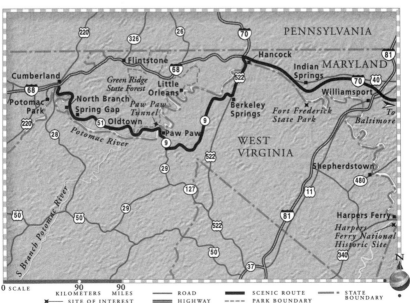

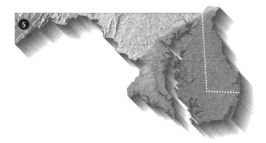

5
WESTERN MARYLAND

In the early 1800s, pioneers in covered wagons made their way through the Allegheny Mountains in western Maryland on their way to a new life in midwestern America. Today western Maryland still holds the allure of escape—escape from the congestion and workaday worlds of greater Baltimore and Washington. In just three hours you can make your way from Baltimore to Cumberland, the gateway to western Maryland.

This is where Marylanders and others go to ski, canoe, raft, hike, bike, and just be outdoors. The region's more than 75,000 acres of forest, parks, lakes, and rivers provide a natural backdrop for a range of outdoor activities. In the winter months, downhill and cross-country skiing beckon weekend travelers. In the summer, Deep Creek Lake, Maryland's largest freshwater lake, teams with boating enthusiasts while rafters and kayakers perfect their skills amidst the white waters of the Savage and Youghiogheny Rivers. In the southwestern corner of the state is Blackbone Mountain, the state's highest point at 3,360 feet above sea level.

Here you can see the forces that were at work in the building of a new nation. In the early 1800s, Cumberland was beginning to establish itself as a transportation and commercial center linking the east with the frontier midwest. By 1842 the Baltimore and Ohio Railroad had reached the city, to be followed eight years later by the Chesapeake and Ohio Canal. By 1880 Cumberland was the second-largest city in the state. Ironically, today's visitors to Cumberland and points beyond are

WESTERN MARYLAND

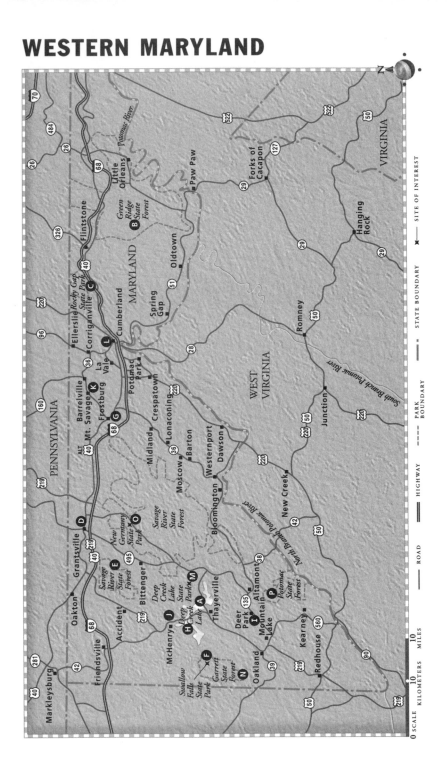

Sights

- Ⓐ Deep Creek Lake
- Ⓑ Green Ridge State Forest
- Ⓒ Rocky Gap State Park
- Ⓓ Spruce Forest Artisan Village and Penn Alps
- Ⓔ Savage River State Forest
- Ⓕ Swallow Falls State Park

Food

- Ⓖ Au Petit Paris
- Ⓗ Chicago's Uno Restaurant and Bar
- Ⓘ Deer Park Inn
- Ⓗ Four Seasons Dining Room
- Ⓙ McClives
- Ⓖ The Old Depot
- Ⓓ Penn Alps Restaurant
- Ⓗ Silver Tree Inn

Lodging

- Ⓚ The Castle
- Ⓓ Elliott House Victorian Inn
- Ⓘ Deer Park Inn
- Ⓙ Lake Pointe Inn
- Ⓛ Rocky Gap Lodge and Golf Resort
- Ⓗ Will o' the Wisp
- Ⓗ Wisp Resort Hotel and Conference Center

Camping

- Ⓜ Deep Creek Lake State Park
- Ⓝ Garrett State Forest
- Ⓑ Green Ridge State Forest
- Ⓞ New Germany State Park
- Ⓟ Potomac State Forest
- Ⓔ Savage River State Forest
- Ⓕ Swallow Falls State Park

Note: Items with the same letter are located in the same town or area.

more apt to be looking to relax, romanticizing the charmed days of canal boats and railroads. For information on activities and sights in Cumberland, see the chapter on the Chesapeake and Ohio Canal.

A PERFECT DAY IN WESTERN MARYLAND

The perfect day in western Maryland largely depends on whether you prefer to relax and soak up the scenery or pursue your outdoor activity of choice, be it in the woods, on a lake, or on a river. Obviously, in their respective seasons skiers will want to be on the slopes, golfers on the green. Still, if you haven't done it before, you might want to explore white-water rafting on the Savage or Youghiogheny Rivers. If you have time at the beginning or end of the day, it's well worth the visit to Swallow Falls State Park, just west of Deep Creek Lake, to experience a pleasant walk in the woods and behold the spectacle of Muddy Creek Falls. At 63 feet it's one of the highest waterfalls in the state. If looking for an alternative to sports, a trip to the Spruce Forest Artisan Village is well worth the drive for the chance to talk to and watch talented craftspeople at work.

SIGHTSEEING HIGHLIGHTS

★★★ **Deep Creek Lake**—A popular destination for vacationers, Deep Creek Lake is Maryland's largest freshwater lake. The man-made lake was built in 1925 as a water source for a hydroelectric plant on the Youghiogheny River. In 1980 the lake was leased to the Maryland Department of Natural Resources to be managed as a public recreational resource. Measuring 12 miles in length, it has a shoreline of 65 miles and covers nearly 3,900 acres. A wide variety of activities beckons visitors to the lake, including boating, waterskiing, fishing, swimming, hiking, sailing, downhill and cross-country skiing, and snowmobiling. Because of the lake's popularity and relative proximity to Washington, Baltimore, and Pittsburgh, visitors should not expect a remote wilderness experience, but instead be prepared for developed, though scenic, atmosphere.
  Details: Route 219, approximately 15 miles south of I-68. To obtain a vacation guide and maps, contact the Deep Creek Lake/Garrett County Promotion Council, 301/334-1948. (1 hour–several days)

★★★ **Swallow Falls State Park**—In the early 1920s, what is now known as Swallow Falls State Park was a favorite camp of pioneer motor tourists Thomas Edison, Henry Ford, and Harvey Firestone. Today this 257-acre mountain park, within close proximity to Deep Creek Lake, contains some of Maryland's most breathtaking scenery, including the state's last virgin forest of giant hemlocks and pines reaching heights of more than 100 feet. The Youghiogheny River flows along the park's borders, passing through shaded rocky gorges and creating rippling rapids. The park's most dramatic sight is Muddy Creek Falls—at 63 feet, it's one of the largest waterfalls in the state. The Canyon Trail, with fern- and wildflower-covered cliffs, mountain laurel, and rhododendron, is considered one of the most beautiful hiking trails in Maryland.

Details: Nine miles northwest of Oakland on County Route 20, four miles beyond the entrance to Herrington Manor State Park. Open dawn to dusk. $1 per car. For further information call 301/334-9180. (1–3 hours)

★★ **Green Ridge State Forest**—Located 22 miles east of Cumberland, Green Ridge State Forest covers 43,000 acres of land in eastern Allegany County. Wildlife is plentiful, including wild turkey, grouse, squirrels, and deer. The Maryland State Forest and Park Service offers self-guided tours designed for you to enjoy the year-round beauty of the state forest lands. The complete tour is approximately 30 miles long. Mountain biking enthusiasts should not miss out on the forest's off-road trails, used for the state mountain-biking championships.

Details: 28700 Headquarters Dr. NE, Flintstone; 301/478-3124. Park headquarters off exit 64 on Interstate 68, approximately eight miles east of Flintstone. Free. (1–3 hours)

★★ **Rocky Gap State Park**—Nestled in a natural saddle created by Evitts Mountain and Martin's Mountain, Rocky Gap State Park covers nearly 3,000 acres and offers rugged mountain scenery along with hiking trails, modern campsites with hookups, boating, fishing, and picnic and play areas. Three swimming beaches and a modern bathhouse adjoin 243-acre Lake Habeeb. Cutting through the park is a mile-long gorge with sheer cliffs, overlooks, rhododendrons, and hemlock forest. A heated chalet that sleeps eight is available year-round for rent.

Details: Take exit 50 from Interstate 68 and travel north; 301/777-2139. Park seven miles northeast of Cumberland on Pennsylvania state line. Free. (1–3 hours)

★★ **Spruce Forest Artisan Village and Penn Alps**—In an era when the vast majority of goods are mass produced half a world away, the Spruce Forest Artisan Village provides a welcome journey back to a time when craftsmanship really meant something. The village is made up of original log cabins that have been moved from other settings. As you stroll through the village you can watch and talk to craftspeople at work, including a spinner, weaver, potter, stained-glass worker, quilt maker, wood sculptor, and bird carver. The fruits of their efforts are also for sale.

Details: Route 40, Grantsville (21 miles west of Cumberland); 301/895-3332. Open Mon–Sat 10–5. Free. (1 hour)

Savage River State Forest—The largest of the state's forests, the Savage River State Forest covers 52,812 acres, much of them classified as northern hardwood. Within the forest is the 350-acre Savage River Reservoir, where canoeists can paddle along more than 17 miles of shoreline

> **Details:** *Route 2, Grantsville; 301/895-5759. Free. (1–3 hours)*

FITNESS AND RECREATION

In addition to the numerous hiking trails that traverse the region's parks, as described earlier, other fitness and recreation options abound in western Maryland. The area surrounding **Deep Creek Lake** is dotted with outdoor sports outfitters renting mountain bikes, fishing, sailing and ski boats, canoes, kayaks, and other outdoor equipment. **High Mountain Sports**, Route 219, McHenry, 301/387-4199, rents mountain bikes. For fishing and boating on the lake, contact **Deep Creek Outfitters**, 1899 Deep Creek Dr., McHenry, 301/387-6977. To explore white-water rafting in the area, contact **Upper Yough Expeditions**, Macadam Road, Friendsville, 301/746-5808. **Precision Rafting**, Main Street, Friendsville, 800/477-3723, offers rafting trips and kayaking instruction. For further information on whitewater activities, call the Garrett County Chamber of Commerce, 301/334-1948.

Near Deep Creek Lake is Marsh Mountain, home of the **Wisp Ski Area**, 290 Marsh Hill Rd., McHenry, 301/387-4911. At 3,080 feet, the mountain provides the setting for the state's only alpine ski resort. Skiers have 23 slopes to choose from and 80 acres of trails, ranging from beginner to difficult. Most are open for night skiing.

FOOD

Despite its rugged surroundings, western Maryland offers a number of worthwhile restaurants, along with casual pubs and eateries where you can unwind after a day of outdoor activities. For restaurants in Cumberland, see the Chesapeake and Ohio Canal chapter.

Just west of Cumberland, in the town of Frostburg, dine in French elegance at **Au Petit Paris**, 86 E. Main St., 301/689-8946. Open for dinner only, Au Petit Paris has been serving high-end French cuisine to local diners for more than 35 years. Specialties include frogs legs, filet of sole meunière, steak au poivre, coq au vin, and chateaubriand. Less expensive and more casual is the **Old Depot**, 19

Depot St., 301/689-1221. The restaurant, housed in a renovated train station originally built in 1891, is operated in conjunction with the Western Maryland Scenic Railroad. Lunches include sandwiches, burgers, soups, and salads while dinner items range from barbecued chicken to grilled shrimp.

If visiting the artisan village in Grantsville, you should plan a meal at the adjacent **Penn Alps Restaurant**, 125 Casselman Rd., 301/895-5985, which offers reasonably priced down-home cooking. The restaurant and gift shop are housed in a remodeled stagecoach inn dating back to 1818. The restaurant's five dining rooms serve Pennsylvania Dutch–style food such as roast pork and hickory-smoked ham, along with sandwiches and salads. The hearty breakfasts are a great value. The extra-large cinnamon buns transport you back to childhood days when frosting calories didn't matter.

The Deep Creek Lake area boasts numerous restaurant options. For those who care, be forewarned that alcoholic beverages are not available on Sundays. One of the more popular casual dining spots, while of the chain variety, offers terrific lake views. **Chicago's Uno Restaurant and Bar**, 19814 Garrett Hwy., Deep Creek Lake, 301/387-4866, has a central fireplace that provides ambiance in the winter months and an outdoor deck that's packed in the summer. The menu, which stays the same all day, consists of salads, soups, sandwiches, deep- and thin-crust pizzas, pasta dishes, and grilled entrées ranging from Mediterranean swordfish to center-cut pork chops.

Nearby, the **Silver Tree Inn**, 564 Glendale Rd., 301/387-4040, offers lakefront views and Italian fare that ranges from moderately priced pasta dishes to more expensive entrées. Open only for dinner, the Silver Tree specializes in seafood dishes including shrimp scampi, crab soufflé, blackened salmon, and broiled lobster tails. Beef, veal, and poultry dishes are also available. Also offering lake views is the **Four Seasons Dining Room** at the Will O'the Wisp motel complex, 20160 Garrett Hwy., 301/387-5501. Breakfasts and lunches, featuring sandwiches, salads, and burgers, are extremely reasonable. Dinners, on the expensive side, include an array of seafood, veal, chicken, beef, and pork dishes. Within close proximity to the Wisp Ski Area is **McClives**, 1375 Deep Creek Dr., McHenry, 301/387-6172. With views of the lake and ski area, McClives has a patio for warm-weather dining and a fireplace lounge that's popular in the winter months. Serving dinner only, McClives offers a range of seafood dishes, including crab cakes and mesquite grilled swordfish, along with meat and pasta dishes. Reservations are not accepted.

For a truly great meal in elegant, candlelit surroundings, reserve a table at the **Deer Park Inn**, 65 Hotel Rd., Deer Park, 301/334-2308, a 15-minute drive south of the Deep Creek Lake area. Chef Pascal Fontaine, formerly executive chef at the Westin Hotel and the Ana Hotel in Washington, prepares country French cuisine, including such mouthwatering dishes as roast rack of lamb with a goat-cheese crust and sun-dried cherry sauce. Hours and days of operation change seasonally, so diners are urged to call ahead and make reservations.

LODGING

A wide range of accommodations is available in western Maryland from farm bed-and-breakfasts, to elegant inns, to inexpensive motels. A few of these, however, come highly overrated, relying more on the area's scenic charms to sell rooms than on the quality of their services and facilities.

The **Rocky Gap Lodge and Golf Resort**, P.O. Box 1199, Cumberland, 301/784-8400 or 800/724-0828, is a full-service resort featuring an 18-hole golf course designed by Jack Nicklaus, as well as a 220-room lodge. Facilities include an indoor/outdoor pool, tennis courts, fitness room, a marina with boat rentals, a private beach, fitness room, whirlpool, and two restaurants. Call for rate information. Tucked away in the town of Mount Savage, five miles north of Frostburg, is **The Castle**, 15925 Mt. Savage Rd., 301/264-4645. This stone house, originally built in 1840, was converted into a replica of Scotland's Craig Castle by Andrew Ramsay, a young entrepreneur who immigrated to the United States from Scotland at the turn of the century. The house, surrounded by a 16-foot stone wall, has lovely gardens and terraces in which to relax. Its six bedrooms, each uniquely decorated, are furnished with period antiques, including four-poster, brass, and sleigh beds. In the summer months, guests may enjoy iced tea and lemonade on the terrace while in the winter a fireplace warms the main parlor. On the weekends rooms run from $95 to $125 from May through October; $85 to $125 in April, November, and December; and $75 to $125 from January through March. A 10-percent discount is given Monday through Thursday nights.

In Grantsville the **Elliott House Victorian Inn**, 146 Casselman Rd., 301/895-4250 or 800/272-4090, is located next door to the Penn Alps Restaurant and Spruce Forest Artisan Village. Built in 1870, the house has been restored and converted into a bed-and-breakfast with three river-view cottages, each with decks. Room rates range from $95 to $130 from May through October and from $75 to $115 from November though April. A minimum two-night stay is required on weekends. Room prices include breakfast at the Penn Alps Restaurant adjacent to the inn. Guests may take advantage of an outdoor hot tub, bicycles, and nature walks on the inn's seven acres along the Casselman River.

In the Deep Creek Lake area there are many lodging alternatives, depending upon your taste, price range, and whether you're looking for a romantic getaway or place for the whole family. For close proximity to winter skiing or summer golfing, try the **Wisp Resort Hotel and Conference Center**, 290 Marsh Hill Rd., Deep Creek Lake, 301/387-5581 or 800/462-9477. While the hotel itself is somewhat dated, chances are you won't be spending much time in your room. In addition to an 18-hole golf course and 23-trail ski area, the hotel has an indoor pool and whirlpool, tennis court, and fitness center. Guest rooms have a queen-size bed, a sofa bed, and a small refrigerator. Suites and mini-suites cost $129 per night during the week and $169 on weekends. Far more economical are the hotel's winter ski packages offering two nights' lodging, a two-day life ticket, two breakfasts, and one dinner for $362 (single) or $237 each (double occupancy).

Overlooking Deep Creek Lake, the **Will o' the Wisp**, 20160 Garrett Hwy., Oakland, 301/387-6990, offers cottages, two motels, and condominium accommodations, all within the same complex. Guests at each have access to the hotel's heated pool, game room, whirlpools, exercise room, sauna, and racquetball facilities. Motel rooms are open only from May through October. Condominium layouts range from a one-bedroom with fireplace to three-bedroom/three-bath units with a kitchen, living room, dining room, and three fireplaces. All are available by the night or by the week, with prices ranging from $70 for a one-bedroom in the off-season (Labor Day until June 14) to $110 during summer months. Larger units run from $128 off-season to $284 in the summer, depending on the number of rooms. Motel rooms run from $49 off-season to $94 during peak months, depending on size.

As an alternative to the area's large hotels, there are a number of bed-and-breakfast accommodations. The **Lake Pointe Inn**, 174 Lake Pointe Dr., McHenry, 301/387-0111 or 800/523-LAKE, is located just 13 feet from the lake's edge and overlooks the Wisp Ski Resort. Built in the late 1800s, the inn underwent an extensive restoration in 1995. Decorated in the Arts and Crafts tradition, the inn has a large stone fireplace and wraparound porch with lake views. An outdoor hot tub is available, along with bicycles, canoes, and kayaks. Rooms run from $128 to $178 during the "in season." Deductions of $15 to $30 are available for those staying off-season; prices depend on whether you're there during the week or on the weekend. A two-night minimum stay is required on weekends and all rates include a hearty breakfast. Therapeutic massages are also available for an additional fee.

Located just south of the lake, the **Deer Park Inn**, 65 Hotel Rd., Deer Park, 301/334-2308, is a restored Victorian mansion, somewhat removed from the hustle and bustle associated with the lake during peak seasons. Built in 1889, the 17-room house was designed by a Baltimore architect as a summer "cottage." Today it is operated as a fine country French restaurant and three-room bed-and-breakfast. Rates run from $98 to $110 and include a full breakfast.

CAMPING

If you're looking to camp near the activities at Deep Creek Lake, **Deep Creek Lake State Park**, Route 2, Swanton, 301/387-5563, has 112 campsites. Roughly 700 feet of beach have been developed, and in the winter the park offers six miles of snowmobile trails. For reservations from Memorial Day through Labor Day, call 301/387-4111. In nearby Oakland, **Garrett State Forest** and **Potomac State Forest** are managed together as a single unit. Together they have 39 primitive campsites. For further information call 301/895-5759. Located within Garrett Forest is **Swallow Falls State Park**, 301/334-9180, featuring 64 improved campsites and five camper-ready campsites.

In Grantsville, **Savage River State Forest**, 301/895-5759, covers more than 52,000 acres and has 42 primitive campsites. Located within the forest is **New Germany State Park**, 301/895-5453, which has 39 campsites and 11 cabins. The park covers 455 acres and has a 13-acre lake. **Rocky Gap State Park**, 301/777-2138, has 278 campsites in nine camping loops with bath houses and hot-water showers; 30 sites provide electricity, and a dumping station is located near the main registration building. Closer to Cumberland, **Green Ridge State Forest**, 301/777-2139, covers 38,811 acres and has 97 primitive campsites.

From Deep Creek Lake, head north on Route 219, which offers pastoral views. At the intersection with Interstate 68, head east. In Grantsville, just off Exit 19, is the 80-foot-long **Casselman River Bridge**. When it was built in 1813, it was the largest span stone arch bridge in America. Nearby is the **Spruce Forest Artisan Village** (see page 101), where you can see local artisans at work in historical log houses carefully moved from surrounding areas. Time permitting, grab a bite to eat at the **Penn Alps Restaurant** (see page 103).

Once back on Route 68, at mile 25 you'll see a sign marking the western edge of the **Chesapeake Bay Watershed**, the boundary line for the Eastern Continental Divide. On the eastern side of the sign, all rivers flow to the Chesapeake Bay and Atlantic Ocean; on the western side they flow to the Mississippi River and eventually the Gulf of Mexico. At Exit 50 is **Rocky Gap State Park** (see page 101), where you can hike the trails or swim in the park's lake Habeeb. Not far off Exit 64 is the **Green Ridge State Forest** headquarters (see page 101), which offers scenic views and 27 miles of hiking trails following narrow ridges and stream valleys. Just past Exit 77 is the

DEEP CREEK LAKE TO HANCOCK

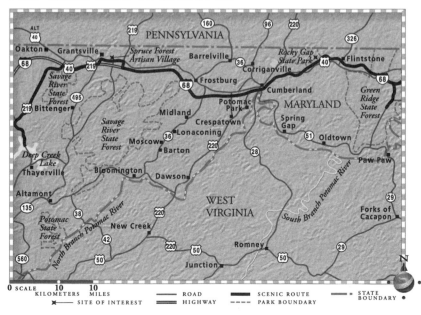

Sideling Hill Exhibit Center. This impressive rock outcrop with great views was carved to make way for Interstate 68. Fossilized plants and seashells show that the site once lay at the bottom of the ocean. The center provides information on local sights and park maps.

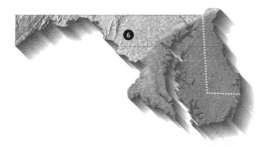

6
FREDERICK COUNTY

Frederick County is distinguished first by its historical significance. Founded in 1745 by English and German settlers, the city of Frederick (then Fredericktown) was established as a frontier town to service the first wagon trains making their way across the Allegheny Mountains. Lewis and Clark stored the provisions for their 1803 expedition in Frederick's Hessian Barracks. A number of crucial Civil War events occurred here. Abraham Lincon addressed the town after the nearby Battle of Antietam. Today the city features a 50-block historic district with noteworthy examples of eighteenth- and nineteenth-century architecture, along with numerous antique shops. Among its more prominent citizens were Francis Scott Key, who wrote "The Star Spangled Banner," and Barbara Fritchie, known for her heroic waving of the Union Flag at Confederate soldiers.

The area also offers abundant outdoor opportunities. To the north are two splendid parks: Cunningham Falls State Park and Catoctin Mountain Park. The first is known best for its 78-foot cascading waterfall, while hidden within the latter is Camp David, the presidential retreat. Both offer miles of hiking trails and scenery well worth the walk, along with fishing, swimming, and canoeing.

A PERFECT DAY IN FREDERICK COUNTY

Begin your day in Frederick County with a visit to the city of Frederick's historic district, where you can admire the architecture and avail yourself

FREDERICK COUNTY

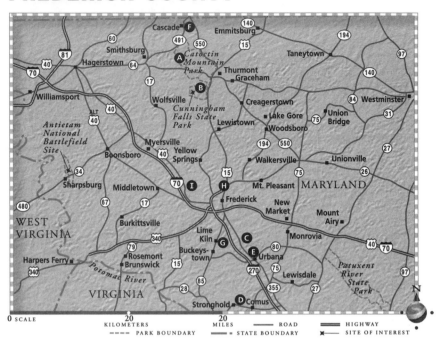

Sights

- Ⓐ Catoctin Mountain State Park
- Ⓑ Cunningham Falls State Park
- Ⓒ Monocacy National Battlefield
- Ⓓ Sugarloaf Mountain

Food

- Ⓓ Comus Inn
- Ⓔ Turning Point Inn

Lodging

- Ⓕ Bluebird on the Mountain
- Ⓖ Catoctin Inn and Conference Center
- Ⓗ Spring Bank
- Ⓔ Turning Point Inn

Camping

- Ⓑ Cunningham Falls State Park
- Ⓘ Gambrill State Park

Note: Items with the same letter are located in the same town or area.

of many antiquing opportunities. To obtain marked maps outlining self-guided tours, stop by the Frederick County Visitor Center, 19 E. Church St., 301/663-8687. While in Frederick, visit the Barbara Fritchie House and Museum and be inspired by the patriotic pluck of a 95-year-old woman. If you have children, the Rose Hill Manor Children's Museum offers a variety of hands-on nineteenth-century activities that engage as well as educate youngsters. If you prefer to spend time outdoors, head to Cunningham Falls State Park, where a relatively short hike will take you to the state's largest waterfall, measuring 78 feet.

SIGHTSEEING HIGHLIGHTS

★★ Barbara Fritchie House and Museum—At the age of 95, Barbara Fritchie is said to have waved a Union flag from her bedroom window as General Stonewall Jackson and his troops marched through town in 1862. Fritchie's patriotic act was immortalized in a poem by John Greenleaf Whittier that appeared in the *Atlantic Monthly* a year later. While the original Fritchie farm was destroyed by flooding, this exact replica was built in 1927 using materials salvaged from the original home that was torn down in 1868.
Details: 154 W. Patrick St., Frederick; 301/698-0630. Open Apr–Sept Thu–Mon 10–4, Oct–Nov weekends 1–4. $2 adults, $1.50 seniors and children under 12. (1 hour)

★★ Catoctin Mountain State Park—Just north of Cunningham Falls State Park (see below), this state park encompasses Camp David, the presidential retreat. Don't bother looking for it; even if you did find it, you'd be met by security officers. The park encompasses 6,000 acres, with 25 miles of hiking trails, many of which lead to outstanding views.
Details: Route 77, Thurmont; 301/663-9388. Catoctin Mountain Park is run by the National Park Service. Free. (1–3 hours)

★★ Cunningham Falls State Park—The park is named for the 78-foot cascading waterfall that draws visitors from around the state. Covering 4,946 acres, the park has 21 miles of hiking trails of varying degrees of difficulty, along with a 43-acre lake for swimming, canoeing, and fishing. Visitors may also check out the **Catoctin Furnace**, a restored historic iron foundry that operated from 1776 to 1903, tapping the area's abundant natural resources.
Details: Route 77, Thurmont; 301/271-7574. Free. (1–3 hours)

★★ **Rose Hill Manor Children's Museum**—Kids can experience early nineteenth-century family life as they play with replicas of old toys, dress up in period costumes, and learn early American games. Hands-on displays demonstrate quilt-making, the carding of wool, the making of biscuits, and the separating of cream. The 1790s era manor, once the home of Thomas Johnson, the state's first elected governor, provides a stellar example of Georgian Colonial architecture. Also on the grounds are a log cabin; icehouse; smokehouse; blacksmith shop; herb, vegetable, and rose garden; orchard; and carriage collection. Guided tours of the house are available.

Details: *1611 N. Market St., Frederick; 301/694-1648. Open Apr–Oct Mon–Sat 10–4, Sun 1–4; Nov weekends 10–4. $3 adults, $2 seniors, $1 under 17. (1 hour)*

★ **Sugarloaf Mountain**—Rising 1,281 feet above the surrounding countryside, Sugarloaf Mountain served as a Union Army signal station during the Civil War. It was in 1862 that a Union soldier posted atop the mountain spotted Confederate forces crossing the Potomac before the Battle of Antietam. After the bloody battle, wounded men from both sides were treated in log cabins that still remain at the base of the mountain. The mountain's shape prompted early pioneers to name it after the "sugar loaves" their wives and mothers prepared for them. Visitors of all ages come to the mountain today to enjoy its splendid views and walking trails. The longest of these trails extends for 5.5 miles across the mountain peak. Shorter hikes with scenic overlooks are also available.

Details: *Comus; 301/874-2024. Open daily 8 a.m. to one hour before sunset. (1–3 hours)*

Frederick County Historical Society Museum—To firmly ground yourself in the area's history, visit the local historical society museum featuring a collection of period furnishings, art, and artifacts. Housed in a restored 1820s Federal-style mansion, the historical society also operates a history and genealogical library here.

Details: *24 E. Church St., Frederick; 301/663-1188. Open Mon–Sat 10–4, Sun 1–4. $2 adults, under 17 free. (1 hour)*

Monocacy National Battlefield—It was here on July 9, 1864, that Union forces, outnumbered three to one, held off a Confederate army on its way to invade Washington, D.C. The fight pitted General Jubal

Early and his army of 18,000 Confederate troops against Union General Lew Wallace and his force of 5,800 men. While Confederate forces won the contest, the Union troops who fought and died here are credited with saving the capital from attack.

Details: 4801 Urbana Pike, Frederick; 301/662-3515. Open Memorial Day–Labor Day 8–4:30, Sept–June Wed and Sun only. (1 hour)

National Museum of Civil War Medicine—Dedicated to telling the medical story of the Civil War, the museum's exhibits display the care of the wounded, caregivers, and medical innovations during the war.

Details: 48 E. Patrick St., Frederick; 301/695-1864. Open Mon–Sat 10–5, Sun 11–5. $2.50 adults, $2 seniors, $1 ages 10–15. (1 hour)

FITNESS AND RECREATION

For walking and biking opportunities along the **Chesapeake Canal** towpath in Frederick County, see the chapter on the C&O Canal. Other great parks for hiking are **Cactoctin National Park** and **Cunningham Falls State Park** (see Sightseeing Highlights, above). The Appalachian Trail can be accessed at three separate locations in Frederick and neighboring Washington Counties: **Washington Monument State Park**, **South Mountain State Park**, and **Greenbrier State Park**, all of which can be reached at 301/791-4767. Outdoor fun can also be had on local waterways. Contact **River and Trail Outfitters**, 301/695-5177, in Knoxville, for information on rafting, tubing, canoeing, and kayaking on the Shenandoah and Potomac Rivers, as well as Antietam Creek.

FOOD

At the base of Sugarloaf Mountain is the **Comus Inn**, 23900 Old Hundred Rd., Comus, 301/428-8593. With spectacular views of the mountain and surrounding farmland, the restaurant rests on a five-acre piece of land once owned by George Washington. Lunches consist of salads, sandwiches, chicken, fish, and beef entrées, as well as vegetarian dishes. Dinners fall within a medium price range and feature pasta, chicken, steak, veal, and seafood. A patio allows for outdoor dining in warm-weather months.

In Frederick, **Brewer's Alley**, 124 N. Market St., 301/631-0089, takes its name from a brewery that operated in Frederick for over 150

FREDERICK

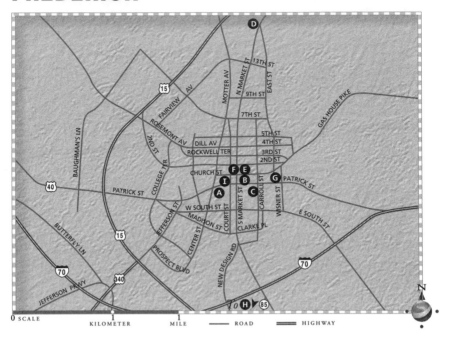

Sights

Ⓐ Barbara Fritchie House and Museum

Ⓑ Frederick County Historical Society Museum

Ⓒ National Museum of Civil War Medicine

Ⓓ Rose Hill Manor Children's Museum

Food

Ⓔ Brewer's Alley

Ⓕ The Province

Ⓖ Tauraso's

Lodging

Ⓗ Frederick Days Inn

Ⓘ Tyler-Spite House

years until it was consumed by fire in 1901. Today's version is housed in a renovated 1873 building. In addition to sampling the restaurant's fine brews, you can eat well. The menu features soups, salads, sandwiches, wood-fired pizzas, pasta; entrées (available after 5 p.m.) include steaks, grilled fish, barbequed chicken, and pork chops.

Nearby is **The Province**, 131 N. Market St., 301/663-1441, serving creative American cuisine with "an international flavor." Specializing in seafood, beef, and lamb dishes, the restaurant is decorated with handmade quilts and snowshoe chairs. For Italian and continental cuisine, try **Tauraso's**, Everedy Square, 6 East St., 301/663-6600. Serving seafood, pasta, beef, and vegetarian dishes, the restaurant also offers a variety of fresh pizzas from its wood-burning oven. Diners may choose between a casual pub atmosphere, formal dining room, or garden patio. Tauraso's is open for lunch and dinner.

Just outside the city, the **Turning Point Inn**, 8406 Urbana Pike, Urbana, 301/874-2421, has an excellent restaurant with an enclosed garden patio overlooking wildflower and rose gardens. It's open for lunch, dinner, and Sunday brunch, and menus feature seafood, roast duck, and beef dishes prepared with local produce and herbs.

LODGING

In and around Frederick, a number of charming inns and bed-and-breakfast accommodations echo the area's historic character. However, if you're looking for cost-saving alternatives to these more quaint lodgings, try the **Frederick Days Inn**, 5646 Buckeystown Pike, 301/694-6600, with rooms ranging from $65 to $75. Within a 10-minute drive of downtown Frederick is **Spring Bank**, 7945 Worman's Mill Rd., 301/694-0440 or 800/400-INNS. Set in an 1880 country home, it has six guest rooms. The price for a room with private bath is $80 (single) or $95 (double). Rooms with a shared bath run from $65 (single) to $80 (double). Room rates include a continental breakfast. Occupying an Edwardian-era home, the **Turning Point Inn**, 3406 Urbana Pike, 301/831-8232, features five guest rooms and two cottages, each decorated with antique reproduction furniture. All rooms have private baths. Rooms in the inn run $75 during the week and $95 on weekends. The smaller of the two cottages, the dairy house, runs $100 during the week and $125 on weekends. The larger carriage house runs $125 to $150. Rates include a country breakfast. Located within Frederick's historic district is the **Tyler-Spite House**, 112 W. Church

St., 301/831-4455. The three-story Federal-style mansion has 13-foot ceilings and working fireplaces in eight rooms. Its nine guest rooms run from $180 to $240 on the weekends and $100 to $150 during the week and include a full breakfast.

In Buckeystown, the **Catoctin Inn and Conference Center**, 3619 Buckeystown Pike, 301/874-5555 or 800/730-5550, occupies a 1780 manor house with additional cottages. Rooms are furnished with antiques and folk art and include amenities such as handmade quilts, fireplaces, and whirlpool tubs. Rooms range from $95 to $175.

Not far from the Pennsylvania border and Catoctin Mountain Park is **Bluebird on the Mountain**, 301/241-4161 or 800/362-9526. The inn has five rooms with private baths, some with working fireplaces and/or Jacuzzis. Room rates run from $105 to $125 and include a continental breakfast. Discounts may apply during the week.

CAMPING

Camping is available at several locations in Frederick County. Located just six miles north of Frederick, **Gambrill State Park** covers 1,137 acres and offers 35 improved campsites, a dumb station, and hiking trails. For reservations, contact the park office, 301/271-7574. Fifteen miles north of Frederick is **Cunningham Falls State Park**. Covering 4,946 acres, the park has two camping areas: the manor area with 31 campsites and the William Houck area with 148 sites. For reservations, contact the park's headquarters, 301/271-7574. Nearby **Catoctin Mountain Park** has 51 RV and tent campsites, 25 cabins, and two Adirondack shelters accessible only on foot. Fees are charged for RV and tent camping and for cabin camping. No hookups are provided and no dump station is available. For further information, contact the park office, 301/663-9388.

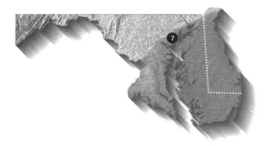

7

BALTIMORE

During the 1970s, Baltimore was widely considered nothing more than an industrial center to be bypassed via the highway. By the 1980s the city had undergone a major transformation, and today it attracts more than 5 million visitors yearly to the most potent symbol of its revival, the bustling Inner Harbor. Nearby, Orioles Statium at Camden Yards, one of major-league baseball's finest facilities, enjoys sell-out crowds in the summer months.

With a population of nearly a million, Baltimore is a big city that retains a small-town atmosphere, mostly owing to the strength and individuality of its neighborhoods. The city's diversity is reflected in a variety of ethnic restaurants and enclaves such as Little Italy. Cultural-ly, Baltimore offers a wealth of options from the Walters Art Gallery to the Baltimore Symphony Orchestra.

The city's rich past is visible in its architectural landscape, espe-cially in neighborhoods like historic Mount Vernon. Established in 1729, Baltimore was named after Maryland's founder: George Calvert, First Lord of Baltimore. It's the city where, during the War of 1812, Francis Scott Key was inspired to write what would become the nation's anthem, "The Star Spangled Banner." Edgar Allen Poe and Babe Ruth were born here. Twentieth-century essayist and critic H. L. Mencken made his home here, as did jazz composer Eubie Blake. Baltimore's streets became widely known to the American public through the popu-larity of the TV series *Homicide*, filmed here. It's a city that's trendy yet cultured, gritty yet gleaming, sophisticated yet accessible.

BALTIMORE

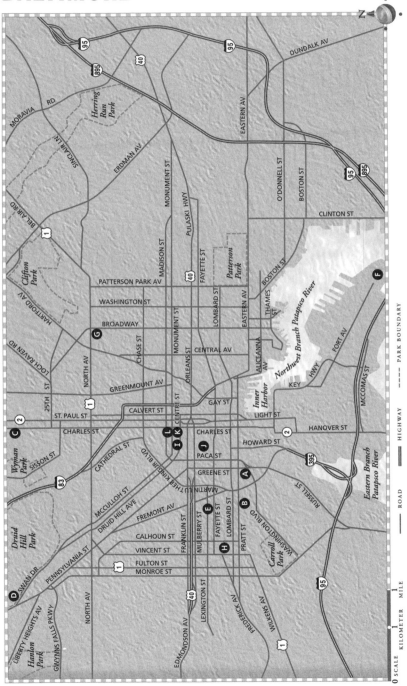

Sights

Ⓐ Babe Ruth Birthplace and Museum

Ⓑ Baltimore and Ohio Railroad Museum

Ⓒ Baltimore Museum of Art

Ⓓ Baltimore Zoo

Ⓔ Edgar Allen Poe House

Ⓕ Fort McHenry

Ⓖ Great Blacks in Wax Museum

Ⓗ H. L. Mencken House

Ⓘ Maryland Historical Society

Ⓙ Lexington Market

Ⓚ Walter's Art Gallery

Ⓛ Washington Monument

A PERFECT DAY IN BALTIMORE

Begin with a visit to the National Aquarium (and, if you have children, to the Port Discovery children's museum). From there, head to the World Trade Center to enjoy panoramic city views from the observation area on the 27th floor. Next door is Harborplace, where it's possible to spend hours wandering through shops and boutiques or listening to outdoor entertainment. After lunch, visit the nearby Maryland Science Center. Then take a walk up Charles Street to the historic Mount Vernon neighborhood, where several great cafés provide refreshment. In the center of Mount Vernon Square is Washington Monument; if you have the energy, walk up its 228 steps. The nearby Walters Art Gallery is worth seeing for its Italian Renaissance architecture as well as for its impressive collection. End your day by taking a water taxi from the Inner Harbor to Fells Point to walk the cobbled streets along the waterfront and enjoy local seafood in one of the area's many restaurants.

SIGHTSEEING HIGHLIGHTS

★★★ **Baltimore Museum of Art**—With more than 100,000 works of art, the Baltimore Museum of Art is the largest museum in Maryland.

The museum is most noted for the Epstein Collection of old master paintings featuring works by Botticelli, Raphael, Titian, Rembrandt, van Dyck, and Goya; and the Cone Collection of French paintings by Manet, Degas, Matisse, Picasso, Cézanne, and others. Also featured are the arts of Africa, Asia, and Oceania. The West Wing for Contemporary Art, devoted primarily to the work of Andy Warhol, holds the world's second-largest collection of paintings by that artist on regular display. After wandering through the museum, enjoy authentic Chesapeake Bay cuisine at **Gertrude's**, located just inside the main entrance. In warm weather, diners may eat outside overlooking the sculpture garden.

Details: 10 Art Museum Dr.; 410/396-7100. Open Wed–Fri 11–5, Sat and Sun 11–6. $6 adults, 18 and under free, $4 seniors and full-time students. (2 hours)

★★★ **Harborplace**—Opened in 1980, this mall was the brainchild of Baltimore native James Rouse, the developer also responsible for converting Boston's Faneuil Hall and New York's South Street Seaport into thriving shopping areas. Harborplace is located in Baltimore's Inner Harbor—the portion of downtown Baltimore that lines the harbor and overlooks the west branch of the Patapsco River. Though many of the city's most popular attractions are located in or near the Inner Harbor, the area is dominated by the two shopping and eating pavilions of Harborplace and by the **Gallery** shops across the street. Covering 85 acres, the Harborplace complex houses more than 200 shops, restaurants, and eateries, and hosts more than 100 entertainment events each year.

Details: Pratt and Light Sts.; 410/332-4191. Both Harborplace and the Gallery open Mon–Sat 10–9, Sun 11–7; Harborplace open to 11 p.m. on Fri and Sat in spring and summer. (1–3 hours)

★★★ **National Aquarium**—Next door on Piers Three and Four is the National Aquarium. Home to more than 5,000 aquatic creatures, the aquarium is considered one of the best in the country and is Maryland's most visited tourist site. Visitors to the aquarium may explore remote regions of the globe from dense rain forests to coral reefs and the ocean depths. Its inhabitants include sharks, dolphins, jellyfish, reptiles, birds, amphibians, and invertebrates. Don't miss the dolphin shows held in the Marine Mammal Pavilion.

Details: 501 E. Pratt St.; 410/576-3800. Open July–Aug daily 9–8;

Mar–June and Sept–Oct daily 9–5, Fri to 8; Nov–Feb daily 10–5, Fri to 8. $14 adults, $7.50 children ages 3–11, $10.50 seniors. (2 hours)

★★★ **Port Discovery, The New Kid-Powered Museum**—In January 1999 one of the most sophisticated children's museums in the nation opened its doors. Interactive exhibits and activities help kids practice the skills necessary to realize their dreams. A host of colorful characters—the Dream Squad—assist young visitors on their journey through the museum. There's Ivan Idea, a creative thinker; Wanda Whye, an explorer; and Annie Action, who knows how to get things done. Museum goers are given the chance to explore ancient Egypt, solve a detective mystery involving the disappearance of an entire family, and, if their timing is right, take part in the production of TV segments in the Studio Works digital TV studio. *Details: 35 Market Pl.; 410/727-8120. Open daily 10–5:30. $10 adults, $7.50 children under 12. (1–2 hours)*

★★★ **Walters Art Gallery**—In the late nineteenth and early twentieth centuries, William T. Walters and his son Henry, both of whom made their fortune in the railroad business, amassed one of the country's largest art collections. In 1909 Henry Walters opened a gallery modeled on a Renaissance Genoese palace to display his collection. Henry Walters died in 1931 and left the museum, with its collection, to the city of Baltimore. Today, the Walters Art Gallery has more than 30,000 works of art spanning 5,000 years. The collection includes art from Ancient Egyptian, Rome, Greek, and Aztec cultures; Renaissance sculpture; Italian, English, and Flemish paintings; Limoges enamels; tapestries; and stained glass. Call ahead to find out about special exhibits. *Details: 600 N. Charles St.; 410/547-9000. Open Tue–Fri 11–4, Sat–Sun 11–5. $6 per person, with free entry Sat–Sun 11–5. (2 hours)*

★★ **American Visionary Art Museum**—Across the harbor from the bustling Harborplace shops, this unique museum showcases a variety of self-taught and largely unknown artists. The museum is the largest of its kind in the United States, featuring artworks created by farmers, housewives, mechanics, retirees, the disabled, the homeless, and the "occasional neurosurgeon." Standing in front of the museum is a colorful 55-foot, 15,000-pound *Whirligig* by visionary farmer and mechanic Vollis Simpson. Its Wildflower Sculpture Garden includes the *Non-Denominational Wedding Alter* by visionary lay naturalist Ben Wilson.

INNER HARBOR

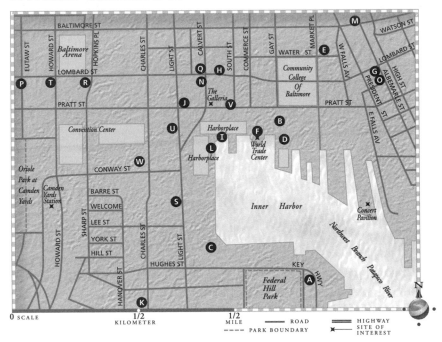

Sights

A American Visionary Art Museum
B Harborplace
C Maryland Science Center
D National Aquarium
E Port Discovery, The New Kid-Powered Museum
F World Trade Center

Food

G Baltimore Brewing Company
H Café Bombay
I Cheesecake Factory
A Joy America Café
J Legal Sea Foods
K One World Café

Food (continued)

L Paolo's
M Patisserie Poupon
N Strand Cybercafe
O Vaccaro's

Lodging

P Baltimore Marriott
Q Brookshire Inner Harbor Suite Hotel
R Days Inn Inner Harbor
S Harbor Court Hotel
T Holiday Inn Inner Harbor
U Hyatt Regency
V Renaissance Harborplace Hotel
W Sheraton Inner Harbor

Note: Items with the same letter are located in the same town or area.

The museum selects a single theme around which entire exhibitions are assembled, so it's wise to call ahead to find out what's being shown. Past exhibitions have included *Wind in My Hair*, a collection of more than 300 diverse paintings, objects, inventions, and flying machines expressing the human desire to fly; and *The End is Near!*, a collection of apocalyptic and post-millenium visions of the twenty-first century. Progressive palates won't want to miss the **Joy of America Café**, located on the top floor of the museum, with views of the harbor and some of the most original, most aesthetic cuisine in all of Baltimore.

> **Details:** *800 Key Hwy.; 410/244-1900. Open Tue–Sun 10–6. $6 adults; $4 seniors, students, and children. (1-2 hours)*

★★ **Baltimore and Ohio Railroad Museum**—The largest railroad museum in the country, the B&O Museum displays more than 80 locomotives and cars in its roundhouse, built in 1884, and throughout the surrounding area. The B&O Railroad was one of the first in the country, beginning regular passenger service in 1830. The museum's entrance is the 1830 Mount Clare Station, the country's first railroad station. Among the exhibits are the world's oldest surviving passenger car, a replica of America's first locomotive—the *Tom Thumb*—and the 1832 steamer, *Atlantic*. The museum also preserves a wealth of railroad memorabilia, including uniforms, clocks, lanterns, and timetables.

> **Details:** *901 E. Pratt St.; 410/752-2490. Open daily 10–5. $6.50 adults, $4 children under 12, $5.50 seniors. (1-2 hours)*

★★ **Baltimore Zoo**—Located just north of downtown Baltimore in Druid Hill, the Baltimore Zoo stands out as an oasis amidst peri-urban surroundings. The zoo's 180 rolling acres are home to more than 1,200 animals, birds, and reptiles from around the world. Its inhabitants include lions, leopards, bears, elephants, gazelles, giraffe, white rhinos, zebras, emus, kookaburras, lion-tailed macaques, blood pythons, and poison-dart frogs. Among its more unusual residents are rare snow leopards and bald eagles that, once injured in the wild, have been nursed back to health by zoo staff. An eight-acre interactive children's zoo allows kids to explore a piece of Maryland wilderness, enter a cave, or ride a merry-go-round. Both adults and children may test their camel riding ability with rides offered, for an additional fee, from Memorial through Labor Day. At the Children's Zoo Farmyard, children can ride a pony on Saturdays from April through October for $1.

Details: Greenspring Ave., Druid Hill Park; 410/396-7102. Open daily 10–4. $8.50 adults, $5 seniors and children ages 2–15. Additional fees for zoo rides. (2 hours)

★★ **Fort McHenry**—Shaped like a giant star, Fort McHenry gained prominence in the War of 1812 when it withstood 25 hours of enemy-fire from a British fleet intent on invading Baltimore. Following the failed invasion, Francis Scott Key, who witnessed the shell-fire from a ship of truce in the harbor, wrote "The Star Spangled Banner" with its reference to "the rocket's red glare" and "bombs bursting in air." The song was officially recognized as the national anthem by Congress in 1931. Every half-hour a 16-minute film is shown chronicling the Fort's history.

Details: Fort Ave.; 410/962-4299. Open daily Sept–May 8–5, June–Labor Day 8–8. $2 per person. (1½ hours)

★★ **Maryland Historical Society**—Among the state treasures housed here are fine examples of early American furniture, the country's largest collection of nineteenth-century silver, and notable historical artifacts, such as the original "Star Spangled Banner" manuscript. Children in

Aerial view of Fort McHenry

National Park Service

particular receive an engaging history lesson, with dioramas and interactive exhibits showcasing the state's history from its first Indian inhabitants to the arrival of English settlers to the Civil War and the industrial era. The Child's World exhibit showcases a large selection of antique toys, dolls, games, dollhouses, and children's furniture.
Details: *201 West Monument St.; 410/685-3750. Open Tue–Fri 10–5, Thu to 8, Sat 9–5, Sun 11–5. $4 adults, $3 seniors and students. (1 hour)*

★★ **Maryland Science Center**—To learn more about Chesapeake Bay history and marine life, visit the Maryland Science Center. With its multitude of hands-on exhibits, the center is also a great place for kids to learn about human anatomy, the creation and transformation of energy, and satellite technology. The museum houses a planetarium and IMAX movie theater where images are shown on a five-story screen.
Details: *602 Light St.; 410/685-5225. Open July–Labor Day Mon–Thu 10–6, Fri–Sun 10–8; Sept–June Mon–Fri 10–5, Sat and Sun 10–6. $9.75 adults, $8 ages 13–18, $7 seniors and children ages 4–12. (2 hours)*

★★ **Mount Vernon**—Just blocks north of the Inner Harbor is historic Mount Vernon, boasting many of Baltimore's architectural and cultural gems. Walking north on Charles Street, you can peruse the area's art galleries and eclectic shops while taking in the nineteenth-century brownstones that surround Mount Vernon Square. In the center of the square stands **Washington Monument**, a towering column rising 178 feet. Begun in 1815 and completed in 1829, it was the first monument in the country to honor George Washington, a 16-foot statue of whom is perched on top. The monument's architect was Robert Mills, who also designed the better known monument to the nation's first president in nearby Washington, D.C. Visitors may climb the Baltimore monument's 228 steps for spectacular views of the city.
Details: *Monument at 600 N. Charles St.; 410/396-0929. Open Wed–Sun 10–4, to 8 on first Thu of every month. $1 suggested donation. (30 minutes–1 hour)*

★★ **World Trade Center**—Just east of Harborplace at Pier Two is the World Trade Center. At 30 stories, it's the highest pentagonal building in the world (the U.S. Pentagon being the largest). From its 27th-floor observation deck, "Top of the World," visitors gain a panoramic view of the city and learn about its history and architecture.

Details: 401 E. Pratt St.; 410/837-4515. Open Mon–Sat 10–5:30, Sun 12–5:30 (with extended summer hours). $3 adults, $2 seniors and children. (30 minutes)

✯ **Babe Ruth Birthplace & Museum**—George Herman "Babe" Ruth was born in a narrow Baltimore row house in 1895. That same house now stands in the shadow of Camden Yards and has been transformed into the Babe Ruth Birthplace & Museum. The museum exhibits highlights from his career with the Boston Red Sox and New York Yankees, including uniforms, bats, gloves, and other memorabilia. Perhaps the most interesting fact to emerge from a visit to the museum is Babe Ruth's tempestuous early years; at age seven he was judged "hopelessly incorrigible" by his parents and sent off to a home for orphans and deliquents. Twelve years later he was "discovered" and began his career with the Orioles. An audiovisual presentation highlights the Babe in action and World Series moments. The museum also pays tribute to the Baltimore Orioles.

Details: 216 Emery St.; 410/727-1539. Open daily Apr–Oct 10–5, to 7 during Orioles' home games; Nov–Mar 10–4. $6 adults, $3 children ages 5–16, $4 seniors. (1 hour)

✯ **Great Blacks in Wax Museum**—This museum chronicles African American history, beginning with ancient Africa and on through slavery, the Civil War, and the Civil Rights era. It's the only museum in the country dedicated to African American heroes and historical legends, including inventors and scientists, as well as political, religious, and educational leaders.

Details: 1601 E. North Ave.; 410/563-3404. Open Jan 15–Oct 15 Tue–Sat 9–6, Sun 12–6; Oct 16–Jan 14 Tue–Sat 9–5, Sun 12–5. $5.75 adults, $5.25 seniors and students, $3.75 ages 12–17, $3.25 ages 2–11. (1 hour)

✯ **H. L. Mencken House**—Remembered as "the sage of Baltimore," the author, editor, and columnist H. L. Mencken lived in a nineteenth-century row house, which is now open to the public. The H. L. Mencken House features many of the writer's possessions and furnishings, including a grand piano. Outside lies a beautiful English row house garden.

Details: 1524 Hollins St.; 410/396-7997. Open Sat 10–5, Sun 12–5. $2 per person. (30 minutes)

Edgar Allan Poe House—Although the poet and short-story writer Edgar Allan Poe lived here for only three years, from 1832 to 1835, the Edgar Allan Poe House is dedicated to his memory. In addition to visiting the room where Poe wrote his first horror story, "Berenice," you can view changing exhibits and a video presentation of the poet's life. Just be wary of the neighborhood.

Details: 203 N. Amity St.; 410/396-7932. Open Wed–Sat 12–3:45. $3 per person. (1 hour)

Lexington Market—To experience the pulse of Baltimore, stop into Lexington Market at lunchtime, when a cornucopia of sounds and smells fills the air. A variety of foods are available, from fresh fish and baked goods to a range of ethnic cuisines—all at reasonable prices.

Details: 400 W. Lexington St.; 410/685-6169. Open Mon–Sat 8:30–6. (1 hour)

PROFESSIONAL AND SPECTATOR SPORTS

Baltimore is a city that takes its professional sports seriously, and none more so than baseball. One of the city's crowning achievements was the opening of **Oriole Park** at Camden Yards, 333 W. Camden St., 410/685-9800. Near the Inner Harbor and easily accessible from the major arteries leading into the downtown area, the stadium is distinguished by its arched brick facade. Tours last approximately an hour and 15 minutes and include a visit to the Orioles' dugout, press box, and scoreboard control room. Call for tour times and costs.

Also located in Camden Yards is **Ravens Stadium**, home of the Baltimore Ravens football team. Completed in Fall 1998, it features the latest in stadium technology, including two of the largest scoreboards in the country. For tickets, call 410/261-RAVE.

Followers of horse racing's famed Triple Crown will recognize Baltimore's **Pimlico Race Course**, Park Heights and Belvedere Avenues, 410/542-9400, as site of the annual Preakness Stakes. Located five miles north of downtown Baltimore, the thoroughbred track is Maryland's oldest and home to the National Jockey's Hall of Fame.

FITNESS AND RECREATION

Within the city proper, outdoor recreation is limited. For nearby parks and biking trails, see the next chapter, "Greater Baltimore." Most downtown hotels offer some sort of exercise facility, and many private clubs supply short-term passes for a fee. The **Downtown Athletic Club**, 210 E. Centre St., 410/332-0906, is one of these, offering squash, racquetball, an indoor pool, and the usual exercise equipment. You can jog along the Inner Harbor promenade, but expect a fair amount of casual foot traffic during nice weather.

FOOD

Baltimore boasts a variety of dining options, from leisurely cafés and vegetarian outposts to a host of ethnic eateries and classic, five-star restaurants. Naturally, seafood is a common theme on most menus. Given the city's strong reputation as a crab capital, these crustaceans show up on nearly every menu in one form or another. Hard-shell crabs are customarily steamed in a spicy broth and served with a small wooden mallet. Be prepared to get down and dirty at any authentic crab house, where they'll likely cover the table with large sheets of paper and let you pound and pick with a vengeance. Crab cakes are also extremely popular, as are sautéed soft-shell crabs. For the best crab cakes, steer clear of large restaurant chains that are likely to serve the frozen, heavy-on-the-bread-crumbs variety. One of the oldest and most popular crab dens is **Obrycki's**, 1727 E. Pratt St., 410/732-6399, in Fells Point. For more than 50 years Obrycki's has introduced newcomers and old-timers alike to the fine art of cracking crabs. Another well-known crab house option is **Gunnings**, 3901 S. Hanover St., 410/354-0085.

Many of the restaurants in the Inner Harbor are of the chain variety (e.g., Hooters and the Hard Rock Café) and vary considerably in quality and ambiance. If you're shopping and want to take in the harbor views, try **Paolo's**, 301 Light St., 410/539-7060, at the Harborplace Light Street Pavilion, for its Californian/Italian fare. A large wood-burning oven fills the air with pleasant aromas and the pizzas, pastas, and complimentary tapenade and breadsticks are quite good. In the Pratt Street Pavilion of Harborplace, the **Cheesecake Factory**, 201 E. Pratt St., 410/234-3990, offers a lively atmosphere as well as reliable service, healthy fare, and big portions. Adjacent to the Gallery shops is **Legal Sea Foods**, 100 E. Pratt St., 410/385-2763, serving a wide variety of seafood. In warm-weather months, diners may take advantage of the restaurant's sidewalk café.

Any number of places in Baltimore offer food that is relatively inexpensive and served in a casual and fun atmosphere. **Louie's**

Bookstore Café, 518 N. Charles St., 410/962-1224, is a local favorite serving everything from sandwiches to grilled salmon. In addition to displaying the latest titles, Louie's offers live classical music or jazz every night and during Sunday brunch. The **Baltimore Brewing Company**, located on the edge of Little Italy, 104 Albemarle St., 410/837-5000, offers a range of microbrews made on the premises, good food with a number of traditional German entrées, and an education on the fine art of making beer for those with an interest. Beer fans may also want to check out the **Brewer's Art**, 1106 N. Charles St., 410/547-6925, with its high ceilings, overstuffed couches, and fireplace. The menu suggests just the right beer or wine to accompany each dish, which range from moderately priced sandwiches and salads to more elaborate entrées. Vegetarians flock to **Margaret's**, 909 Fells St., 410/276-5605, in Fells Point for healthy, meatless cuisine at a reasonable price. The **Wild Mushroom**, 641 S. Montford Ave., 410/675-4225, serves a variety of mushroom dishes, such as wild mushroom ravioli and portabello burgers, along with 'shroomless fare in a lively environment.

If you have the money and want to spend it, a number of truly fine restaurants in town will give you the chance. A personal favorite is the **Joy America Café**, 800 Key Hwy., 410/244-6500, located at the top of the Visionary Arts Museum. The café offers views of Baltimore Harbor and dishes that are in themselves works of art. For superb, upscale fare, try **Charleston**, 1000 Lancaster St., 410/332-7373. Another excellent choice is **The Orchid**, 419 N. Charles St., 410/837-0080, offering a blend of artfully presented French and Asian cuisine. The **Brass Elephant**, 924 N. Charles St., 410/547-8480, in Mount Vernon specializes in northern Italian cuisine. Its white tablecloths, carved mantels, and leaded glass windows all contribute to the elegant atmosphere. Nearby is **Restaurant Tio Pepe**, 10 E. Franklin St., 410/539-4675, long cited as one of Baltimore's finest. Tio Pepe serves fine Spanish cuisine in a setting that mirrors old Spain. While the food is excellent, the wait to get in, even with a reservation, can dampen your spirit even as it enhances your appetite. The **Polo Grill**, located within the Inn at the Colonnade, 4 W. University Pkwy., 410/235-8200, offers excellent food in an elegant atmosphere.

Baltimore also showcases tastes from around the world in a wide variety of ethnic restaurants that are generally quite affordable. The section of Charles Street north and south of the Washington Monument is known for its international cuisine options. The

BALTIMORE

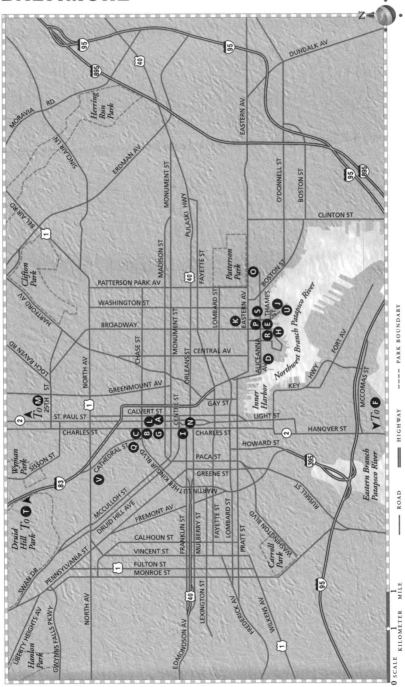

Food

Ⓐ Bombay Grill

Ⓑ Brass Elephant

Ⓒ Brewer's Art

Ⓓ Charleston

Ⓔ Daily Grind

Ⓕ Gunnings

Ⓖ The Helmand

Ⓗ Lista's

Ⓘ Louie's Bookstore Café

Ⓙ Margaret's

Ⓚ Obrycki's

Ⓛ The Orchid

Ⓜ Polo Grill

Ⓝ Restaurant Tio Pepe

Ⓞ Wild Mushroom

Ⓟ Ze Mean Bean Cafe

Lodging

Ⓠ Abercrombie Badger Bed and Breakfast

Ⓡ Admiral Fell Inn

Ⓢ Celie's

Ⓣ Cross Keys Inn

Ⓜ Doubletree Inn at the Colonnade

Ⓤ Inn at Henderson's Wharf

Ⓥ Mr. Mole

Note: Items with the same letter are located in the same town or area.

Helmand, 806 N. Charles St., 410/752-0311, is known for its unusual Afghan fare and pleasant dining environment with colorful folk costumes decorating the walls. The menu features delicately spiced dishes, including *kabuli* (marinated chunks of lamb tenderloin), *aushuk* (Afghan ravioli), and *banjan borawni* (pan-fried eggplant with yogurt garlic sauce). **Café Bombay**, 114 E. Lombard St., 410/539-2233, and its sister restaurant, the **Bombay Grill**, 2 E. Madison St., 410/837-2973, serve up authentic Indian cuisine, including lamb, crab, chicken, and vegetarian dishes. At lunchtime, both restaurants serve an extensive buffet. For excellent Mexican food in a lively, colorful atmosphere with water views, try **Lista's**, 1637 Thames St., 410/327-0040, in Fells Point.

Café life thrives in Baltimore; many low-key spots offer a place to sit and scan the headlines, listen to live music, drink lattes, and people-watch. Downtown, a block from Harborplace, is the **Strand**

CyberCafé, 105 E. Lombard St., 410/625-8944, serving innovative sandwiches and salads that you can enjoy while reading the paper or surfing the Net. In Federal Hill, the **One World Café**, 904 S. Charles St., 410/234-0235, is a popular hangout among locals featuring sidewalk tables and an outside courtyard. In Fells Point, **Ze Mean Bean Café**, 1739 Fleet St., 410/675-5999, mirrors European café life with a cozy atmosphere and menu featuring homemade borscht, pierogis (slavic dumplings), *holupki* (cabbage stuffed with ground beef), potato pancakes, and a wide assortment of pastries and cakes. The café provides a popular venue for local folk and jazz artists. Also in Fells Point is the **Daily Grind**, 1726 Thames St., 410/558-0399, another popular local hangout.

For the best desserts in town, there are two spots not to be missed. **Vaccaro's**, 222 Albemarle St., in Little Italy, displays a vast assortment of mouthwatering Italian pastries, including some of the world's largest and best chocolate éclairs. There's a dining area for those who can't wait long enough to take it home. Equally delectable is the nearby **Patisserie Poupon**, 820 Baltimore St., open Tuesday through Saturday. Their pastries, small works of art, are served at some of Baltimore's finest restaurants. While the bakery primarily runs a take-out business, coffee is served and a couple of small tables accommodate those who wish to stay.

LODGING

Baltimore's Inner Harbor abounds with hotels to suit a variety of budgets. Most of the downtown hotels are of the chain variety. The majority of those listed below are within walking distance of the Harborplace shops and Camden Yards. Prices vary according to the season and availability of rooms, with rates peaking in the summer months. Discounts and special weekend rates often apply. Beginning with less expensive lodgings, try the **Days Inn Inner Harbor**, 100 Hopkins Pl., 410/576-1000 or 800/329-7466. While the front lobby and rooms are a bit dated, there is a health club. Room rates are $79 to $149 (single) and $89 to $159 (double). Close by is the **Holiday Inn Inner Harbor**, 301 W. Lombard St., 410/685-3500 or 800/465-4329, with 375 guest rooms. The hotel features Baltimore's largest indoor pool, along with an exercise facility and sauna. Rates range from $115 (single or double) in the winter months to $139 in the summer.

In the mid-range of downtown hotels is the **Sheraton Inner**

Harbor, 300 S. Charles St., 410/962-8300 or 800/325-3535. Near the Baltimore Convention Center, the Sheraton offers rates between $129 and $245, depending on the season and availability. The **Hyatt Regency,** 300 Light St., 410/528-1234 or 800/233-1234, occupies a modern glass building with a six-story atrium lobby. In addition to a fully equipped exercise facility, the Hyatt features two tennis courts, a basketball court, outdoor pool, and jogging path. Rooms range from $145 to $220, with suites available for $350 to $1,400. The **Baltimore Marriott,** located at the intersection of Eutaw and Pratt Streets, 410/962-0202 or 800/228-9290, offers a health club, exercise room, saunas, and whirlpools. During the off-season, rooms can be had for $119 ($109 on weekends). During peak months, rooms run $179 ($169 on weekends) with breakfast included. At the time of this writing, the **Brookshire Inner Harbor Suite Hotel** was preparing for renovation. Located at 120 East Lombard Street, 410/625-1300 or 800/647-0013, the Brookshire mainly consists of suites with a bedroom, living room, and refrigerator. Rates fluctuate daily and range from $190 to $238 with occasional specials.

Any list of high-end, luxury lodging in the Inner Harbor should begin with the **Harbor Court Hotel,** 550 Light St., 410/234-0550 or 800/824-0076. Rooms are elegantly decorated with reproductions of English antiques. Suites include mahogany, four-poster canopy beds, and six-foot marble baths. Rooms with a view of the city or courtyard are $295 ($310 double); suites run from $500 to $2,500. Adjacent to the Gallery at Harborplace is the **Renaissance Harborplace Hotel,** 202 E. Pratt St., 410/547-1200 or 800/468-3571. The hotel's spacious rooms are nicely decorated and offer views of the harbor or city skyline. Facilities include an indoor pool, roof deck, and health club with sauna and whirlpool. During the winter months, rooms range from $149 to $199; the rest of the year rates run from $199 to $265.

If you're looking to experience the city's historic architecture from the inside, there are a number of bed-and-breakfast options; however, these vary in distance from the bustling harborfront. Several B&Bs are listed below. For further referrals, including smaller B&Bs with two to three rooms, contact **Amanda's Bed & Breakfast Reservation Service,** 1428 Park Ave., Baltimore, 410/225-0001.

Occupying a brick townhouse in the waterfront community of Fells Point is **Celie's,** 1714 Thames St., 410/522-2323 or 800/432-0184. Celie's seven rooms come in a variety of sizes and offer different features, such as a whirlpool tub, fireplace, skylight, and private balcony. Some overlook an inner courtyard; others have harbor views (and a view of the police-station set used in *Homicide*). Prices range from $100 to $200 depending on the room and occupancy. Some rooms require a two-night minimum stay on weekends. Smoking is not permitted inside; children must be 10 years of age or older.

A five-minute drive north of the Inner Harbor is the **Abercrombie Badger Bed and Breakfast**, 58 W. Biddle St., 410/244-7227. Each of its 12 rooms is unique, with creative flourishes like stenciled walls, four-poster beds, and decorative fireplaces. You stand a good chance of sharing the breakfast room with visiting performers associated with the Meyerhoff Symphony Hall or Lyric Opera House, both just a short distance away. Prices start at $79 for a single room with a twin bed to $105 to $135 for a room with a queen bed and private bath. Reserved parking is available and public transportation plentiful. Smoking is not allowed. Neither are children if they're under 10.

A sister-inn to the Abercrombie is **Mr. Mole**, 1601 Bolton St., 410/728-1179, a personal favorite. Located in the nearby historic community of Bolton Hill, Mr. Mole takes its name from the character in the popular children's tale *The Wind in the Willows*. Built in 1870, the house is furnished with eighteenth- and nineteenth-century antiques. Rooms and suites are distinctively—and impeccably—decorated. Rates start at $97 for a room with a queen bed, sitting area, and private bath, and go up to $125 to $155 for a two-bedroom suite. Rates include a large Dutch-style breakfast, garage parking, and a direct-dial telephone.

Just a short drive (or harbor taxi ride) from the Inner Harbor is Fells Point, offering several distinctive inns as alternatives to downtown hotel chains. Numerous eateries and small shops are scattered throughout Fells Point, known for its cobbled streets and nightlife, which can produce a fair amount of noise on summer weekends. Just across the street from the waterfront is the **Admiral Fell Inn**, 888 S. Broadway, 410/522-7377 or 800/292-4667. This historic eighteenth-century hotel originally served as a seamen's hostel. Today it's known for its emphasis on quality and as a place where guests can enjoy afternoon tea, Federal-period furnishings, an English-style pub, and on-site restaurant. Rooms run $135 in the off-season and $195 during peak months; rates include free parking and a continental breakfast.

Slightly removed from the heart of Fell's Point is the **Inn at**

Henderson's Wharf, 1000 Fell St., 410/522-7777 or 800/522-2088. Built in 1894 as a tobacco warehouse, the inn lies on a point of land jutting into the harbor, offering harbor views and sea breezes. Rooms start at $160 with views of the harbor or a garden courtyard. While there is no restaurant on site, many of the restaurants in nearby Little Italy offer free transportation to and from their doors.

If you're looking to escape the busy downtown and waterfront areas altogether, options just to the north are still close enough to make these areas easily accessible. Near Johns Hopkins University is the **DoubleTree Inn at the Colonnade**, 4 W. University Pkwy., 410/532-6900. The DoubleTree has an indoor swimming pool and fitness room, offers complimentary shuttle service downtown, and welcomes guests with freshly baked chocolate chip cookies upon check-in. Rooms range from $119 to $149 for a junior suite. Be sure to ask for any weekend specials. A little further north, just off the major downtown expressway, Route 83, is the **Cross Keys Inn**, 5100 Falls Rd., 410/532-6900. Set within a gated community, the inn offers a quiet, relaxed, rustic setting, along with access to the sophisticated shops and boutiques of the Village of Cross Keys. The inn has a health club and outdoor pool and offers free shuttle service to the Inner Harbor. Rooms run from $109 to $150 depending on the season and occupancy rates.

NIGHTLIFE

Baltimoreans have long supported a thriving performing arts scene. The city not only boasts accomplished local talent but draws national and international performers as well. Tickets and information regarding performances at many of the venues listed below can be obtained by contacting the Baltimore Visitors Center, 301 E. Pratt St., 410/752-TICS. The **Joseph Meyerhoff Symphony Hall**, 1212 Cathedral St., 410/783-8000, is home to the Baltimore Symphony Orchestra and provides a sophisticated venue for visiting jazz, classical, and pop artists. Nearby, the **Lyric Opera House**, 140 W. Mount Royal Ave., 410/783-8000, features performances by the Baltimore Opera Company from October to May. **CenterStage**, 700 N. Calvert St., 410/332-0033, presents critically acclaimed productions ranging from Shakespeare to more avant-garde performances. The nation's oldest school of music, the Peabody Conservatory of Music, 1 E. Mount Vernon Pl., 410/659-8124, hosts more than 60 events from September through May featuring the

Peabody Symphony Orchestra and student performers. Downtown, the **Morris Mechanic Theater**, 1 N. Charles St., 410/752-1200, provides a venue for the latest in touring musicals, dramas, and dance performances.

With several universities and colleges, Baltimore is a young town with lots going on in the evenings. Much of the action centers around Fells Point. A number of the pubs in the area have live music ranging from folk to rock to blues. For information on who's playing where, consult the *City Paper*, Baltimore's free alternative newspaper, or the *Baltimore Sun*'s Thursday "Weekend" section. For an elegant and sophisticated evening out, try the **Explorer's Club** at the Harbor Court Hotel, 550 Light St., 410/234-0550. Its walls and furniture echo the African bush. A pianist performs every night, with a complete jazz band on Friday and Saturday nights. Jazz enthusiasts should also check out **Buddies Pub and Jazz Club**, 313 N. Charles St., 410/332-4200, Wednesday through Saturday nights. For blues and progressive rock, check out who's playing at **8x10**, 8 E. Cross St., 410/625-2000. For more of a grunge scene (complete with a coffin as a coffee table), try the **Good Luv Bar**, 2322 Boston St., 410/558-2347. For an artsy experience, head to **Club Charles**, 1724 N. Charles St., 410/727-8815. Some of the best comedy in Baltimore can be heard at the **Comedy Factory Outlet**, Lombard and Light Sts., 410/659-7527.

8

GREATER BALTIMORE

You'll find protected parklands, stately homes and gardens, and historic towns such as Ellicott City located less than a half-hour from Baltimore's Inner Harbor. While the area surrounding the city has experienced the pressures of development, you can still take country roads past sprawling horse farms and stands where you can pick up fresh produce in the summer. A number of great restaurants have cropped up around the city, catering to suburbanites with demanding tastes.

Here you can witness the grandeur of the region's past. This chapter describes several historic homes whose architectural styles and interior furnishings have been carefully preserved. Just west of Baltimore, the quaint streets of historic Ellicott City are lined with eighteenth- and nineteenth-century stone and brick buildings that house a variety of restaurants and specialty, antique, and art shops. If nature is what you're after, a number of parks in the area will take you far from city congestion in less than a half-hour's drive. Sports such as golf, tennis, horseback riding, biking, and canoeing are all within easy reach.

A PERFECT DAY IN GREATER BALTIMORE

Begin with a visit to Homewood House, where you can also view the campus of Johns Hopkins University. Afterward, head north to the Baltimore beltway (Route 695), exiting on Delaney Valley Road; you'll immediately see signs to the Hampton National Historic Site Mansion. A tour of Hampton will give you a solid knowledge of the

GREATER BALTIMORE

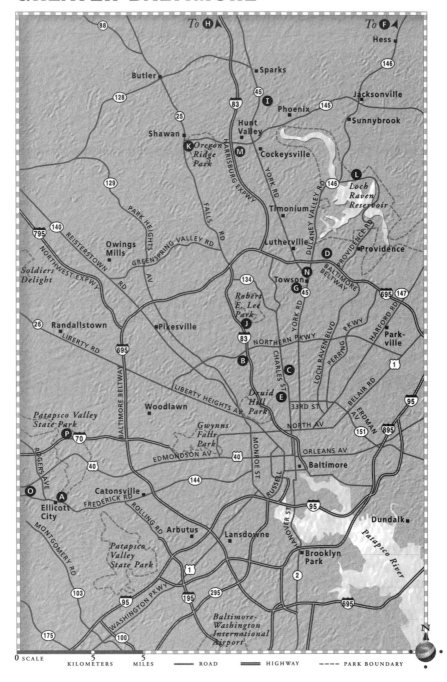

To **H** ▲   To **F** ▲

Hess ■

88

Butler ■   ■ Sparks   146

128   45

25   83   **I**   Phoenix   145   Jacksonville ■

Shawan ■   Hunt   ■ Sunnybrook
    Valley

129   **K** *Oregon*   **M**   ■ Cockeysville
    Ridge
    Park   **L**

146   *Loch*
    Raven
    Reservoir

Timonium ■

140   Owings   Lutherville ■   **D**   ■ Providence
795   Mills

Soldiers   134   Towson ■   **N**
Delight   **G** 45   695 147

26 Randallstown ■   *Robert*   York RD   Park-
    ■ Pikesville   *E. Lee*   *Park*   ville
    J
    LIBERTY RD   695   83   NORTHERN PKWY   1
    B   CHARLES ST   **C**

    LIBERTY HEIGHTS AV   *Druid*   **E**   95
    Woodlawn ■   *Hill*   33RD ST
    Park   NORTH AV
Patapsco Valley   *Gwynns*   151   895
State Park   *Falls*
    P 70   *Park*   ORLEANS AV
    40   EDMONDSON AV   40   ■ Baltimore
    144
    O   Catonsville ■   RUSSELL ST   95
    A   FREDERICK RD   Dundalk ■
Ellicott
City   Arbutus ■   ■ Lansdowne   *Patapsco*
    Patapsco   *River*
    Valley   ■ Brooklyn
    State Park   1   Park   2

    103
    95   195   295   695
    175   100   *Baltimore-*
    Washington
    International
    Airport

    N
    ▲

0 SCALE   5   5
    KILOMETERS   MILES   ━━ ROAD   ▰▰▰ HIGHWAY   ---- PARK BOUNDARY

Sights

Ⓐ B&O Railroad Museum

Ⓑ Cylburn Arboretum

Ⓒ Evergreen House

Ⓓ Hampton National Historic
Site Mansion

Ⓔ Homewood House Museum

Ⓕ Ladew Topiary Gardens and
Manor House

Food

Ⓖ Café Troia

Ⓐ Ellicott Mills Brewing
Company

Ⓗ Manor Tavern

Ⓘ Milton Inn

Ⓙ Mount Washington Tavern

Food (continued)

Ⓚ Oregon Grille

Ⓖ Paolo's

Ⓛ Peerce's Plantation

Ⓐ PJ's

Lodging

Ⓜ Embassy Suites

Ⓜ Marriott Hunt Valley Inn

Ⓝ Sheraton Baltimore Inn

Ⓞ Turf Valley Resort &
Conference Center

Camping

Ⓟ Patapsco Valley State Park

Note: Items with the same letter are located in the same town or area.

post-Revolutionary history of the area. Afterward head to historic Ellicott City, where you can have lunch, stroll the streets, and visit the B&O Railroad Museum. A brochure describing a self-guided walking tour of Ellicott City's historic district is available at many area shops.

SIGHTSEEING HIGHLIGHTS

★★ **B&O Railroad Museum**—In 1830 America's first steam engine, the *Tom Thumb*, made its way to the then-terminus of the Baltimore and Ohio Railroad in Ellicott City. Today a restored freight house has been made into a museum, offering a model railroad display of the first 13 miles of the line and a restored 1927 caboose. On display are the sta-tionmaster's quarters, a waiting room, a ticket office, and a freight house.
   Details: *2711 Maryland Ave., Elliott City; 410/461-1944. Open*

Memorial Day–Labor Day Wed–Mon 11–4, rest of the year Fri–Mon 11–4.
$3 adults, $1 children under 12, $2 seniors. (1 hour)

★★ **Evergreen House**—Listed on the National Register of Historic
Places, Evergreen House is a 48-room, Italianate mansion set on 26
acres just north of Baltimore proper. Built in the 1850s by the
Broadbent family, it was then purchased by the Garrett family, who
lived there from 1878 to 1942. Highlights include collections of post-
Impressionist paintings, Japanese netsuke, Tiffany glass, and rare books.
The house was bequeathed to Johns Hopkins University in 1942.
Details: 4545 N. Charles St., Baltimore; 410/516-0341. Open
Mon–Fri 10–4, Sat–Sun 1–4. $6 adults, $5 seniors, $3 students. (1 hour)

★★ **Hampton National Historic Site Mansion**—At the time it was
completed in 1790, Hampton was one of the largest and most luxuri-
ous homes in America. Built by Charles Ridgely, who made his fortune
in ironmaking, shipping, trading, and agriculture, the mansion and its
grounds tell a rich story of American business and commerce from the
perspective of successive generations of one family.

The house itself reflects classic Georgian symmetry. Its main
three-story structure is balanced by smaller wings on either side. The
interior is imbued with strong classical influence, along with the later
addition of Victorian features. At one time the property included over
24,000 acres, accommodating an ironworks, grain crops, beef cattle,
coal mining, marble quarries, and mills. The iron furnace produced a
variety of products from pig iron to artillery pieces used by George
Washington's army. Running the furnace required extensive labor,
which was provided at different times by indentured servants, slaves,
convicts, day laborers, and British prisoners of war. In 1948 the mansion and 43 acres were designated a national historic site. Today the
property is administered by the National Park Service.
Details: 535 Hampton Ln., Towson; 410/823-1309. Open daily 9–5.
Tours given on the hour and take 45 minutes. $5 person. (1 hour)

★★ **Homewood House Museum**—Located on the Johns Hopkins
University campus, Homewood House is a beautiful Federal-style mansion built in 1801 by Charles Carroll, a signer of the Declaration of
Independence, as a wedding present for his son. At the time, it was the
centerpiece of a 130-acre estate. A trip to downtown Baltimore then
would have taken over an hour by carriage; now it takes but a few min-

utes. The two-story, brick house has porticos at two entrances. The interior is decorated with eighteenth- and early-nineteenth-century furnishings and decorations, including pieces owned by the Carroll family. *Details: 3400 N. Charles St., Baltimore; 410/516-5589. Open Tue–Sat 11–4, Sun 12–4. Tours given on the hour and half hour. $6 adults, $3 students and seniors. (1 hour)*

★★ **Ladew Topiary Gardens and Manor House**—Covering 22 acres, the Ladew Topiary Gardens were designed by artist and fox-hunting enthusiast Harvey Smith Ladew. The property features flower gardens, including a formal rose garden, water garden, and cottage garden, along with some of the country's finest sculptured topiary trees and shrubs. Displayed inside the manor house are Ladew's collection of English antiques, paintings, and fox-hunting and equestrian memorabilia. *Details: 3535 Jarrettsville Pike, Monkton; 410/557-9466. House and gardens open mid-Apr–Oct Mon–Fri 10–4, Sat and Sun 10:30–5, with 45-minute tours given on the hour; Memorial Day–Labor Day gardens and café open to 8 on Thu. Garden only: $6 adults, $1 children under 12, $5 seniors and students. House and gardens: $8 adults, $2 children under 12, $7 seniors and students. (1–2 hours)*

Cylburn Arboretum—A lovely estate set on 76 acres, Cylburn provides a welcome escape with gardens, trails, a hands-on nature museum, and a horticultural reference library. Built by Jesse Tyson, a wealthy Baltimore industrialist, the home was completed in 1888. Today you can wander through grounds featuring magnolias, Japanese maples, flowering perennials, herbs, and a variety of other carefully maintained plantings and gardens. *Details: 4915 Greenspring Ave., Baltimore; 410/367-2217. Open dawn–dusk. Free. (1 hour)*

FITNESS AND RECREATION

Baltimore is fortunate to be surrounded by several parks, making country walks, mountain biking, and hiking easily accessible. Located north of the city, the area surrounding **Loch Raven Reservoir** makes for nice walks. Loch Raven Road, paralleling the reservoir, is closed to automobiles on weekends and attracts biking and in-line skating enthusiasts. **Oregon Ridge State Park**, also located north of Baltimore on

Beaver Dam Road in Cockeysville, has a nature center, a lake with a beach for swimming, and walking trails. **Gunpowder Falls State Park** has more than 100 miles of hiking trails, trout streams, and tidal fishing. Just west of the city along the Patapsco River, **Patapsco State Park** has five separate recreation areas with walking trails, biking, kayaking, and canoeing opportunities.

For biking, there's the **Baltimore and Annapolis Trail** running for 13.3 miles through open spaces and woodlands from Glen Burnie to Annapolis. Also popular is the **Northern Central Railroad Hike and Bike Trail,** which runs for 21 miles along the old Maryland-Pennsylvania Railroad line. The trail begins at Ashland Road, just east of York Road, and heads north to the Pennsylvania border. Parking is available at seven access points. For further information, contact Gunpowder Falls State Park, 410/592-2897.

FOOD

High-quality dining is not hard to find in the suburbs surrounding Baltimore, if you know where to go. Located in the small hamlet of Mount Washington, just north of the city, the **Mount Washington Tavern,** 5700 Newbury St., 410/367-6903, is a lively spot where you can find good food and drink without having to spend a lot. The tavern, especially popular among local yuppies, features a variety of beer from around the world, along with a large selection of American microbrews. Menu items include a wide range of creative sandwiches, soups, burgers, salads, and seafood, along with higher-priced dinner entrées such as grilled Atlantic salmon and jumbo lump crab cakes.

Just north in Towson, **Paolo's,** 1 W. Pennsylvania Ave., 410/321-7000, is part of a chain that manages to serve delicious salads, pizzas, and pasta dishes at reasonable prices in an upbeat, contemporary atmosphere. The "California Italian" menu also includes higher-priced seafood, chicken, beef, and veal entrées. For truly authentic regional Italian fare, try **Café Troia,** 28 W. Allegheny Ave., 410/337-0133.

The horse country north of Baltimore boasts a number of taverns and restaurants with their own historic charm. **Peerce's Plantation,** 12450 Dulaney Valley Rd., Phoenix, 410/252-3100, is located next to Loch Raven Reservoir. Serving lunch, dinner, and Sunday brunch, Peerce's specializes in steak and seafood dishes and is noted for its Maryland crab soup. In good weather, the outdoor patio can't be beat. The **Manor Tavern,** 15819 Old York Rd., Monkton, 410/771-8155, is

a favorite resting spot among the *aprés*-hunt set. The tavern features
more formal dining areas, along with a rustic barroom and light fare.
For a truly special meal, the **Milton Inn**, 14833 York Rd.,
410/771-4366, offers a memorable, if expensive, dining experience set
within an old stone country mansion. The menu features seafood, beef,
and Maryland specialties. Serving exceptional food in a rustic setting is
the **Oregon Grille**, 1201 Shawan Rd., Hunt Valley, 410/771-0505.
The restaurant is housed in an early-nineteenth-century building
located next to Oregon Ridge State Park. Hunting prints, horse sad-
dles, and bridles decorate the first floor while Vanity Fair and New
Yorker magazine covers adorn the walls upstairs. The Grille is open for
lunch, dinner, and Sunday brunch. Men are required to wear jackets
for the evening meal. Dinners are exquisitely prepared, consisting of
beef, lamb, pork, chicken, and seafood dishes, with a healthy dose of
grilled foods.

In Ellicott City, the **Ellicott Mills Brewing Company**, 8308
Main St., 410/313-8141, is located in a 1904 stone building that served
for decades as a lumber store. Its revamped interior features high ceilings, copper-topped tables, and a view of the restaurant's brewing facilities. Lunches consist of a variety of appetizers, salads, and sandwiches,
which are also available throughout the evening. Dinner entrées
include steak, chicken, seafood, and several unique items such as wild
boar in a beer sauce and grilled buffalo steaks. Across the street, **PJ's**,
8307 Main St., offers outdoor dining in warm weather and fireside dining in colder months. Lunches include salads, burgers, pasta, sandwiches, and a variety of entrées. Lighter fare is also available at dinner,
along with more extensive chicken, beef, and seafood entrées.

LODGING

North of Baltimore are a number of hotels and motels of the chain
variety that may save you some money over the higher-priced in-town
alternatives. In Towson, the **Sheraton Baltimore North**, 903 Dulaney
Valley Rd., 410/321-7400 or 800/325-3535, is within walking distance
of a popular mall, movie theaters, and restaurants. A large, corporate-
feeling hotel, it has the benefits of a pool, exercise room, sauna, and
Jacuzzi. Rooms range from $109 to $179, depending on the time of
year and occupancy rates.

Further north, in Hunt Valley, the **Embassy Suites**, 213
International Circle, 410/584-1400 or 800/EMBASSY, is cheerfully

decorated, with a plant-filled inner atrium. Its 223 suites each have a bedroom, living room with sofa bed, microwave, wet bar, refrigerator, and coffeemaker. The hotel also has an indoor pool, exercise room, and restaurant. Rooms run from $109 to $155. Nearby is the **Marriott Hunt Valley Inn**, 245 Shawan Rd., 410/785-7000. The 392-room inn features an indoor swimming pool, fitness room, and sauna, along with several dining facilities. Rooms range from $99 to $129.

Located on the outskirts of Ellicott City, the **Turf Valley Resort & Conference Center**, 2700 Turf Valley Rd., 410/465-1500 or 800/666-TURF, offers a sprawling resort atmosphere with golf, tennis, basketball, volleyball, softball, an outdoor swimming pool, and exercise facilities. Its 220 rooms and suites each have terraces. Rates range from $120 to $415. Be sure to ask about any special packages or discounts.

CAMPING

Camping is available just west of Baltimore at **Patapsco Valley State Park**. Covering 12,699 acres, the park spreads out along the Patapsco River. The park is divided into five separate recreation areas with camping available at only two of these: Hilton and Hollofield. There are 84 improved campsites all together, and electric hookups and a dump station at the Hollofield area only. The Hilton area is open Friday through Sunday only. For reservations, contact the park office, 8020 Baltimore National Pike, Ellicott City, 410/461-5005.

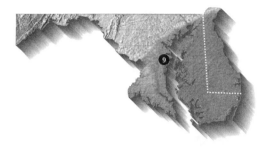

9
ANNAPOLIS

From the picturesque sailboats gracing its harbor to the myriad restaurants and pubs lining its streets, Annapolis is a place where you can relax and immerse your senses. Sea breezes and the sound of halyards hitting sailboat masts remind you that you're in one of the country's most popular sailing capitals. The appearance of delicately spiced crab cakes on most area menus tells you that you're on the Chesapeake Bay.

Founded in 1650, Annapolis is a town steeped in history. For nine months following the Revolutionary War, it served as the first peace-time capital of the United States. It was here that the Treaty of Paris, in which Great Britain formally recognized U.S. independence, was ratified. The city has one of the highest concentrations of eighteenth-century mansions, churches, and public buildings in the country. In fact, the entire mid-city region is a national historic district. Visitors may tour the state capitol, sign up for a walking tour of the city, or take in one or several carefully restored historic homes at their own pace. If looking to dine in a historic atmosphere, you can choose among several taverns and restaurants that once hosted colonial travelers. For a look at naval history, visit the campus of the U.S. Naval Academy, a vital part of Annapolis for more than 150 years.

To really experience Annapolis, try seeing it from the water aboard any number of sail and motor craft. Choose between an hour-long tour of the harbor and an entire day on the Chesapeake Bay. Several sailing schools offer lessons in the city's most popular and visible pastime.

ANNAPOLIS

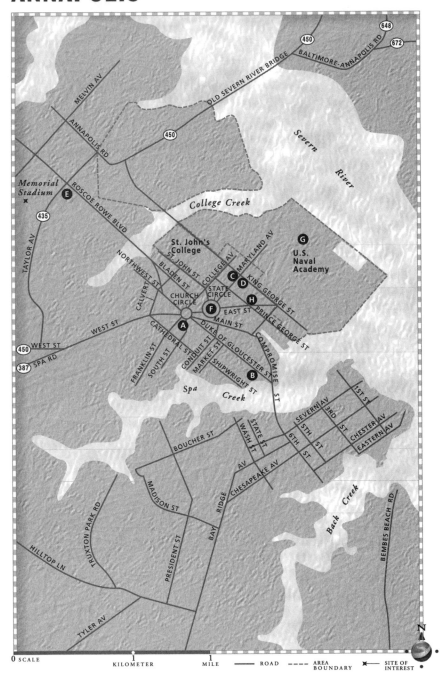

MELVIN AV

ANNAPOLIS RD

450

OLD SEVERN RIVER BRIDGE

450

648

672

BALTIMORE-ANNAPOLIS RD

Severn

River

Memorial
Stadium

E

ROSCOE ROWE BLVD

College Creek

435

TAYLOR AV

NORTHWEST ST

St. John's
College

ST. JOHN ST

BLADEN ST

COLLEGE AV

MARYLAND AV

G

U.S.
Naval
Academy

CALVERT ST

CHURCH
CIRCLE

C

D

KING GEORGE ST

STATE
CIRCLE

H

F

A

EAST ST

PRINCE GEORGE ST

WEST ST

WEST ST

450

WEST ST

387

SPA RD

CATHEDRAL ST

FRANKLIN ST

SOUTH ST

DUKE OF GLOUCESTER ST

CONDUIT ST

MARKET ST

MAIN ST

SHIPWRIGHT ST

COMPROMISE ST

B

Spa

Creek

BOUCHER ST

WASH ST

STATE ST

SEVERN AV

5TH ST

6TH ST

3RD ST

1ST ST

CHESTER AV

EASTERN AV

AV

MADISON ST

BAY RIDGE

CHESAPEAKE AV

Back

Creek

BEMBES BEACH RD

TRUXTON PARK RD

HILLTOP LN

PRESIDENT ST

TYLER AV

N

0 SCALE   1 KILOMETER   1 MILE   —— ROAD   - - - - AREA BOUNDARY   ✕ SITE OF INTEREST ●

Sights

Ⓐ Banneker-Douglass Museum

Ⓑ Charles Carroll House

Ⓒ Chase-Lloyd House

Ⓓ Hammond Harwood House

Ⓔ Helen Avalynne Tawes Garden

Ⓕ Maryland State House

Ⓖ United States Naval Academy

Ⓗ William Paca House and Garden

A PERFECT DAY IN ANNAPOLIS

Begin your day in Annapolis with a visit to the Maryland State House, the oldest U.S. capitol in continuous use and a prominent city landmark. Afterward, you may want to take a formal tour of the city's historic district, or spend time on your own touring one or several of the city's historic homes. Highly recommended is the William Paca House and Garden. For lunch, walk down to the harborfront where you can take in the views while eating at one of the many area restaurants. In the afternoon walk the grounds of the U.S. Naval Academy, stopping into the museum and chapel. If time, budget, and weather permit, an afternoon boat tour is highly recommended for truly appreciating this Chesapeake Bay city.

GETTING TO KNOW HISTORIC ANNAPOLIS

For a good orientation to the city, stop by the **Visitors Center** on City Dock, operating from April through October. Also helpful is the **Historic Annapolis Foundation Museum Store & Welcome Center**, 77 Main St., 410/268-5576, which, in addition to exhibits on the area's history, offers a self-guided, audio-cassette walking tour of over 15 of the city's historic sites. Historic walking tours of the city are available through **Annapolis Walkabout**, 223 S. Cherry Grove Ave., 410/263-8253. Tours leave from the visitors center at 10 a.m. and 11:30 a.m. on Saturday and Sunday from April through October, or you can call ahead and reserve a tour at a different time. **Three**

Centuries Tours, 410/263-5401, also offers walking tours twice a day in season. **Chesapeake Marine Tours Inc.**, 410/268-7600, offers narrated boat tours and day trips to the Eastern Shore.

SIGHTSEEING HIGHLIGHTS

★★★ **Maryland State House**—Built between 1772 and 1779, the Maryland State House is the oldest U.S. state capitol in continuous legislative use. It was here that the Treaty of Paris was ratified bringing the Revolutionary War to an end. The dome of the building, the largest of its kind constructed entirely of wood, is made of cypress beams and is held together by wooden pegs. Exhibits depict life in Annapolis during colonial times. Free guided tours are offered at 11 a.m. and 3 p.m.

Details: State Circle; 410/974-3400. Building open daily 9–5. Visitors center open Mon–Fri 9–5, Sat and Sun 10–4. Free. (30 minutes)

★★★ **United States Naval Academy**—Founded in 1845, the United States Naval Academy, the U.S. Navy's undergraduate professional college, occupies a beautiful 300-acre campus overlooking the Severn River. As many of its original structures were demolished at the turn of the century, what you'll see is an impressive array of Beaux-Arts buildings designed by Ernest Flagg. For a brief orientation, stop into the **Armel-Leftwich Visitors Center** at the Halsey Field House, just inside Gate 1. Here you can watch a 12-minute introductory video and plan your next steps. In addition to strolling around or driving through the campus, you'll want to visit the **U.S. Naval Academy Museum**, located in Preble Hall. On display is a large collection of paintings, ship models, weapons, medals, and naval memorabilia. Also of interest is the **Naval Academy Chapel** with its 200-foot dome and stained-glass Tiffany windows commemorating naval heroes. Beneath the chapel is a crypt containing the remains of John Paul Jones, the great naval leader of the American Revolution.

Details: King George and Randall Sts.; 410/263-6933. Grounds open daily 9 a.m.–sunset; museum open daily 9–5, crypt open daily 9–4:30. Free. (1–2 hours)

★★★ **William Paca House and Garden**—This historic mansion, built between 1763 and 1765, was home to lawyer William Paca, signer of the Declaration of Independence and Revolutionary-era governor of

Maryland. Paca lived in the 37-room house until 1780. In the nineteenth century it was used as a boardinghouse with additions subsequently added. Slated for demolition in the 1960s, the house was saved by preservationists who undertook an extensive restoration process. Today, many of its rooms are decorated with furnishings reflecting the time in which its first owner lived. The house is surrounded by a two-acre formal garden with five terraces, a fish-shaped pond, a Chinese Chippendale bridge, and a wilderness garden.

Details: 186 Prince George St.; 410/263-5553. Open Mon–Sat 10–4, Sun 12–4. Call for hours in Jan and Feb. $5 house only, $4 garden only, $7 house and garden; children ages 6–18 half price. (1 hour)

★★ **Banneker-Douglass Museum**—The Banneker-Douglass Museum, named after two prominent black residents of Annapolis—Benjamin Banneker and Frederick Douglass—is dedicated to portraying the historical and cultural experiences of African Americans in Maryland. Housed in the former Mt. Moriah Church, built in 1874, the museum's collection includes historical and archaeological artifacts, African and African American art, rare books, and oral history tapes. Exhibits focus on African American arts and culture.

Details: 84 Franklin St.; 410/974-2893. Open Tue–Fri 10–3, Sat 12–4. Free. (1 hour)

★★ **Charles Carroll House**—Located on the grounds of St. Mary's church is the Charles Carroll House, built in 1721. The house was the birthplace and home of Charles Carroll of Carrollton, one of the wealthiest men in the colonies and the only Roman Catholic to sign the Declaration of Independence.

Details: 107 Duke of Gloucester St.; 410/269-1737. Open Fri and Sun 12–4, Sat 10–2. Tours $5 adults, $4 seniors, $2 students ages 12–17. (1 hour)

★★ **Hammond-Harwood House**—Built from 1774 to 1776, the Hammond-Harwood House is considered one of the finest examples of Georgian architecture in the country. The house is famous for its center doorway flanked by tall Ionic columns. The house is based on a five-part plan consisting of a main house connected to two wings by one-story passageways. Inside, elaborate carved woodwork and plaster ornamentation can be found on doorways, windows, and fireplaces. The house is furnished with period pieces from 1760 to 1800.

Annapolis and Anne Arundel County CVB

Charles Carroll House

Details: *19 Maryland Ave.; 410/269-1714. Open Mon–Sat 10–4, Sun 12–4. $5 adults, $3 students and children. Combination ticket to Hammond-Harwood House and William Paca House and Garden (see above) $10 adults. (1 hour)*

✿ **Chase-Lloyd House**—Across the street from the Hammond-Harwood House (see above) is the Chase-Lloyd House, a three-story Georgian brick townhouse. Built in 1769 by Samuel Chase, a signer of the Declaration of Independence, the house is known for its fine interior detail.
   Details: *22 Maryland Ave.; 410/263-2723. Open Mon–Sat 2–4. $2 per person. (30 minutes)*

✿ **Helen Avalynne Tawes Garden**—To get a feel for Maryland's diverse natural environments, visit the Helen Avalynne Tawes Garden, a six-acre botanical garden featuring a range of scenic representations from the forested mountains of western Maryland to the sand dunes of the Eastern Shore.
   Details: *580 Taylor Ave. at the Tawes State Office Building; 410/974-3717. Open Mon–Fri dawn–dusk. Free. (1 hour)*

FITNESS AND RECREATION

Water sports are king in Annapolis. Windsurfing lessons and rental equipment are available from **East of Maui**, 2303E Forest Dr., 410/573-9463. Canoes, paddeleboats, sailboats, and powerboats can be rented at **Quiet Waters Park Boat Rentals**, Hillsmere Dr., 410/267-8742. Sailboat cruises and sailboat lessons are also widely available. The **AYS Sailing School**, 7416 Edgewood Rd., 410/267-8181, offers full-service charter and sailing instruction on sailboats ranging from 28 to 46 feet long. The **Annapolis Sailing School**, 601 Sixth St., 410/267-7205, offers basic instruction, boat rentals, and sailing vacations. **Chesapeake Sailing School**, 7074 Bembe Beach Rd., 410/269-1594, also provides lessons for all ages and sailboat charters from 22 to 43 feet.

For biking, walking, and running, the **Baltimore & Annapolis Trail** stretches for 13 miles from Glen Burnie to Annapolis, passing through forests, farmland, and urban and suburban neighborhoods. A map and brochure are available at the park's headquarters, Earleigh Heights Rd., Severna Park, 410/222-6244.

FOOD

Good restaurants are easy to find in Annapolis. What follows is a diverse selection of some of the more popular spots. Dinner reservations are recommended at most area restaurants during peak summer months.

Billed as a coffeehouse and wine bar, there's more to **49 West** than meets the eye. Located at 49 West St., 410/626-9796, this popular meeting spot is open from 7:30 a.m. to midnight on weekdays and until 2 a.m. on weekends. The breakfast menu consists of egg dishes, waffles, bread, muffins, and scones. During the remainder of the day a variety of appetizers, soups, salads, and sandwiches are available (and yes, alcohol is served). The work of a different artist is featured each month, and live music is played Tuesday through Sunday evenings, including classical, jazz, blues, and folk.

The downtown harbor area is filled with restaurants; in the summer months these can get quite crowded, resulting in occasionally lackluster service. Not more than a stone's throw from the harbor itself is the **Middleton Tavern Oyster Bar and Restaurant**, 2 Market Space, 410/263-3323. The eighteenth-century tavern serves traditional

ANNAPOLIS

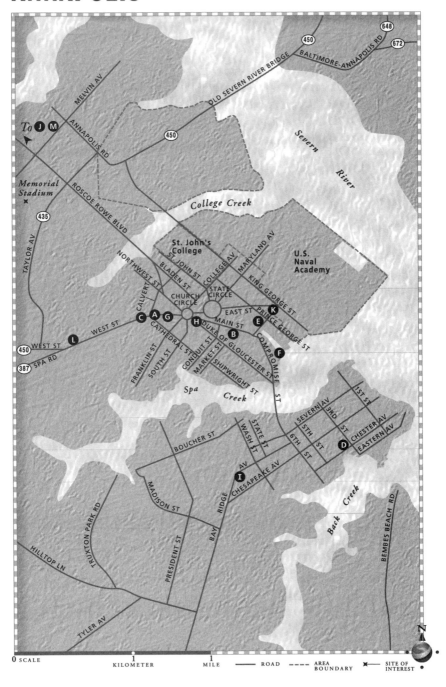

Food

Ⓐ 49 West

Ⓑ Café Normandie

Ⓒ Ciao

Ⓓ Davis' Pub

Ⓔ Middleton Tavern Oyster Bar
and Restaurant

Ⓕ Pusser's Landing

Ⓖ Ram's Head Tavern and
Fordham Brewing Company

Ⓗ Treaty of Paris

Ⓘ Wild Orchid Café

Lodging

Ⓙ Barn on Howard's Cove

Ⓚ Gibson's Lodgings Bed
and Breakfast

Ⓗ Historic Inns of Annapolis

Ⓛ Loews Annapolis Hotel

Ⓕ Marriott Waterfront

Camping

Ⓜ Capital KOA Campground

Note: Items with the same letter are located in the same town or area.

Maryland fare, including crab soup, spiced shrimp, and stuffed rock-fish, and has a raw-oyster bar. A sidewalk café is available for warm-weather dining while a fireplace inside takes the chill off of cold winter days. A great spot for a casual lunch or dinner and great harbor views is **Pusser's Landing**, 80 Compromise St., 410/626-0004, located in the Marriott Waterfront Hotel. Known for its creative rum concoctions, Pusser's offers classic pub fare with a Caribbean twist. Lunches include Tortola black bean soup, Grenadian tuna and lentil salad, and West Indian turkey sandwiches. Dinner entrées range from coconut fried shrimp to a Caribbean chicken burrito. The **Ram's Head Tavern and Fordham Brewing Company**, 33 West St., 410/268-4545, is an English-style tavern serving more than 170 beers from around the world, along with its own microbrews. The tavern serves lunch and dinner and is now offering live music four to six nights a week. For a memorable crab cake in a low-key, neighborhood atmosphere, try **Davis' Pub**, 400 Chester Ave., 410/268-7432. With views of Back Creek, the pub offers outdoor dining in warm weather. Menu items range from some of the best burgers in town to crab cake and shrimp platters, along with blue plate specials featuring pot roast and turkey dinners.

For reasonably priced French fare in a casual, rustic setting, try **Café Normandie**, 185 Main St., 410/263-3382. The café serves breakfast, lunch, and dinner, and specializes in such French favorites as crêpes, omelettes, baked brie, country pâté, and *salade niçoise*. **Ciao**, 51 West St., 410/267-7912, offers an intimate setting with a Mediterranean flair. Lunches consist of reasonably priced sandwiches and salads, while dinners feature a creative blend of tastes from Italy, France, and the Middle East. Entrées range from Spanish paella and Mediterranean meatloaf to artichoke and sundried tomato ravioli.

Housed in a renovated 1920s Eastport home (five minutes from downtown Annapolis), the **Wild Orchid Café**, 909 Bay Ridge Ave., 410/268-8009, specializes in creative American cuisine. The café, with an outdoor patio for warm-weather dining, is open for lunch and dinner Tuesday through Friday, and for breakfast on weekends. Lunches consist of soups, salads, sandwiches, and entrées. Dinners fall into the mid price range and feature an extensive seafood selection, along with poultry, duck, and beef.

For elegant dining in an eighteenth-century setting, try **Treaty of Paris**, 58 State Circle, 410/216-6340, located at the Maryland Inn. Dinners consist of delicately prepared seafood, beef, lamb, and poultry, including such dishes as Maryland stuffed rockfish and roast rack of lamb Grenoble. Sunday brunches are especially popular.

LODGING

In addition to being a state capital, Annapolis could well be considered a bed-and-breakfast capital. There are literally dozens of them. Located next door to the U.S. Naval Academy, **Gibson's Lodgings Bed & Breakfast**, 110 Prince George St., 410/268-5555, is made up of three historic houses with a total of 21 rooms. A range of room types are available from those with private or shared baths to suites. Rates run from $68 to $125 and include a full continental breakfast and parking.

Just outside of the city is the **Barn on Howard's Cove**, 500 Wilson Rd., 410/266-6840. Set on 6.5 wooded acres, this lovely B&B is a converted 1850 horse barn overlooking the Severn River. The inn features a deep-water dock and canoe. Its two guest accommodations, one a suite, the other a room with private bath, go for $100 and $90 respectively.

Conveniently located in the city's historic district, the **Historic Inns of Annapolis**, 58 State Circle, 410/263-2641 or 800/847-8882, consists of three inns near one another. Reservations for each of these inns can be made by calling the one central number. Each has been carefully restored and furnished with reproduction antiques. Together they feature 128 guest rooms, all with private baths, ranging from $135 to $285. While many of the 44 guest rooms at the **Maryland Inn** date back to the Revolutionary era, its wooden porches reflect Victorian tastes. Facing the Colonial Gardens on one side and the State House on the other, the **Governor Calvert House** has both colonial and Victorian features. Overlooking the governor's mansion and the State House, the brick **Robert Johnson House** is actually three houses, with 25 rooms, that have been fully restored.

For all the conveniences of a modern full-service hotel, try **Loews Annapolis Hotel**, 126 West St., 410/263-7777 or 800/23LOEWS. Located within walking distance of the historic district and waterfront, the hotel features a sky-lit atrium lobby, spacious rooms, and a complimentary continental breakfast. Also available is an athletic facility with stationary equipment. Room rates begin at $99 in the off-season and go up as high as $229. Suites are also available for $149 to $329. You can't beat the location of the **Marriott Waterfront**, 80 Compromise St., 410/268-7555 or 800/336-0072, for harbor views and easy accessibility to area sights. The hotel's 150 guest rooms are spacious and include two telephones, ironing boards and irons, modem hookups, and a complimentary morning newspaper. An exercise room is also available. Rooms range from $159 to $199 and are slightly higher for a waterfront view.

CAMPING

Open from April to November, the **Capital KOA Campground**, 768 Cecil Ave. North, Millersville, 410/923-2771, has full-service camping accommodations for recreational vehicles and tents, along with log cabins, picnic areas, and recreational services.

NIGHTLIFE

Offering live music to suit a range of tastes is **49 West**, 49 West St., 410/626-9796. The café features classical, jazz, blues, folk, and the occasional guitar or fiddle player on various nights of the week. The **Ram's Head Tavern**, 33 West St., 410/268-4545, shows national acts most nights of the week. You can listen to live jazz on Thursday, Friday, and Saturday nights at the **King of France Tavern**, 16 Church

Circle, 410/263-2641, located at the Maryland Inn. The tavern has a warm and welcoming ambiance with low ceilings, stone walls, and brick floors. Located close to the waterfront, the **Middleton Tavern**, City Dock, 410/263-3323, offers acoustic music nightly and blues on Sunday nights.

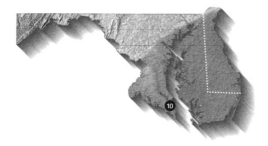

10
SOUTHERN MARYLAND

R oughly 15 million years ago, whales came to bear their young in the shallow seas that covered what is now southern Maryland. Today visitors to the area re-create the past as amateur archaeologists. Sifting through the sand at Calvert Cliffs State Park, it's not unusual to discover sharks' teeth and other fossils dating back to the Miocene period. The cliffs stretch on for 30 miles and range in height from 40 to 100 feet. Nearby, at the Battle Creek Cypress Swamp, an elevated boardwalk takes you through a forest of towering cypress trees in a swamp environment reminiscent of the days when mammoths roamed the region.

Southern Maryland is replete with opportunities to explore the past and enjoy the great outdoors. At the Calvert Marine Museum, you can trace the Chesapeake Bay's maritime history, watch otters play, or board a 100-year-old "bugeye" boat for a tour of the nearby harbor. Maryland's colonial history is preserved in historic St. Marys City, where archaeologists in the 1970s began piecing together the early history of the state's first capital.

Proximity to the bay and several excellent parks enable visitors to enjoy a variety of outdoor sports—from fishing for striped bass aboard a charter to windsurfing in the waters just off Solomons. Spots to hike, bike, and view local flora and fauna abound. For those more interested in the built environment, the Calvert Cliffs Nuclear Power Plant is open to visitors year-round.

SOUTHERN MARYLAND

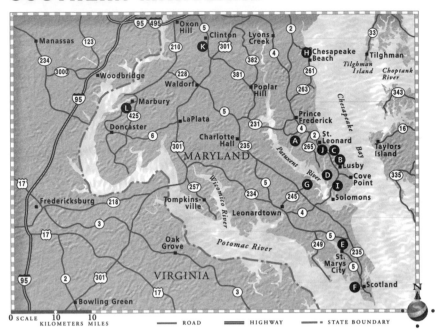

Sights

Ⓐ Battle Creek Cypress Swamp Sanctuary

Ⓑ Calvert Cliffs Nuclear Power Plant

Ⓑ Calvert Cliffs State Park

Ⓒ Flag Ponds Nature Park

Ⓓ Jefferson Patterson Park and Museum

Ⓔ Historic St. Marys City

Ⓕ Point Lookout State Park

Ⓖ Sotterly Plantation

Food

Ⓗ Rod 'n' Reel

Ⓗ Smokey Joe's Grill

Lodging

Ⓘ Holiday Inn Select Solomons

Ⓙ Mantoaka Beach Cabins

Camping

Ⓚ Cosca Regional Park

Ⓕ Point Lookout State Park

Ⓛ Smallwood State Park

Note: Items with the same letter are located in the same town or area.

A PERFECT DAY IN SOUTHERN MARYLAND

Begin your day in southern Maryland with a visit to the Jefferson Patterson Park and Museum, set on more than 500 acres of wooded farmland overlooking the Patuxent River. Here you can learn about the early history of the state and enjoy a pleasant walk through the fields and by the river. Then drive south to Calvert Cliffs State Park. Here follow a two-mile hiking trail that takes you down to the beach, where you can comb the sand for fossils and shark teeth. In the afternoon, you might opt to wander the streets of Solomons. This quaint town features a number of art galleries, small boutiques, and restaurants. Be sure to visit the Calvert Maritime Museum to learn about the creatures that inhabit the Chesapeake Bay and the watermen who have made a living on the bay for centuries.

SIGHTSEEING HIGHLIGHTS

★★★ **Jefferson Patterson Park and Museum**—Set on 512 acres of woods and farmland overlooking the Patuxent River, the Jefferson Patterson Park and Museum is a great place to learn about the history and archaeology of Maryland or simply walk and enjoy the outdoors and river views. Mrs. Jefferson Patterson donated the property to the State of Maryland in 1983. Previously it had served as a model farm for raising tobacco, soybeans, corn, and Aberdeen cattle. The visitors center hosts changing exhibits on local culture and history, along with a permanent exhibit, "12,000 Years in the Chesapeake," that chronicles the region's inhabitants beginning with Ice Age animals up through successive hunter-gatherer, early agricultural, and plantation societies. Archaeological finds on exhibit include a mastodon molar, primitive knives, Native American pottery fragments, and colonial items. In addition, a farm exhibit building houses a 20,000-pound steam traction engine and a demonstration garden where you can compare Native American, colonial, and nineteenth-century crops and planting techniques specific to southern Maryland. Two trails teach visitors about local wildlife, crops, and the evolution of the surrounding landscape.

Details: 10515 Mackall Rd., St. Leonard; 410/586-0050. Open Apr 15–Oct 15 Wed–Sun 10–5. Free. (2 hours)

★★ **Battle Creek Cypress Swamp Sanctuary**—Here you can conjure up images of Maryland some 100,000 years ago, when swamps covered much of the area and saber-toothed tigers and mammoths roamed the land. Protected in this 100-acre nature reserve is the northernmost stand of bald cypress trees in the United States. These tall conifers, which can live for some 3,000 years, are related to California's redwoods. The trees emerge from the water-covered landscape, rising up more than 100 feet. A quarter-mile elevated boardwalk leads you through the forest to perhaps catch a glimpse of a white-tailed deer, muskrat, possum, turtle, frog, or a number of bird species. The nature center houses a variety of interactive exhibits, demonstrations, and audio-visual presentations. Children will especially enjoy guessing the sounds of various animals, making their own animal tracks, and checking out the albino snapping turtle—one of only seven in the world.

Details: Route 506, off Route 4, just south of Prince Frederick; 410/535-5327. Open Apr–Sept Tue–Sat 10–5, Sun 1–5; Oct–Mar until 4:30 p.m. on the same days. Free. (1 hour)

★★ **Calvert Cliffs State Park**—Stretching for 30 miles from North Beach to Solomons, the Calvert Cliffs range from 40 to 100 feet high and contain shells and fossils that were once on the floor of the shallow ocean that covered southern Maryland during the Miocene epoch (15 to 20 million years ago). The 1,460-acre park has several trails, averaging two miles in length, leading down to the beach where you can hunt for shark's teeth and other fossils. Access to the cliffs is banned due to the danger of landslides.

Details: Route 2/4, Lusby; 410/888-1410. Open Fri–Sun 10–6 (schedule for rest of week varies). $3 per car. (1–2 hours)

★★ **Calvert Maritime Museum**—The Calvert Maritime Museum offers an engaging educational experience without being the least bit overwhelming. Visitors can learn about creatures native to the Chesapeake Bay region—both now and millions of years ago. The high-ceilinged main exhibition hall details the region's maritime history and contains life-size examples of business and pleasure boats. A 15-tank "Estuarium" displays the diverse plant and animal life in the bay. Children enjoy sifting through sand and gravel for shark teeth and other fossils in the Discovery Room. Outside you can watch river otters at play or walk along the museum's salt marsh habitat, home to various crab species, herons, and egrets. Also on the museum's grounds is the **Drum Point Lighthouse**, a squat, hexagonal house perched on six legs. Built in 1883, the lighthouse was moved here in 1975 and is

Calvert Maritime Museum in Solomons

open to the public. Visitors may also opt to take a cruise on a converted 1899 bugeye sailboat.

Details: Route 2/4 at Solomons Island Rd., Solomons; 410/326-2042. Open daily 10–5. $5 adults, $4 seniors, $2 children 5–12. (1–2 hours)

★★ **Flag Ponds Nature Park**—For a pleasant hike through the woods or walk along the Chesapeake shoreline try Flag Ponds Nature Park. The park takes its name from the blue flag iris, a wildflower that dominates the landscape in warmer weather, along with columbine and rose mallow. Three hiking trails of varying lengths (the shortest being a half-mile) take you through the woods to the sandy beach. Here you can hunt for shark teeth or other ancient fossils. The park includes two ponds, a fishing pier on the Chesapeake Bay, and a visitors center with wildlife displays.

Details: Look for signs on Route 4, 10 miles south of Prince Frederick; 410/586-1477. Open Memorial Day–Labor Day Mon–Fri 9–6, Sat and Sun 9–8; rest of the year weekends only 9–6. $6 per person Memorial Day through Labor Day; $3 per person off-season. (1–2 hours)

★★ **Historic St. Marys City**—It was in 1634 that roughly 140 settlers sailed across the Atlantic on two ships, the *Ark* and the *Dove*, and created a settlement at St. Marys City. St. Marys City would become the first capital of Maryland, until 1695, when the legislature moved to Annapolis. Thereafter the city disappeared from maps and history books for more than two centuries. In the early 1970s an archaeological/reconstruction effort was undertaken to rediscover the past. Today historic St. Marys City serves as an 800-acre outdoor museum with exhibits that showcase the history, archaeology, and natural history of the area. The **Godiah Spray Plantation** demonstrates what life was like on a seventeenth-century tobacco plantation. Visitors may even take part in household and garden chores. **Farthings Ordinary** is a reconstructed seventeenth-century inn. The **Old State House**, a reproduction of the original 1676 building, contains historical exhibits and is the setting for trials and other living history re-creations. The *Maryland Dove*, on the water behind the State House, is a replica of the small square-rigged boat that brought early settlers and cargo to Maryland.

Details: Off Route 5, St. Marys City; 301/862-0990 or 800/SMC-1634. Open mid-Mar–Nov Wed–Sun 10–5. Visitors center and archaeology exhibit open year-round. $7.50 adults, $3.50 children ages 6–12, $6 seniors and students. (2–3 hours)

✯ **Calvert Cliffs Nuclear Power Plant**—Supplying one-third of Maryland's electricity, the Calvert Cliffs Nuclear Power Plant operates a visitors center that educates visitors about the region's natural history, the production of nuclear power, and safety precautions. The rustic building housing the plant's educational outreach component, a former tobacco barn, stands in stark contrast to the cement and steel of the nuclear facility itself. Perched on a cliff overlooking the Chesapeake— from which it derives its cooling water—the plant's "scenic overlook" offers commanding views of the bay. While potentially eerie for the nuclear-wary, elements of the plant's public education/PR campaign are commendable.

Details: 1650 Calvert Cliffs Parkway (10 miles south of Prince Frederick, just off of Route 4), Lusby; 410/495-4673. Open daily 10–4. Free. (30 minutes)

✯ **Point Lookout State Park**—Located on the peninsula that forms the southern tip of Maryland's Western Shore, Point Lookout State Park is bounded by the Chesapeake Bay and Potomac River. The 500-acre state park maintains nature trails, a swimming beach, fishing pier, picnic area, and year-round camping facilities. During the Civil War more than 20,000 Confederate soldiers were imprisoned at nearby Fort Lincoln; nearly a quarter of them died from exposure, starvation, and disease. A small museum in the park provides background on this tragic event.

Details: Route 5, Point Lookout; 301/872-5688. Park open daily 8 a.m.–dusk; museum open Memorial Day–Labor Day daily 10–6, May on weekends only 10–5. $2 access to beach and picnic area. (1 hour)

✯ **Sotterly Plantation**—You need not travel to the Deep South to visit an authentic former tobacco plantation. Overlooking the Patuxent River, Sotterly Manor House is the only eighteenth-century plantation in Maryland open to the public. The house is the oldest example of post-in-ground architecture in the United States (meaning that it is supported by cedar timbers driven straight into the ground, rather than by a foundation). In warm-weather months, visitors may tour the manor house itself and admire the hand-carved Chippendale staircase and Georgian shell alcoves. There's even a secret closet that was built to hide children from pirates. The grounds feature an eighteenth-century warehouse, smokehouse, restored slave cabin, and plantation school.

Details: Route 245, Hollywood; 800/681-0850 or 301/373-2280.
Grounds open year-round Tue–Sun 10–4; Manor House tours May–Oct
Tue–Sun 10–4. House tour $7 adults, $5 children 6–14; $2 donation
requested for touring grounds. (1–2 hours)

FITNESS AND RECREATION

Hiking, swimming, and birdwatching opportunities are available at
Calvert Cliff State Park and **Flag Ponds Nature Park** (see
Sightseeing Highlights, above). Fishing is a popular pastime in
Southern Maryland, with a number of charter fishing services available.
In Chesapeake Beach contact **Rod 'n' Reel Charter Fishing**,
800/233-2080 or 301/855-8450. **Seaside Charters**, 301/855-4665, also
offers day fishing trips. In Solomons **Bunky's Charter Boats, Inc.**,
410/326-3241, offers group charters and skiff rentals. For additional
charter options, contact **Solomons Charter Captain Association**,
800/831-2702 or 410/326-4251.

FOOD

Because of its proximity to the Chesapeake, the cuisine of southern
Maryland centers on great seafood, although most menus offer other
options. In Chesapeake Beach the **Rod 'n' Reel**, Route 261 and Mears
Avenue, 410/257-2735, offers views of a marina and Chesapeake Bay
beyond. Established in 1946, the restaurant is a local institution offering seafood buffets on Friday and Saturday nights and brunch on
Saturday and Sunday mornings. While it has a distinctly "older" feel,
the history of the place makes it work. The menu features a variety of
seafood and shellfish; crabs are a specialty. Lunches include soups,
sandwiches, burgers, crab cakes, and mixed seafood platters. At dinnertime you can choose from moderately priced salads to fresh rockfish,
lobster, and surf and turf combinations. Capping it all off is a giant
bingo room upstairs with large windows overlooking the bay, where
patrons of all ages try their luck six nights a week. Next door is
Smokey Joe's Grill, 410/257-2427, specializing in ribs, chicken, and
steaks. In warm-weather months, an outdoor café just outside the
doors of the Rod 'n' Reel serves light meals overlooking the water.
    Solomons offers a number of worthwhile restaurants from which
to choose. The **CD Café**, 14350 Solomons Island Rd., 410/326-3877,
has just 12 tables, a pleasant atmosphere, and nicely prepared food

SOLOMONS

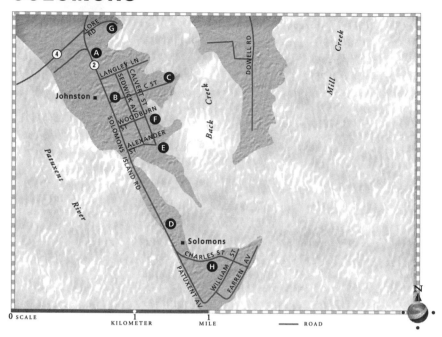

Sights

Ⓐ Calvert Maritime Museum

Food

Ⓑ CD Café

Ⓒ Dry Dock

Ⓓ Lighthouse Inn

Lodging

Ⓔ Back Creek Inn

Ⓕ By-the-Bay Bed & Breakfast

Ⓖ Comfort Inn Beacon Marina

Ⓗ Solomons Victorian Inn

suiting a range of budgets. Lunches consist of homemade soups, creative salads, original sandwiches, and hot dishes such as cajun shepherd's pie. Dinners include soups, salads, pasta dishes, and entrées such as honey-blackened salmon.

Open for dinner and Sunday brunch, the **Dry Dock**, located in Zahniser's Marina at the end of C Street, 410/326-4817, offers spectacular views of the Back Creek and marina. Its relatively small size adds to its charm, but during summer you'll need to reserve a table as much as three days in advance. The menu changes daily to take advantage of the freshest fish available. Entrées, on the expensive side, include such delectable seafood items as mahimahi with a dijon brie sauce, blackened salmon, braised pork tenderloin, and prime rib au jus.

Also offering waterfront views is the **Lighthouse Inn**, 14636 Solomons Island Rd. S., 410/326-2444 (which, despite its name, does not accommodate overnight guests). The tastefully decorated restaurant has a cheerful contemporary feel and a bar that is actually a one-third-scale skipjack, complete with a raised sail. Serving dinner only (except on Sundays, when lunch is available), the restaurant features chicken, beef, and seafood dishes, including scallops champignon, fried oysters, and crab imperial. In warm-weather months, lighter, more casual meals are available on an adjoining deck.

LODGING

As most of southern Maryland's finer sights are clustered in the southernmost portion of the region, this is where many of the most interesting accommodations lie, particularly in and around Solomons Island, which also offers great restaurants and shopping. But if you're looking for a rustic escape without camping, try the **Matoaka Beach Cabins**, P.O. Box 124, St. Leonard, 410/586-0269, located 12 miles north of Solomons. Formerly a private girls' camp, the cabins are set on 40 acres that include a vineyard, hiking trails, and beachfront. The six-person cabins rent from April through October for $145 to $170 for two nights, $360 to $445 per week. Bring your own linens, blankets, cooking, and eating utensils.

Solomons has several relatively inexpensive hotels of the chain variety, as well as cozy bed-and-breakfasts. The **Holiday Inn Select Solomons**, 155 Holiday Dr., 410/326-6311 or 800/356-2009, has 326 rooms, including larger suites with kitchenettes and Jacuzzis. Many of the rooms overlook the creek leading into the Patuxent River. The hotel offers an outdoor pool, health club with sauna, and tennis facilities. Golfing, boating, sailing, and fishing opportunities are available nearby. Rooms run $94 Sunday through Friday and $99 on Saturday nights. Nearby is the **Comfort Inn Beacon Marina** at the end of Lore Road, 410/326-6303 or 800/228-5150. Many guests arrive by motor- or sailboat, taking advantage of the inn's 186-slip marina, which itself affords picturesque views. The inn, with outdoor pool and hot tub, is within walking distance of many area attractions. Rooms run from $69 to $87 and include a continental breakfast.

Several bed-and-breakfasts situated in Victorian homes, each within walking distance of galleries, boutiques, and restaurants, afford opportunities to admire the area's historic architecture. The **Solomons Victorian Inn**, 125 Charles St., 410/326-4811, is set in the former home of Clarence Davis, a reknowned builder of early twentieth-century sailing yachts. The inn's eight bedrooms each have a private bath. In the mornings, guests enjoy a full breakfast overlooking the harbor. Rooms range from $90 to $175; rates are reduced during cold-weather months for stays longer than one night. As its name suggests, the **By-the-Bay Bed & Breakfast**, 14374 Calvert St., 410/326-3428, is situated on Back Creek and is accessible by boat. In the evenings, guests can sit by the water's edge or relax on a swing on the inn's wrap-around porch. Inside, the Victorian theme is echoed in flowery wallpaper and furnishings from the early 1900s. Rooms range from $75 to $95 and include a full breakfast.

With water views and a lovely garden, the **Back Creek Inn**, at the corner of Alexander and Calvert Streets, 410/326-2022, is a personal favorite. Built in 1880, the inn, originally a waterman's home, now serves as a seven-room B&B. A hot tub overlooking the bay is available to guests, along with bicycles for touring the island. A pier with two slips makes the inn accessible to those coming by water. Rooms run from $95 to $145 for a cottage with fireplace, screened in porch, and water view. A full breakfast is included.

CAMPING

Southern Maryland has several camping areas. One of the most popular, **Point Lookout State Park**, 301/872-5688, is located at the tip of St. Marys County at the junction of the Potomac River and Chesapeake Bay. The 525-acre park has a visitors center, 143 campsites, full hookups, a camp store, a boat launch, a fishing pier, and swimming and picnicking areas. Also providing access to the Potomac River is **Smallwood State Park**, 301/888-1410, in Marbury. Covering 624 acres, Smallwood was once the home of General William Smallwood, a Revolutionary War officer and former governor of Maryland. His house, located in the park, is open to the public. The park has 16 campsites with electric hookups, a fishing pier, boat ramps, 50 boat slips, canoeing, and picnicking facilities. **Cosca Regional Park**, 410/868-1397, is located two miles south of Clinton and has a 15-acre lake for boating and fishing. The park has 23 campsites (open year-round) with electrical and water hookups; hiking, biking, and horse trails; tennis courts; softball and baseball fields; paddleboats; and a nature center.

MARYLAND'S EASTERN SHORE

One of the state's greatest treasures, Maryland's Eastern Shore satisfies a range of visitors, from those seeking to get away from it all to those looking for a lively summer scene. The neon signs and shopping outlets of Ocean City stand in marked contrast to the windswept dunes and sea grass of nearby Assateague Island, famous for its wild ponies. The area ia also easy to access. A 4.3-mile drive over the Chesapeake Bay Bridge, just outside Annapolis, deposits visitors on the Eastern Shore, which is bounded by the Chesapeake Bay to the west and the Atlantic Ocean to the east. Sprawling farms, fishing villages, and historic towns are scattered throughout the region. Some of the most popular destinations, such as Easton and St. Michaels, are a mere 90-minute drive from Baltimore.

Sporting opportunities—such as golfing, fishing, windsurfing, sailing, biking, canoeing, and hiking—abound. Peaceful retreats such as the Blackwater Wildlife Refuge afford visitors a glimpse at some of the region's diverse wildlife: Canada geese, ducks, blue heron, ospreys, and endangered species such as the Delmarva fox squirrel and bald eagle. While migrating birds find refuge here, other areas of the Eastern Shore have long drawn sportsmen and -women to its prime sport-fishing and duck- and goose-hunting destinations. Seasonal festivals and celebrations are common throughout the year; annual events such as the Wildfowl Festival in Easton attract some 20,000 bird-art enthusiasts to the area.

The Eastern Shore's rich history remains accessible today in its

MARYLAND'S EASTERN SHORE

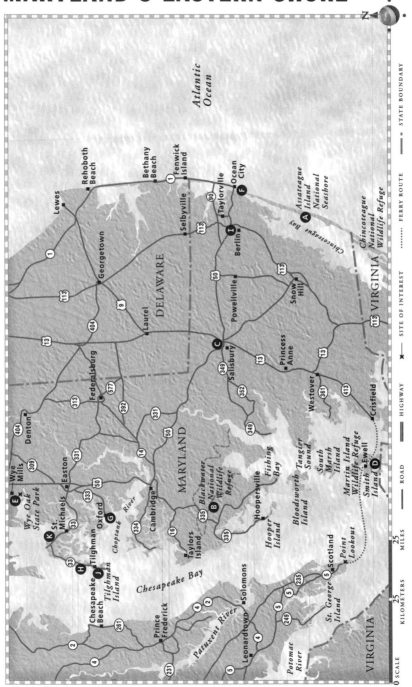

Sights

Ⓐ Assateague Island National Seashore and State Park

Ⓑ Blackwater National Wildlife Refuge

Ⓒ Salisbury Zoological Park

Ⓓ Smith Island

Ⓔ Ward Museum of Wildfowl Art

Ⓔ Wye Mill

Food

Ⓕ Bayside Skillet

Ⓕ The Hobbit

Ⓕ Hotel California

Ⓖ Pope's Tavern

Ⓖ Robert Morris Inn

Ⓗ Tilghman Island Inn

Lodging

Ⓘ Atlantic Hotel

Ⓙ Black Walnut Inn

Ⓘ Merry Sherwood Plantation

Ⓖ Oxford Inn

Ⓖ Robert Morris Inn

Ⓗ Tilghman Island Inn

Ⓚ Wades Point Inn on the Bay

Camping

Ⓐ Assateague Island National Seashore

Ⓐ Assateague State Park

Note: Items with the same letter are located in the same town or area.

many restored houses, churches, and museums, where you can learn about the region's early Native American inhabitants, colonial settlements, and the connection between humans and the surrounding bay.

A PERFECT DAY ON MARYLAND'S EASTERN SHORE

How you plan a perfect day on the Eastern Shore depends on where you're starting from and how much time you're willing to spend in the car. Within a 90-minute drive of Baltimore are the quaint towns of Easton and St. Michaels, where you can enjoy a day of wandering through galleries and shops, eating fresh seafood, and exploring local sights. In St. Michaels, stop into the Chesapeake Bay Maritime Museum to learn about the region's history.

If you're more interested in experiencing the beauty of nature and don't mind the drive, head to Assateague Island, where miles of beachfront have been carefully preserved and wild ponies roam free. Or visit Cambridge and Blackwater National Wildlife Refuge, where you can quietly take in the park's abundant wildlife either by walking one of its trails or driving the 3.5-mile Wildlife Drive. If you time your trip right, you might end it with a spectacular sunset view.

SIGHTSEEING HIGHLIGHTS

★★★ **Assateague Island National Seashore and State Park**—Wild ponies roam free amidst the dunes and sea grass of Assateague Island. But that's not all: The island is a popular destination for migrating ducks and geese, along with herons, egrets, terns, and the piping plover, a threatened species. In the summer months, thousands of humans descend on the island to take advantage of swimming, biking, hiking, fishing, picnicking, and camping opportunities. The 37-mile-long barrier island consists of three major public areas: the Assateague Island National Seashore, managed by the National Park Service; Assateague State Park, managed by the Maryland Department of Natural Resources; and Chincoteague National Wildlife Refuge (on the Virginia side), managed by the U.S. Fish and Wildlife Service. Assateague's wild horses are the descendants of domestic horses that were brought to the island as early as the seventeenth-century by Eastern Shore farmers eager to avoid mainland taxes and fencing laws. Visitors are urged not to touch or feed the ponies who have been known to kick and/or bite. The National Park Service offers guided walks, children's programs, and demonstrations daily in the summer and on weekends in fall and spring.

Details: 7206 National Seashore Ln., Berlin; 410/641-3030. Visitors center open daily 9–5; park open 24 hours. $4 for cars, $2 per person for bicycles and pedestrians. (1–4 hours)

★★ **Blackwater National Wildlife Refuge**—Be sure to bring binoculars to really appreciate the diverse animal life protected here. Established in 1933 to protect migratory birds, the refuge consists of more than 23,000 acres of tidal salt marsh, freshwater ponds, mixed evergreen and deciduous forest, and small amounts of cropland. It remains one of the principle wintering spots for Canada geese, whose numbers swell to more than 35,000 in November, the peak of the migration season. The best time for viewing waterfowl in the refuge is mid-October through mid-March. In addition to geese, more than 20 duck species migrate here. Bald eagles, blue heron, and ospreys are also common to the area, along with mammals such as deer, raccoons, rabbits, fox, and the endangered Delmarva fox squirrel. Exhibits and films, as well as trail maps, are available at the visitors center. In addition to hiking trails, a 3.5-mile wildlife drive winds through the woods and alongside the marshes, enabling visitors to take in the scenery from car or bike.

Details: 2145 Key Wallace Dr., Cambridge; 410/228-2677. Visitors center open Mon–Fri 8–4, Sat and Sun 9–5. Wildlife Drive open year-round dawn–dusk. $3 for cars, $1 for pedestrians and cyclists. (1 hour)

★★ **Chesapeake Bay Maritime Museum**—The history of the Chesapeake Bay is showcased within an 18-acre compound known as the Chesapeake Bay Maritime Museum. Nine exhibition buildings feature displays on how the bay came into being, its role in American history, and how it has shaped the lives of those who live near it. Included are more than 80 traditional watercraft, along with a waterfowl exhibition that displays carved decoys and stuffed birds. Visitors can catch a glimpse of the life of a lighthouse keeper while touring the fully restored 1879 Hooper Strait Lighthouse, a hexagonal structure perched on six legs that once warned sailors they were nearing dangerous shoals.

Details: Mill St., St. Michaels; 410/745-2916. Open summer 9–6, spring and fall 9–5, winter 9–4. $7.50 adults, $3 children ages 6–17, $6.50 seniors. (1 hour)

★★ **Smith Island**—Named after Captain John Smith, who explored the Chesapeake Bay in 1608, Smith Island is actually three islands that form an area eight miles long and four miles wide. Settled in 1657, the island remains steeped in traditions three centuries old with islanders speaking in the manner of their seventeenth-century ancestors. A morning or afternoon visit allows you to walk around the island and take advantage of local seafood specialties. The Smith Island Center offers a 20-minute film, exhibits of watermen's boats and tools, and information on local history and the environment.

Details: To get there, try Smith Island Cruise Ships, 410/425-2771, departing from Crisfield. For other ferry services, call the Somerset County Tourism Office, 800/521-9189. Smith Island Center, 410/425-3351, is just down the road from the county dock; open April–Oct Thu–Sun 12–4; $2 adults, under age 12 free. (3 hours)

Thomas Fletcher

Boat dock on the Eastern Shore

✪ **Historical Society of Talbot County**—Housed in a Federal-style townhouse in downtown Easton, the Historical Society of Talbot County features a three-gallery museum with changing exhibitions and guided tours of two restored houses: the James Neall House built in 1810 and the Joseph Neall House built in 1795. Guided walking tours of the area are offered through the museum.

Details: 25 S. Washington St., Easton; 410/822-0773. Open Tue–Sat 11–3 (closed Sat in Feb and Mar); tours at 11:30 and 1:30. Tour or exhibit $3 adults, $2 children 6–12; combined tour and exhibit $5 adults, $4 children. (1 hour)

✪ **Old Third Haven Quaker Meeting House**—Set off Easton's main street in a tranquil environment, the Old Third Haven Quaker Meeting House, with its simple design and well-worn wooden pews, is in keeping with its long-standing purpose. Built in 1682, the meeting house is one of the oldest framed houses of worship still in use in the United States and played a strong role in the establishment of Quakerism in America.

Details: 405 S. Washington St., Easton; 410/822-0293. Open daily 9–5. Meetings Sun 10 a.m. and Wed 5:30 p.m. (30 minutes)

✪ **Ward Museum of Wildfowl Art**—Bird enthusiasts won't want to miss the Ward Museum of Wildfowl Art in Salisbury, a 30,000-square-foot structure showcasing bird carvings as well as wildfowl sculpture and painting. Reputedly the most comprehensive collection of wildfowl carving in the world, the museum is located near Ocean City, home to the World Championship Carving Competition held each April. The museum's Decoy Study gallery traces more than 100 years of regional decoys while the Ward Brothers Workshop showcases the work of these famed local artisans. Visitors may also tour re-created marshlands and tune their ears to duck and geese calls.

Details: 909 S. Schumaker Dr., Salisbury; 410/742-4988. Open Mon–Sat 10–5, Sun 12–5. $7 adults, $3 students, preschoolers free, $5 seniors. (1 hour)

Salisbury Zoological Park—Local wildlife as well as North and South American animal species can be seen at the Salisbury Zoo, reputedly one of the finest small zoos in the country. The 12-acre, completely outdoor zoo is home to bears, monkeys, prairie dogs, alligators, lions, panthers, llamas, bison, and a variety of waterfowl. The zoo features 18 species of mammals, 52 species of birds, six reptile species, and two amphibian species.

Details: 755 S. Park Dr., Salisbury; 410/548-3188. Open Mon–Fri 8–4:30, Sat–Sun 8–7. Free. (1 hour)

Wye Mill—Built in 1682 and powered by a waterwheel, Wye Mill opens its doors to the public seven months of the year. Visitors can purchase the cornmeal, whole wheat, and buckwheat flour that is produced here. Nearby is Maryland's State Tree: **Wye Oak.** The largest white oak in the United States, the tree is estimated to be more than 450 years old and stands 95 feet high. Surrounding the tree is a 29-acre public park with picnic tables.

Details: Route 662, Wye Mills; 410/827-6909. Open mid-Apr–mid-Nov Mon–Fri 10–1, Sat and Sun 10–4. Free. (30 minutes)

FITNESS AND RECREATION

To rent bikes in St. Michaels, try **St. Michaels Town Dock Marina**, 305 Mulberry St., 410/745-2400. You can also rent small motor craft at the marina. Canoes and aquabikes can be rented at **St. Michaels Harbour Inn** and **Marine Aqua Center**, 101 N. Harbor Rd., 410/745-9001. For fishing charters on Tilghman Island, contact **Harrison's Sport Fishing Center**, 21551 Chesapeake House Dr., 410/886-2121. Duck and goose hunting is a popular past-time on the Eastern Shore because of the thousands of migratory game birds that make their way here in cold-weather months. For assistance with organizing a hunting trip, contact **Albright's Sportsman's Travel Service**, 36 Dover Rd., Easton, 410/820-8811. A prime golf destination in Easton is **Hog Neck Golf Course**, 10142 Old Cordova Rd., 410/822-6079.

Recreational opportunities abound in Ocean City, starting with its 10 miles of beachfront for swimming, surfing, and other water sports. For water sport equipment, including jet skis and windsurfers, try **Bahia Marina**, between 21st and 22nd Sts. on the bay, 410/723-2124, or Bay Sports, 22nd St. and the bay, 410/289-2144. To rent bikes, contact **Mike's Bikes** on First St., 410/289-4637, or **Continental Cycle**, 73rd and Coastal Hwy., 410/289-4637. For information on the area's myriad golfing opportunities, contact **Ocean City Golf Getaway**, 6101 Coastal Hwy., 800/4OC-GOLF or 410/723-5207.

If you're more interested in natural, as opposed to man-made

ST. MICHAELS

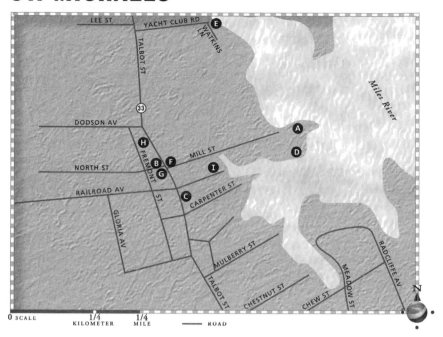

Sights

Ⓐ Chesapeake Bay Maritime Museum

Food

Ⓑ 208 Talbot

Ⓒ Carpenter Street Saloon

Ⓓ Crab Claw

Ⓔ Inn at Perry Cabin

Ⓕ Poppi's

Ⓖ Suddenly Last Summer Café & Grill

Lodging

Ⓔ Inn at Perry Cabin

Ⓗ Parsonage Inn

Ⓘ Victoriana Inn

Note: Items with the same letter are located in the same town or area.

sights, **Captain Bill Bunting's Angler Nature Cruise**, 410/289-7424, operates dolphin and whale watches, along with day long fishing trips, and one-hour sightseeing cruises. For deep sea fishing and offshore nature cruises, you can also step aboard the *O.C. Princess*, 410/213-0926 or 800/457-6650, a 90-foot boat offering both evening and all-day cruises.

FOOD

The Eastern Shore has some excellent fine-dining establishments and casual seaside eateries where you can enjoy a great view and local seafood. The following restaurants are listed from least to most expensive and are grouped according to the town in which they're located.

In Easton try **Legal Spirits**, 42 E. Dover St., 410/820-4100. Located in the Avalon Theatre building, built in 1921, the restaurant's bar is distinguished by its art-deco carving. Photographs of famous gangsters decorate the walls, along with the heads of a stuffed moose, deer, elk, and bear. The lunch menu includes creative sandwiches featuring grilled portobello mushrooms, fried oysters, and crab cakes. Dinners range from inexpensive salads to entrées such as pan-seared rockfish and baked salmon with curried pineapple and banana crust. A block away is the **Washington Street Pub**, 20 N. Washington St., 410/822-9011, a fun spot with exposed brick walls, a pressed-tin ceiling, and an extra-long bar. A variety of salads, sandwiches, soups, and burgers are available, along with dinner entrées including swordfish and Southwestern-style chicken. For more upscale dining there's the **Hunter's Tavern**, 100 E. Dover St., 410/822-1300, at the Tidewater Inn. The walls are decorated with wildfowl paintings, duck decoys, and beautifully carved geese. The dimly lit, rustic-feeling bar is especially nice. Lunches include a variety of salads, sandwiches, and entrées, including a crab melt and Chesapeake oysters with chips. The dinner menu features an assortment of beef, lamb, duck, chicken, and seafood entrées.

A wide variety of eating options exists in St. Michaels. For a casual breakfast or lunch, try **Poppi's**, 207 N. Talbot St., 410/745-3158. You can dine outside on the front porch or inside enjoying the eclectic nautical decor and authentic lunch counter. Homemade muffins and desserts are baked on the premises. Lunches consist of your basic soups, salads, burgers, fried seafood, and sandwiches. Open for breakfast, lunch and dinner, the **Carpenter Street Saloon**, 113 S. Talbot St., 410/745-5111, is housed in an 1874 building. This is basic, inexpensive food served in a casual atmosphere. To experience the Eastern Shore at its most authentic, try the **Crab Claw**, Navy Point, 410/745-2900. Here you can sit on an open deck, drink a cold beer, roll up your sleeves, and dig into a pile of spicy, steamed crabs. For those not up to that particular challenge, salads, steamed shellfish, fried seafood, and steak are also served. Be forewarned: They don't take credit cards.

One can only assume Clint Eastwood eats pretty well, which is only one (relatively small) reason to visit **Suddenly Last Summer Café & Grill**, 106 N. Talbot St., 410/745-5882. Owner and chef Perry Thomas relocated to St. Michaels from Carmel, California, where he was Eastwood's chef. The atmosphere is lively and colorful with bright yellow walls and contemporary paintings. Specializing in continental cuisine with a California twist, Thomas serves up a variety of sandwiches, salads, pasta, and seafood dishes for lunch, and a tantalizing array of dinner items, including duck with a peppercorn sauce, medallions of pork, and seared scallops on black squid-ink pasta. Limited outdoor dining is available and live music is offered on occasion.

Featuring innovative gourmet cuisine, **208 Talbot**, 208 Talbot St., 410/745-3838, is one of the finest restaurants in the region. Housed in an 1870 structure, it retains a historic charm with fireplaces, exposed brick walls, wooden beams, and brick floors. Open Wednesday through Sunday for dinner only and Sunday brunch, entrées range from mahimahi served on a bed of couscous to New Zealand rack of lamb. On weekends the five-course menu is available at a fixed price only. In the busy season it's best to make reservations far in advance. Equally upscale is the restaurant at the **Inn at Perry Cabin**, 308 Watkins Ln., 410/745-2200. Lunch and dinner are served in the impeccably decorated dining room overlooking the Miles River or just outside on the terrace. Lunches range from a turkey club to onion-crusted rockfish with herb mashed potatoes. Come with a big appetite and credit card for dinner, which consists of five mouthwatering courses at a fixed price.

On Tilghman Island, the best food is at the **Tilghman Island Inn**, 21384 Coopertown Rd., 410/886-2141. With a dining room and deck overlooking the water, guests arrive both by car and boat. Soups, sandwiches, and special plates are available at lunch; dinner consists of six to eight entrées that change regularly. Breakfast is also available.

In Oxford, for more casual fare, try **Pope's Tavern**, 504 S. Morris

St., 410/226-5005, located within the Oxford Inn. The tavern has a simple pub atmosphere and an ornate tin ceiling. Lunches feature soups, salads, fried oysters, and sandwiches; dinners include much of the same, along with steak, seafood, and beef dishes. Outdoor dining is available on the inn's front porch. A bit more upscale is the restaurant at the **Robert Morris Inn**, P.O. Box 70, 410/226-5111, where James Michener reputedly came on occasion to savor the inn's crab cake recipe. The inn's historic charm is represented in the dining area in three framed murals, exposed beams, a slate floor, and fireplace. Crab cakes are served in a variety of ways at lunch and dinner, along with other seafood items, chicken, and beef.

In Ocean City, the **Bayside Skillet**, 77th Street and Coast Highway, 410/524-7950, is a popular spot for breakfast, lunch, or dinner. Open 24 hours a day, its pink and white exterior makes it hard to miss. The restaurant, with outdoor deck, specializes in a variety of omelettes, crêpes, and frittatas. For a lively atmosphere, try the **Hotel California**, 120th Street and Coastal Highway, 410/524-7776. Housed in a pink stucco, Mission-style structure, the restaurant serves a variety of pasta, chicken, and seafood dishes, and features an oyster bar and grill with a wide selection of beers on tap. **The Hobbit**, 101 81st St., 410/524-8100, named after Tolkien's classic, is decorated with murals depicting scenes from the novel. The gift shop sells related items. The main dining room, serving a variety of high-end seafood, beef, and chicken dishes, overlooks the Assawoman Bay and surrounding marshland. Lighter, less expensive fare is available in the bar and café. Reservations are highly recommended.

LODGING

The Eastern Shore offers many accommodations options, from pastel-colored seaside motels to deluxe luxury inns reknowned for pampering their guests. The accommodations described below are grouped according to the town or region in which they're located, and then by price range from moderately priced to expensive.

Several of the larger hotel chains operate less expensive accommodations in Easton. Rooms at the **Holiday Inn Express**, 8561 Ocean Gateway, 410/819-6500 or 800/HOLIDAY, run $79 to $99. The hotel has an indoor pool, hot tub, and exercise room. The **Days Inn**, Route 50 East (mile 67), 410/822-4600 or 800/DAYS INN, is just outside downtown Easton and has an outdoor pool. Rooms run from $56 to $88.

EASTON

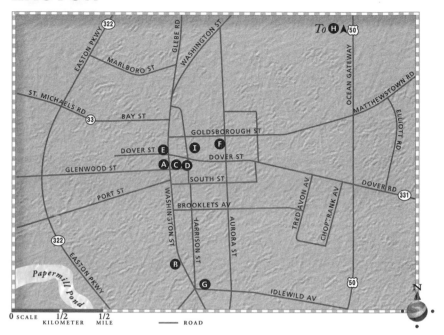

Sights

A Historical Society of Talbot County

B Old Third Haven Quaker Meeting House

Food

C Legal Spirits

D Hunter's Tavern

E Washington Street Pub

Lodging

F Bishop's House

G Chaffinch House

H Days Inn

H Holiday Inn Express

I Tidewater Inn

Note: Items with the same letter are located in the same town or area.

Because of its rich history, Easton has a number of bed-and-breakfasts set in Victorian homes. Built in 1880, the **Bishop's House**, 214 Goldsborough St., 410/820-7290 or 800/223-7290, was once the home of the Bishop of the Diocese of Easton. Located minutes from downtown Easton, the house was converted into a bed-and-breakfast in 1988 and features six rooms, most with private baths. One room features an antique sleigh bed and private bath with double whirlpool; another has a queen-size bed with a carved headboard, reading alcove, and private bath. Rates run $75 to $100 ($10 more for double occupancy) and include a hot breakfast. A two-night minimum stay is required on holidays and weekends. Distinguished by its octagonal tower and wraparound front porch, the **Chaffinch House**, 132 S. Harrison St., 800/861-5074, has six rooms, each with private bath. Rooms run from $85 to $110 and include a full breakfast.

For all the conveniences and privacy of a large hotel, try the **Tidewater Inn**, 100 E. Dover St., 410/822-1300 or 800/237-8775. Located in downtown Easton, the four-story brick inn is furnished with antique reproductions and has an outdoor pool. Rates begin at $85 for a room with two twin beds during the winter months to $90 to $350 in the summer and fall.

Nearby St. Michaels offers a wealth of lodging possibilities. Located on the main street of town, the **Parsonage Inn**, 210 N. Talbot St., 410/745-5519 or 800/394-5519, was built in 1883 and served as the parsonage to the Union Methodist Church from 1924 to 1985. The nicely landscaped Victorian brick home has a front porch with white wicker furniture. Each room is furnished with a queen or king brass bed with Laura Ashley linens and Queen Anne cherry reproduction furniture. Three bedrooms have wood-burning fireplaces. Rooms run from $120 to $160 (with a $20 discount Monday through Thursday nights) and include breakfast. Tucked away in a quiet neighborhood just blocks from the main street is the **Victoriana Inn**, 205 Cherry St., 410/745-3366. The house is surrounded by an expansive lawn and overlooks the Miles River. Guests can sit and enjoy the view from several scattered Adirondack chairs. The inn's five rooms are painted in rich hues and are tastefully decorated. Several have four-poster beds. Not all rooms have private baths. Rates run from $125 to $175 and include a full breakfast.

On the outskirts of Easton is the award-winning **Inn at Perry Cabin**, 308 Watkins Ln., 410/745-2200 or 800/722-2949—consistently rated one of the finest inns in the country. Set on a 25-acre estate, the 1812 manor house was purchased and renovated in 1989 by Sir Bernard Ashley, co-founder of the Laura Ashley Company. In keeping with the aims of its founder, the inn is styled after an English country home with beautiful gardens and plenty of common spaces for relaxing; playing chess, checkers, cribbage; or merely reading the newspaper. Each of the inn's 41 rooms is impeccably decorated with colorful fabrics and antique and reproduction furniture. Some have fireplaces; others have lofts with telescopes for focusing on the nearby wetlands. The rambling inn and its elegant restaurant overlook the Miles River. Amenities include an indoor pool, exercise room, and sauna and steam room. Rates run from $195 to $595 for a master suite and include a full English breakfast, afternoon tea, and fresh fruit and mineral water in each room. Special weekend packages are also available.

If you really want to experience the beauty of the bay away from tourist distractions, two inns are well worth checking out for their views alone. **Wades Point Inn on the Bay**, located five miles south of St. Michaels at the end of Wades Point Road, 410/745-2500, has served as a guest resort for more than 100 years. The inn, situated on a point of land surrounded on three sides by the bay, is set on 120 acres of fields and woodland. Rooms run from $95 to $230, with a two-night stay required on weekends and holidays. A full continental breakfast is included. Offering equally breathtaking scenery is the **Black Walnut Inn,** located at the tip of Tilghman Island at the end of Route 33, 410/886-2452. Set on a point of land surrounded by the bay, this is the closest you can get to the Chesapeake without leaving the shore. If you're lucky, one of the inn's resident Chesapeake Bay retriever's will greet you upon arrival. Located within a 57-acre wildlife sanctuary, the inn features a hot tub, swimming pool, tennis court, and hammocks poised for catching the sunset. Its seven guest rooms each have a private bath. Far from a Laura Ashley–type environment, the inn has a rustic, homey feel. Rooms run from $120 to $140 with a full continental breakfast.

Also on the island is the **Tilghman Island Inn,** 21384 Coopertown Rd., 410/886-2141 or 800/866-2141. The inn, overlooking Knapps Narrows, has a contemporary feel and is accessible to visitors arriving by land or sea. Amenities include tennis courts, a pool, and one of the best restaurants in the area with water views. Rooms run from $95 to $125 during the week and $120 to $150 on weekends and include a continental breakfast.

In Oxford, the **Oxford Inn**, 510 S. Morris St., 410/226-5005, is within walking distance of the harbor and historic district and has a wide front porch for enjoying late-afternoon breezes. The 11-room inn accommodates families with children and most rooms have private baths. Room rates are $80 to $140. At the opposite end of town, the historic **Robert Morris Inn**, 410/226-5111, has rooms dating back to 1710. In 1730 it was bought by Robert Morris, whose son, in addition to helping finance the American Revolution, was among the signers of the Declaration of Independence and the U.S. Constitution. In addition to the main building, the inn operates the nearby **Sandaway Lodge**, located on two acres of waterfront property with a private beach. Rooms at the inn range from $90 to $180. Lodge accommodations run $120 to $240.

Not far from Assateague Island is the **Merry Sherwood Plantation** in Berlin, 8909 Worcestor Hwy., 410/641-2112. Built in 1859, the restored Victorian mansion, set on 18 acres, is surrounded by lovely gardens designed by people at *Southern Living* magazine. Inside, the inn boasts an elegant ballroom, a dining room with a grand chandelier, and eight bedrooms, each furnished with Victorian antiques. A wraparound veranda shades guests in warm-weather months. During the peak season rooms run $150, off-peak they're $95. Located in Berlin's town center is the **Atlantic Hotel**, 2 N. Main St., 410/641-3589 or 800/814-7672. Built in 1895, the inn was placed on the National Register of Historic Places in 1980. Rooms run $85 to $150 during the summer months, $65 to $120 in the off-season.

CAMPING

On the Atlantic side of the Eastern Shore, camping is available at Assateague Island. **Assateague State Park** covers 756 acres with two miles of ocean frontage. The park's campground features bathhouses with hot showers and flush toilets. Any size camping unit can be accommodated (dump station only; no hookups). A small camp store and snack bar are open in the summer. During the winter campgrounds may be closed. Summer reservations are available for a full week only by calling 410/641-2120. The **National Park Service** also operates two campgrounds on the island: Oceanside with 104 sites and Bayside with 48 sites. Oceanside is operated year-round while Bayside is open late spring to early fall. Primitive outdoor facilities include chemical toilets, drinking water, and cold showers. Any size camping unit can be accommodated (dump station only; no hookups). A campsite reservation system is in place from May 15 through October 31. Call 410/641-3030 for further information. Sites are on a first-come, first-served basis the rest of the year.

On the Chesapeake Bay in Crisfield is **Janes Island State Park**. Covering 3,124 acres, the park has 104 improved campsites (40 with electric hookups) hot showers, a dump station, four cabins, and a camp store. For reservations contact the park office at 410/968-1565. Camping is also available at **Pocomoke River State Park** in Snow Hill. The park has two sections: Milburn Landing and Shad Landing. Combined they have 250 improved campsites. Electric hookups are available at Shad Landing. Reservations are necessary for Shad Landing May through September; call the park office at 410/632-2566.

Just south of Denton is **Martinak State Park**, 410/479-1619. Located at the confluence of the Choptank River and Watts Creek, the park is believed to have been the site of an Indian village. Covering 107 acres, the park has 63 improved campsites, a dump station, one cabin, and boat launch facilities.

NIGHTLIFE

The more popular tourist destinations on the Eastern Shore boast nightlife that includes bars, restaurants, and live music offerings during the summer. In Easton the **Washington Street Pub**, 20 N. Washington St., 410/822-9011, is a popular hangout in the evenings. To enjoy a more cultural experience, find out what's playing at the **Avalon Theatre**, 40 E. Dover St., 410/822-0345, an art-deco theater offering year-round musical and theatrical performances. In St. Michaels, **Yesteryears**, 200 Talbot St., 410/745-6206, features live music in the summer months on weekend nights, including blues, folk, jazz, and light rock. The **Town Dock**, 125 Mulberry St., 410/745-5577, also features entertainment and dancing for the "over-30 crowd" on weekends from mid-May through October.

On Tilghman Island, the **Tilghman Island Inn**, 21384 Coopertown Rd., 410/886-2141, offers live piano music on weekend nights when its lounge is transformed into a New York–style cabaret. Ocean City offers the widest range of nightlife options. The **Under 21 Club**, the Boardwalk at Worcester Street, 410/289-6331, attracts the ultra-young set with a DJ and nonalcoholic refreshment. The **Purple Moose**, 108 S. Boardwalk, 410/289-6953, is a popular spot featuring a variety of live music as well as deejayed fare. **Tiffany's**, 24th and Philadelphia Streets, also features live bands for those who like to rock well into the night.

Scenic Route: St. Michaels to Tilghman

Follow Route 333 south from Easton to the quaint town of **Oxford**.
Depending on the time of day, you may want to stop into the Robert
Morris Inn for a crab cake. According to James Michener, the inn's
crab cake recipe is among the finest anywhere. From Oxford, board
the Oxford Bellevue Ferry, 410/745-9023, which crosses the Tred
Avon River. First launched in 1683, it's the country's oldest privately
operated ferry service, with departures roughly every 20 minutes in
March through mid-December. Call ahead for further details on hours
of operation. Once in **Bellevue**, take a right on Ferry Neck Road—
that will put you on Bellevue Road. Follow Bellevue until it intersects
with Royal Oak Road and take a left. From here follow signs to Route
33, which will take you to the lovely town of **St. Michaels**, where you
can tour the shops and enjoy terrific seafood at rustic spots like the
Crab Claw, 410/745-2900.

From St. Michaels take Route 33 west to **Tilghman Island**.
Sprawling horse farms, country estates, and water views on either
side of the highway distinguish the 18-mile trip. On one side of the
highway is the Chesapeake Bay, on the other are views of Harris

ST. MICHAELS TO TILGHMAN

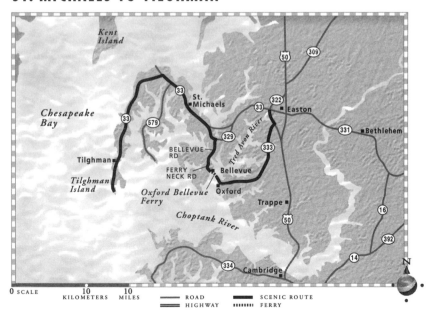

Creek. After crossing the Knapp Narrows, you'll be on Tilghman Island, which is still relatively unaffected by the commercialism that has impacted nearby areas. Route 33 then turns into Black Walnut Road. Follow it through the town of Tilghman to the end of the island, where you'll see breathtaking views of the Chesapeake Bay. If you have time and can plan in advance, consider staying at the **Black Walnut Inn**, 410/886-2452, at the tip of Tilghman Island. The inn sits is surrounded by the Chesapeake Bay on three sides, offering spectacular views and a relaxed atmosphere. From Tilghman Island, you'll want to follow Route 33 back to Saint Michaels and onward to your next destination. ◪

12
TOP OF THE BAY

The coastal towns surrounding the upper reaches of the Chesapeake Bay each exhibit their own historic character, though some have more to offer than others. Chesapeake City, located on the Chesapeake and Delaware Canal, is a jewel of a historic town providing a relaxing escape. Its mixture of nineteenth-century buildings, water views, antique shops, and craft galleries make it a pleasant place to stroll and enjoy a delicious meal overlooking the water.

The drive from Chesapeake City to Chestertown takes you through miles of scenic farmland dotted by lovely old houses. Founded in 1706 on the banks of the Chester River, Chestertown boasts a rich history reflected in the eighteenth-century brick houses gracing many of its streets. In 1774 the spirited citizens held their own revolt against England's tea tax, casting overboard tea that had been brought into port aboard a British brigantine. Every Memorial Day the town reenacts this historic event during the Chestertown Tea Party Festival.

If you have a particular interest in birds, hunting, and the folk art of making decoys, visit the Havre de Grace Decoy Museum. With more than 1,500 decoys, the museum chronicles the evolution of the craft and use of decoys. If tanks and guns are more your passion, the U.S. Army Ordnance Museum in Aberdeen displays the world's foremost collection of military ordnance, along with a 25-acre tank and artillery park.

For a natural escape, visit the Susquehanna State Park or Elk Neck State Park, both of which have hiking trails and waterways that are well suited for canoeing.

TOP OF THE BAY

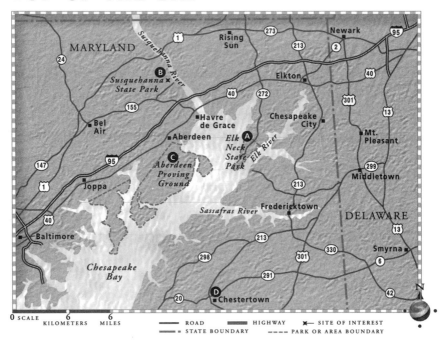

Sights

Ⓐ Elk Neck State Park

Ⓑ Susquehanna State Park

Ⓒ U.S. Army Ordnance Museum

Food

Ⓓ Imperial Hotel

Ⓓ Ironstone Café

Ⓓ Old Wharf Inn

Lodging

Ⓓ Imperial Hotel

Ⓓ White Swan Tavern

Camping

Ⓐ Elk Neck State Park

Ⓑ Susquehanna State Park

Note: Items with the same letter are located in the same town or area.

A PERFECT DAY AT THE TOP OF THE BAY

Begin your day with a visit to Susquehanna State Park and the Steppingstone Museum if it's open (weekends only May through October). The museum is a complex of restored farm buildings that evoke farm life around the turn of the century. Travel next to Chesapeake City, where you can have lunch overlooking the Chesapeake and Delaware Canal and visit the canal museum. After strolling the streets of this small town, which in recent years has undergone a painstaking restoration, continue south to Chestertown. The beautiful drive takes you through small towns and picturesque farmland. In the afternoon you can get acquainted with the town's historic charms either by simply walking around or by stopping at the Chamber of Commerce, 400 S. Cross St., 410/778-0416, to pick up a copy of the walking-tour brochure.

SIGHTSEEING HIGHLIGHTS

★★ **Chesapeake & Delaware Canal and Museum**—Connecting the Delaware River with the Chesapeake Bay, the Chesapeake & Delaware Canal stretches for 14 miles from Chesapeake City to Delaware City. Construction of the canal began in 1804 as a means of improving the transportation of goods between Philadelphia and Baltimore. After a series of financial obstacles, the canal was finally completed in 1829. Today 40 percent of all ship traffic in and out of the Port of Baltimore passes through the canal. The canal's history is carefully exhibited at the Chesapeake & Delaware Canal Museum; interactive videos and a television monitor identify the locations of ships as they travel the canal. Also on display are the original waterwheel and steam engines.
Details: Second St. and Bethel Rd., Chesapeake City; 410/885-5621. Open Apr 15–Oct Mon–Sat 8–4:15, Sun 10–6; rest of the year Mon–Sat 8–4:15. Free. (1 hour)

★★ **Susquehanna State Park**—Covering 2,639 acres, Susquehanna State Park is located on the Susquehanna River just north of Havre de Grace. In addition to hiking trails and picnic facilities, the park is home to several historic landmarks. Built in 1794, the **Rock Run Grist Mill** is a four-story, water-powered mill that houses a collection of milling-related machinery. **Steppingstone Museum** is a nineteenth-century farm displaying turn-of-the-century rural arts and industries.

Demonstrations are made by a blacksmith, weaver, wood carver, a dairy maid, and a decoy artisan. The 13-room **Mansion House**, open to the public, was built in 1804 by John Carter.

Details: Route 155, three miles north of Havre de Grace; 410/557-7994. Grist Mill, Steppingstone Museum, and Mansion House open summer weekends and holidays. Free. For further information, call 410/939-2299. (1–2 hours)

☆ **Havre de Grace Decoy Museum**—Havre de Grace was once known as the decoy capital of the world because of the number of master decoy carvers who lived, studied, or were affiliated with the town over the years. To preserve this uniquely American folk art form, the Havre de Grace Decoy Museum was established to document and interpret wildfowl decoys and their role in the cultural heritage of the Chesapeake Bay. Each year more than 30,000 people visit the museum or take part in its Decoy Festival, held in May.

Details: 215 Giles St., Havre de Grace; 410/939-3775. Open Mon–Fri 9–5. $4 adults, $2 seniors and children. (1 hour)

Concord Point Lighthouse—Erected in 1827, the Concord Point Lighthouse in Havre de Grace, protecting boats in the Upper Chesapeake Bay from maritime hazards, is distinguished as one of the oldest lighthouses in continuous operation on the East Coast. Although now under automatic control, until 1928 the lighthouse was manned by the O'Neill family. John O'Neill received the honor in recognition of his defense of Havre de Grace against the British in the War of 1812. On summer Sunday afternoons you can climb 30 feet up to the top for great views of the bay and river.

Details: Concord and Lafayette Sts., Havre de Grace; 410/939-9040. Open May–Oct Sun 1–5. Free. (30 minutes)

Elk Neck State Park—Located nine miles south of the town of North East, Elk Neck State Park covers 2,188 acres of heavily wooded bluffs, marshland, and sandy beach. The park has hiking trails, swimming, fishing, and boat rentals, along with a visitor center and camp store.

Details: 4395 Turkey Point Rd., North East; 410/287-5333. Open 8 a.m.–dusk. Free, but $2 parking fee for beach access. (1–3 hours)

U.S. Army Ordnance Museum—One of the world's foremost collections of military ordnance is on display at the U.S. Army Ordnance

Museum at the Aberdeen Proving Ground. The museum includes more than 8,000 artifacts ranging from small arms to tanks and artillery pieces. Outside, a 25-acre tank/artillery park displays 225 items. **Details:** *Aberdeen Proving Ground, exit 85 off I-95; 410/278-3602. Open daily 10–4:45. Free. (1 hour)*

FITNESS AND RECREATION

Susquehanna State Park and **Elk Neck State Park** (see Sightseeing Highlights, above) both offer a variety of hiking trails, some with water views. To experience the bay around Havre de Grace under sail, contact **Havre de Grace Sailing Services**, Tidewater Marina, 410/939-2869, which offers sailing lessons, charters, and rental boats from 19 to 37 feet. If you'd rather someone else do the work, step aboard the *Martha Lewis*, 800/406-0766, a 49-foot sailing craft built in 1955. No reservations are necessary; call for tour times and dates of operation. To charter a boat for local fishing excursions, contact **Penn's Beach Marina**, 410/939-2060, which rents 15-foot fiberglass boats.

One of the best ways to explore Chestertown and its surroundings is by bike. For bike rentals, try **Bikework**, 410/778-6940. For golfing in the area, contact **Mears Great Oaks Landing Resort and Conference Center**, 800/LANDING, an executive nine-hole course. River tours are available through **Chester River Tour Boat and Charters**, 410/778-0088.

FOOD

Seafood is naturally the most common menu item in the upper bay region. Listed below are restaurants located in Havre de Grace, Chesapeake City, and Chestertown, each grouped by location and then by price range, beginning with the least expensive.

In Havre de Grace, the **Crazy Swede**, 400 N. Union St., 410/939-5440, is distinguished by its bright blue awning. In warm weather you can dine on an outdoor patio. Lunches consist of soups, salads, sandwiches, and burgers, while dinner entrées feature a range of seafood, beef, veal, chicken, and lamb dishes. Sunday brunch is also available from 10 a.m. to 2 p.m. **MacGregor's**, 331 St. John St., 410/939-3565, overlooks the Susquehanna River. Lunches include sandwiches, grilled chicken dishes, burgers, and entrées such as shrimp quesadillas. Dinners fall into the medium price range with seafood,

HAVRE DE GRACE

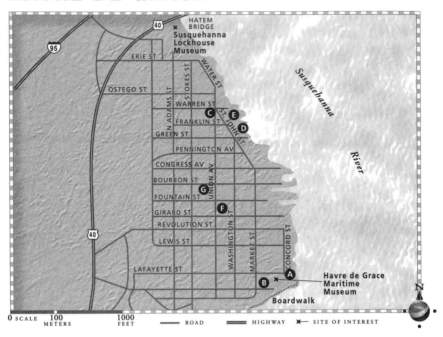

Sights

- **A** Concord Point Lighthouse
- **B** Havre de Grace Decoy Museum

Food

- **C** Crazy Swede
- **D** MacGregor's
- **E** Tidewater Grille
- **F** Vandiver Inn

Lodging

- **G** Spencer-Silver Mansion
- **F** Vandiver Inn

Note: Items with the same letter are located in the same town or area.

poultry, beef, and the requisite Maryland crab cakes. Less expensive, lighter fare is also available at dinnertime. Nearby is the **Tidewater Grille**, 300 Franklin St., 410/939-3313. With an outdoor deck overlooking the Susquehanna, the Tidewater features live music in the summer months. Lunches consist of salads, sandwiches, burgers, and entrées such as the popular "Crab Tidewater" dish. Dinners include pasta, seafood, grilled steaks and chicken, and veal dishes. Serving dinner by reservation only on Fridays and Saturdays, the **Vandiver Inn**, 301 S. Union Ave., 410/939-5200, offers an elegant Victorian dining room with a menu that changes weekly but typically offers fresh seafood, beef, and poultry.

In Chesapeake City, **Schaefer's Canal House**, Bank St., North Chesapeake City, 410/885-2200, has large windows on three sides offering pleasant views of the Chesapeake and Delaware Canal. The restaurant's nautical theme is reinforced by a 300-pound blue marlin mounted in the main dining room. Lunches include soups, sandwiches, and seafood entrées. Dinners range from medium-priced to expensive and include beef, chicken, veal, duck, and a variety of seafood dishes. Directly across the canal, the **Chesapeake Inn Restaurant & Marina**, 605 2nd St., 410/885-2040, also offers commanding views of the waterway. Murals featuring historic scenes of Chesapeake City decorate the walls. Lunches consist of a variety of soups, salads, sandwiches, pizzas, and pasta. Dinners fall in the medium price range with homemade pasta, seafood, chicken, beef, and veal entrées.

For a truly special evening, reserve a table at the **Bayard House Restaurant**, 11 Bohemia Ave., 410/885-5040. You can't beat the views or the ambiance of this historic restaurant, which dates back to the 1780s. Dining rooms are separated on three levels and feature period decoration, needlepoint tapestries, and horse prints. In warm-weather months, outdoor dining is available overlooking the water. Lunches consist of creative salads such as pecan chicken with fried oysters, along with pasta dishes and a range of mouthwatering entrées. Dinners include a variety of fresh seafood dishes—blackened, grilled, pan-seared, stuffed, broiled, and otherwise artfully prepared—along with beef, pasta, and poultry.

In Chestertown, try the **Ironstone Café**, 236 Cannon St., 410/778-0188, serving French and Italian cooking with an Eastern Shore flair. The **Old Wharf Inn** at the foot of Cannon Street, 410/778-3566, is also open for lunch and dinner and serves seafood, steaks, and chicken. Open for dinner only, the **Imperial Hotel**, 208

High St., 410/778-5000, has an elegant atmosphere and features contemporary American cuisine including chicken, beef, duck, and seafood entrées.

LODGING

A variety of small inns and bed-and-breakfast accommodations are scattered throughout the upper bay region. In Havre de Grace, the **Spencer-Silver Mansion**, 200 S. Union Ave., 410/939-1097 or 800/780-1485, is set in a large stone Victorian home built in 1896. The main house has four guest rooms, each furnished with walnut and mahogany Victorian antiques. In addition, a two-story stone carriage house features a whirlpool bath, spiral staircase, living room with a working fireplace, and kitchenette. Room rates range from $70 to $140 and include a gourmet breakfast. The **Vandiver Inn**, 301 S. Union Ave., 410/939-5200 or 800/245-1655, is a three-story Victorian mansion built in 1886 and listed on the National Historic Register. Its eight guest rooms, many with fireplaces, are decorated with period antiques. Room rates range from $75 to $105 and include a full breakfast.

In Chesapeake City, the **Chesapeake City B&B** at Schaefer's Canal House, Bank St., 410/885-2200, operates six colonial-style cottages of varying sizes. "Mischief" offers a small sitting area with a refrigerator downstairs and two adjoining bedrooms upstairs; while "Shamrock" features a den, dining room, kitchen, and three bedrooms. A favorite with honeymoon couples, and offering water views, is "McNulty." While individual rooms are available for as little as $40, cottages rent for $100 to $225 depending upon occupancy. Prices include breakfast. Located in the heart of Chesapeake City, the **Inn at the Canal**, 104 Bohemia Ave., 410/885-5995, is a Victorian-era home featuring six bedrooms, each with a private bath. Room rates range from $75 to $105 and include a full breakfast. The nearby **Blue Max Inn**, 300 Bohemia Ave., 410/885-2784, was built in 1854 by Jack Hunter, who wrote a book by the same name. The inn's seven rooms each have a private bath and are handsomely decorated with period furniture. Two of the front rooms have private porches for relaxing on warm summer evenings. Prices range from $85 to $120 and include a full four-course breakfast.

In Chestertown, the **White Swan Tavern**, 231 High St., 410/778-2300, is centrally located; parts of the building date back to

CHESAPEAKE CITY

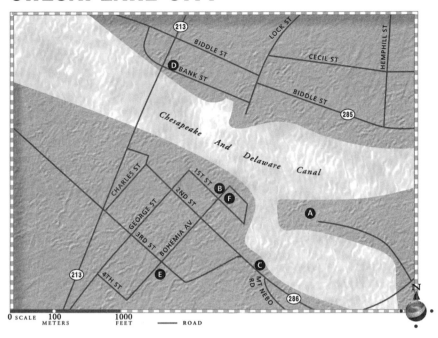

Sights

Ⓐ Chesapeake & Delaware Canal and Museum

Food

Ⓑ Bayard House Restaurant

Ⓒ Chesapeake Inn Restaurant and Marina

Ⓓ Schaefer's Canal House

Lodging

Ⓔ Blue Max Inn

Ⓓ Chesapeake City B&B

Ⓕ Inn at the Canal

Note: Items with the same letter are located in the same town or area.

1733. Its six guest rooms and suites vary in size and decor, and feature canopy beds, fireplaces, and adjoining sitting rooms. Rates range from $100 to $150 and include a full continental breakfast. Built in 1903, the **Imperial Hotel**, 208 High St., 410/778-5000, is located in Chestertown's historic district. Accommodations range from deluxe guest rooms to suites to a full carriage house. Rooms are decorated with authentic period furnishings. Rates range from $100 to $125 for a deluxe room to $200 to $300 for one- and two-bedroom suites. A continental breakfast is included and mid-week discounts are frequently available.

CAMPING

Susquehanna State Park offers 75 improved campsites, along with hiking and horseback riding trails, a boat launch, and places to fish and flatwater canoe. Reservations are necessary on weekends and holidays from Memorial Day through Labor Day. Reservations can be made by contacting the park office, 3318 Rocks Chrome Hill Rd., Jarrettsville, MD 21084; 410/557-7994. Camping is also available at **Elk Neck State Park**, with 302 improved campsites, cabins, full hookups, a dump station, and camp store. For reservations, contact the park office, 4395 Turkey Point Rd., North East, MD 21901; 410/287-5333.

13
WILMINGTON AND THE BRANDYWINE VALLEY

Much of Wilmington can be summed up in a name: du Pont. The du Pont name graces one of the tallest buildings in town and the largest and grandest hotel. It was in the early nineteenth century that Eleuthere Irenee du Pont de Nemours and his two sons came to Wilmington and established a factory, Hagley Mills, for the production of gunpowder on the banks of the Brandywine River. History aided the du Ponts; increasing amounts of gunpowder were needed to clear land and fight wars. The du Ponts would play a strong role in Wilmington's development as an industrial and financial hub. Today the DuPont Chemical company, headquartered in Wilmington, continues to be a boon to the local economy.

Not to be missed are the lovely estates and rolling countryside just north of the city. Just six miles away is Winterthur, the 175-room former home of Henry Francis du Pont, who preserved many of the best examples of early American art and antiques for the public to enjoy. The surrounding gardens are spectacular to behold, particularly in spring. Nearby is Hagley Mills, where you can walk along the banks of the Brandywine and learn about nineteenth-century life through demonstrations in a series of restored buildings.

Bring your credit cards—Delaware is known as a mecca for tax-free shopping. More than half of all Fortune 500 companies have incorporated here as a result of the state's tax treatment of corporations.

BRANDYWINE VALLEY

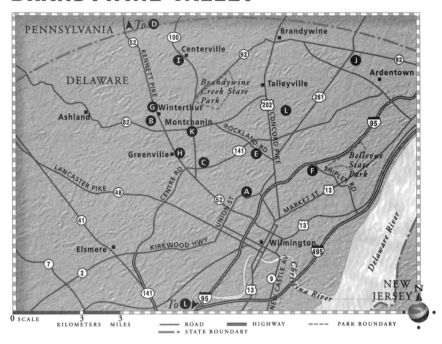

Sights

- **A** Delaware Museum of Art
- **B** Delaware Museum of Natural History
- **C** Delaware Toy and Miniature Museum
- **C** Hagley Museum
- **D** Longwood Gardens
- **E** Nemours Mansion and Gardens
- **F** Rockwood Museum
- **G** Winterthur Museum and Gardens

Food

- **H** Brandywine Brewing Company
- **I** Buckley's Tavern
- **J** Harry's Savoy Grill
- **K** Krazy Kats
- **H** Pizza by Elizabeths

Lodging

- **K** Inn at Montchanin Village

Camping

- **L** Lums Pond State Park

Note: Items with the same letter are located in the same town or area.

A PERFECT DAY IN WILMINGTON AND THE BRANDYWINE VALLEY

Begin your day with a tour of the Winterthur Museum and Gardens. Winterthur is sufficiently large in scope that you could begin and end your day here and see only a fraction of its contents. You may wish to have lunch at the museum's well-appointed cafeteria or venture forth to one of the other nice restaurants in the area. Afterward you can learn more about the early history of the region at Hagley Mills or cross the Pennsylvania state line to Longwood Gardens. In the early evening it's worth stopping into the Hotel du Pont for a walk around its grand interior. You might also want to check out what's playing at the Grand Opera House.

SIGHTSEEING HIGHLIGHTS

★★★ **Hagley Museum**—Set along the shores of the Brandywine River, the Hagley Museum features the original du Pont gunpowder mills, estate, and gardens, covering more than 240 acres in all. Here you can learn about nineteenth-century life. Working models in the Millwright Shop demonstrate the production of black powder. A walk through the Gibbons House, located in a restored worker's community, shows how a worker's family lived, the foods they ate, and what their home environment looked like. Nearby, in the one-room schoolhouse their children would have attended, lesson demonstrations are given. At the restored 1880s machine shop, volunteers show visitors how the equipment works. Visitors may also tour Eleutherian Mills. Completed in 1803, it was the first du Pont family home built in America. The Georgian-style residence—with Empire-, Federal-, and Victorian-era furnishings—reveals the tastes and lives of successive generations who resided there. The authentic nineteenth-century French garden reflects E. I. du Pont's love of botany and gardening. Additional demonstrations include a massive water wheel and vintage steam engine.

Details: Route 141, Wilmington; 302/658-2400. Open daily mid-Mar–Dec 9:30–4:30, year-round Sat and Sun 9:30–4:30. Guided bus tours weekdays Jan–Mar at 1:30. $9.75 adults, $3.50 children 6–14, $7.50 seniors and students. (2 hours)

★★★ **Longwood Gardens**—Just over the state border in Pennsylvania, Longwood Gardens was once the country estate of industrialist

Pierre S. du Pont, who personally designed the gardens from 1907 until 1954. Today Longwood encompasses 1,050 acres of gardens, woodlands, and meadows, including 20 outdoor gardens, four acres of greenhouses, and 11,000 different types of plants. Throughout the year the gardens host a number of special events such as flower shows, gardening demonstrations, children's programs, concerts, and recitals. Dining is available in the Terrace Restaurant.

Details: Route 1, Kennett Square, Pennsylvania; 610/388-1000 or 800/737-5500. Outdoor areas open Apr–Oct daily 9–6, rest of year daily 9–5; conservatory opens at 10. $12 adults, $6 children ages 16–20, $2 ages 6–15. (2 hours)

★★★ **Nemours Mansion and Gardens**—Built from 1909 to 1910 by Alfred I. du Pont, Nemours Mansion was modeled after a Louis XVI–style chateau. Surrounded by 300 acres of gardens and woodlands, the mansion was named after the site of the du Pont ancestral home in north-central France. The mansion's 102 rooms contain European antiques, oriental rugs and tapestries, and paintings dating back to the fifteenth century. Also on display are vintage automobiles, a billiard room, and a bowling alley. The French gardens, considered among the finest in America, extend almost a third of a mile from the house.

Details: 1600 Rockland Rd., Wilmington; 302/651-6912. Entrance to estate by reservation only. Guided tours available May–Nov Tue–Sat at 9, 11, 1, and 3; Sun at 11, 1, and 3. Tours include rooms on three of the mansion's floors as well as a bus tour through the estate's gardens. Admission, by tour only, is $10. For reservations, write the Reservations Office, Nemours Mansion and Gardens, P.O. Box 109, Wilmington, DE 19899. (2 hours)

★★★ **Winterthur Museum and Gardens**—At a time when most home furnishings come mass-produced and are designed with cost-efficiency rather than quality and longevity in mind, a visit to the Winterthur Museum inspires awe in the craftsmanship of yesteryear. Winterthur houses the world's foremost collection of American decorative arts, a dazzling array of more than 89,000 objects including furniture, textiles, architectural elements, tools, needlework, prints, and paintings. The collection focuses on the finest examples of American craftmanship made between 1640 and 1860. The collection is presented in almost 200 period room settings and room displays. Henry Francis du Pont, the museum's founder, assembled the collection over a period of many years and decided in the late 1940s to turn Winterthur into a museum and garden for the "education and enjoyment of the American public." Winterthur officially opened its doors to the public in 1951, and the collection continues to grow. The 60-acre garden of native and exotic plants surrounding Winterthur is a site to behold, no matter what the season. In addition to the museum and gardens, Winterthur operates a library and conservation laboratory. Visitors may also enjoy breakfast, lunch, Sunday brunch, and afternoon tea at the Visitor Pavilion or light snacks at the Cappuccino Café. The museum store sells outstanding reproduction furniture, accessories, plants, and gifts.

Details: Route 52, 6 miles northwest of Wilmington; 302/888-4600 or 800/448-3883. Open Mon–Sat 9–5, Sun 12–5. Garden open until dusk. $8 adults, $4 children ages 5–11, $6 seniors. General admission includes access to galleries and garden. Guided introductory tours and one- and two-hour decorative arts tours available for additional fee; make reservations well in advance. (2–3 hours)

★★ **Delaware Museum of Art**—The Delaware Museum of Art is home to the Bancroft Collection of English pre-Raphaelite paintings, considered one of the most important in the country. The museum's

Nemours Mansion and Gardens

Delaware Tourism Office

permanent collection also includes paintings by American artists such as Thomas Eakins, Winslow Homer, Maxfield Parrish, John Sloan, Howard Pyle, Edward Hopper, and the Wyeths. Changing exhibits, lectures, and classes are also offered.

Details: 2301 Kentmere Pkwy., Wilmington; 302/571-9590. Open Tue–Sat 10–5, Sun 12–5. $5 adults, $2.50 students, $3 seniors. (1 hour)

★★ **Grand Opera House**—Listed on the National Register of Historic Places, the Grand Opera House is one of the finest examples of cast-iron architecture in the country. The 1,100-seat facility hosts a range of events, including stand-up comedy; classical, jazz, pop, and big-band music; and dance. It is also home to the Delaware Symphony Orchestra and Opera Delaware. Past appearances have been made by four-time Grammy winner Lou Rawls, folk singer Nanci Griffith, the Demon Drummers of Japan, and the Canadian Brass.

Details: 818 N. Market St., Wilmington; 302/658-7897. Call ahead for a schedule of upcoming events. (30 minutes to view opera house)

★★ **Rockwood Museum**—Built in 1851 by merchant-banker Joseph Shipley, the Rockwood Estate is set on 72 acres and provides a noteworthy example of Rural Gothic architecture. The house is furnished with English, continental, and American decorative arts from the seventeenth to nineteenth centuries. The house, along with the porter's lodge, gardener's cottage, and barn, is surrounded by six acres of exotic foliage.

Details: 610 Shipley Rd., Wilmington; 302/761-4340. Open Mar–Dec Tue–Sun 11–4, rest of year Tue–Sat 11–4. Guided tours only. $5 adults, $4 seniors, $1 children ages 5–16. (1 hour)

Delaware Museum of Natural History—Exhibits at the museum include a visit to an African waterhole, a walk over the great barrier reef, a look at extinct and vanishing birds, and an introduction to animals found in Delaware. Hands-on exhibits in the museum's Discovery Room enable children to learn while playing games, looking through microscopes, conducting experiments, and solving puzzles. Several times daily the museum's 300-seat theater shows films on a wide variety of natural history subjects.

Details: Route 52 (Kennett Pike), five miles northwest of Wilmington; 302/658-9111. Open Mon–Sat 9:30–4:30, Sun 12–5. $4 adults, $3 seniors and children ages 3–17. (1 hour)

Delaware Toy and Miniature Museum—Dollhouse enthusiasts will enjoy the Delaware Toy and Miniature Museum with its collection of more than 100 dollhouses and rooms, along with dollhouse miniatures, dolls, toys, trains, boats, and planes. The collection spans the eighteenth to twentieth centuries and includes both American and European works.

Details: Route 141, adjacent to the Hagley Museum, Wilmington; 302/427-8698. Open Tue–Sat 10–4, Sun 12–4. $5 adults, $3 children, $4 seniors. (1 hour)

FITNESS AND RECREATION

Located three miles north of Wilmington, **Brandywine Creek State Park** has an 18-hole golf course, an equestrian center with stables, hiking and biking trails, and a nature center. Brandywine Creek, which flows through the center of the park, also allows for fishing, canoeing, and tubing. The 795-acre park boasts the state's first two nature preserves: Freshwater Marsh and Tulip Tree Woods, a stand of 190-year-old tulip poplars. Also relatively close by is **Carpenter State Park**, 15 miles to the southwest of Wilmington and three miles north of Newark. The 1,164-acre park has a nine-hole golf course, equestrian center, hiking trails, ice skating, and snowmobile and cross-country skiing trails.

FOOD

Wilmington and the surrounding area present a variety of eating options from casual pubs to ethnic restaurants to more highbrow, fine-dining establishments. On nearly everyone's list of favorite casual pubs in Wilmington is the **Washington Street Ale House**, 1206 Washington St., 302/658-ALES. The pub's renovated interior features exposed brick walls decorated with historic photographs of the city, decks, and more than ten television screens for sports fans. In addition to a variety of appetizers, soups, sandwiches, and pizzas, the restaurant serves basic entrées such as meatloaf, blackened salmon, and cajun chicken, all reasonably priced.

Also popular is **Kid Shelleen's**, 14th and Scott Sts., 302/658-4600. This oftentimes rowdy restaurant and saloon is a favorite gathering place among both necktied accountants and Levi-clad singles. Choose your spot—at the bar, in a booth, or at a table. Lacking good

WILMINGTON

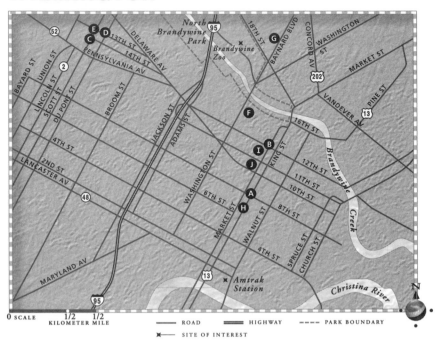

Sights

Ⓐ Grand Opera House

Food

Ⓑ Hotel du Pont
Ⓒ Kid Shelleen's
Ⓓ Silk Purse & Sow's Ear
Ⓔ Tavola Toscana
Ⓕ Washington Street Ale House

Lodging

Ⓖ Boulevard Bed and Breakfast
Ⓗ Brandywine Suites Hotel
Ⓘ Courtyard by Marriott
Ⓑ Hotel du Pont
Ⓙ Sheraton Suites Wilmington

Note: Items with the same letter are located in the same town or area.

company you can always check out the day's sporting events on TV. The menu features affordably priced, no-frills fare including salads, grilled burgers, pasta dishes, and meat, seafood, and chicken entrées. Just outside the city proper is the **Brandywine Brewing Company**, 3801 Kennett Pike, Greenville, 302/655-8000. Distinguished as Delaware's first brewery, this is a prime spot for lunch, dinner, or a beer and pretzel fix. High ceilings, leather booths, and tastefully mounted televisions over the bar give the restaurant a casual, contemporary feel. Complementing the great beer selection are a variety of homemade mustards and horseradish, apple butter, and fresh-from-the-oven pretzels. The creative lunch and dinner menu offers a variety of pizzas, salads, sandwiches, burgers, and pasta dishes. Sandwiches include black-bean veggie burgers and cajun catfish; entrées range from bratwurst and sauerkraut to grilled wild boar and roast duck. If you fancy the brews, you can take home a half-gallon "growler" for under $10.

Just up the street in the Greenville Crossing mall is **Pizza by Elizabeths**, 4019A Kennett Pike, Greenville, 302/654-4478. Small, casual, and comfortable, Elizabeths serves salads and gourmet pizza from its wood-burning oven with delectable toppings ranging from goat cheese to grilled duck. Open for lunch and dinner, Elizabeths also serves wine and beer.

Another popular local hangout north of the city is **Buckley's Tavern**, 5812 Kennett Pike, Centerville, 302/656-9776. This former tollhouse, with a bar, cozy booths, and fireplace, serves lunch, dinner, and Sunday brunch. Lunches consist of soups, creative salads, sandwiches, and entrées like wild-mushroom torte, shepherd's pie, and apple wood-smoked salmon. Dinners are equally original and suit a variety of price ranges.

For a great meal in a fun, contemporary atmosphere, try the **Silk Purse and Sow's Ear**, 1307 N. Scott St., 302/654-7666. Open for dinner only, the restaurant offers two dining experiences depending on your tastes. The Silk Purse, located on the lower floor, is slightly more formal, while upstairs, the Sow's Ear is whimsically decorated with stenciled walls, chili-pepper lights, and painted floors. The blended American/continental cuisine features a creative array of seafood, beef, and lamb dishes. For authentic northern Italian cuisine head to **Tavola Toscana**, 1412 N. DuPont St., 302/655-8001. Toscana serves Tuscan specialties, emphasizing grilled meats and seafood, hand-rolled pastas, fresh herbs, and sauces. The restaurant operates a nearby take-out shop where you can purchase fresh breads, gourmet entrées to go, and decadent desserts.

If you can afford to spend more for a big-deal meal, try **Harry's Savoy Grill**, 2020 Naaman's Rd. (Route 92), Wilmington, 302/475-3000. Photographs of famous "Harry's" such as Dirty Harry, Harry Belafonte, Debby Harry, and Harry Truman decorate the walls. The ceiling in the main dining room is littered with playing cards, tossed there by magician "Harry Houdini," who makes weekly visits. Harry's draws big crowds with its lively yet upscale decor, gas lights, and reknowned prime rib. Lunches include a variety of salads, sandwiches, and grilled selections ranging from steak béarnaise to seafood mixed grill. The dinner menu features less expensive sandwiches and pasta dishes, along with entrées like pork chops with Jack Daniel's apple pan gravy and crab cakes with wasabi cream.

Just outside of the city at the Inn at Monchanin Village is **Krazy Kats**, Route 100 and Kirk Rd., Monchanin, 302/888-2133. Open for breakfast, lunch, and dinner, Krazy Kats specializes in eclectic cuisine using fresh local ingredients. Decorating the walls are whimsical animal portraits; a zebra print dominates the upholstery. This is fine dining in a fun, upscale atmosphere. A typical evening meal might include sautéed escargot followed by veal medallions in a roasted garlic and sage demi-cream.

For truly elegant dining, the **Hotel du Pont**, 11th and Market Sts., 302/594-3100, operates two fine restaurants. The **Brandywine Room** serves American traditional cuisine in a quiet setting with intimate booths, a fireplace in one room, hand-carved wood paneling, and works by Brandywine Valley artists. To start, choose from appetizers such as artichoke and crabmeat struedel. Sample dinner entrées include ginger-crusted salmon, *porcini*-dusted tuna, and several meat and chicken dishes. The hotel's famous **Green Room** has an aura of opulence with its soaring ceiling, golden chandeliers, and rich forest-green decor. Specializing in French continental cuisine, the restaurant's dinner offerings range from pomegranate-glazed duck to baked salmon with a horseradish crust.

LODGING

Conveniently located downtown and reasonably priced is the **Brandywine Suites Hotel**, 707 N. King St., 302/656-9300 or 800/756-0070. The hotel's 49 rooms, surrounding an atrium lobby, were recently renovated. Each has a bedroom, living area, and minibar, and is tastefully furnished with antique reproductions. Hotel staff are friendly and well versed in area offerings; a high-quality restaurant is on the premises. Rates are $99 on the weekend and $129 to $169 during the week. Parking is available across the street for an additional fee.

If you're looking to experience Wilmington from an authentic historic home, check into the **Boulevard Bed and Breakfast**, 1909 Baynard Blvd., 302/656-9700. Built in 1913 and located in a tree-lined historic district, the Boulevard is a three-story brick house with neo-classical, Federal, and turn-of-the-century features. Its six rooms are decorated with family furnishings, antiques, and handicrafts. The living room and library each have a fireplace. Breakfast is served in the sun-drenched living room or screened-in porch. Room rates run from $60 to $65 for a shared bath and $70 to $80 for a private bath. Breakfast is included.

Downtown Wilmington features several of the larger hotel chains, each in the mid-priced range. The **Sheraton Suites Wilmington**, 422 Delaware Ave., 302/654-8300 or 800/325-3535, has 230 suites, each with a minibar. Amenities include an indoor swimming pool and exercise facility. Rooms run from $109 to $175, depending on the time of week and availability. Parking is available for an additional fee. Be sure to inquire about weekend packages. The **Courtyard by Marriott Wilmington**, 1102 West St., 302/429-7600 or 800/321-2211, has quiet, spacious rooms with refrigerators and offers an exericise facility. Rooms run from $69 to $134, with an additional parking fee.

If money is no object, then by all means reserve a room at the **Inn at Montchanin Village**, Route 100 and Kirk Rd., Montchanin, 302/888-2133 or 800/COWBIRD. Located near the Hagley Museum and other area sights, the inn is made up of 11 buildings that once comprised most of the village of Montchanin. In the mid-1850s the village was home to laborers who worked at the DuPont powder mills and nearby factories. The impeccably restored property is now listed on the National Register of Historic Places. The inn's 37 guest rooms, located in nine separate buildings, are decorated with selected period and reproduction furniture and contain marble baths. Individual rooms run from $150 to $170, suites from $180 to $325. Breakfast is included.

Dominating downtown Wilmington is the **Hotel du Pont**, 11th and Market Sts., 302/594-3100 or 800/441-9019. Opened to much fanfare in 1913, over the years the hotel has hosted heads of state, sports figures, corporate giants, and celebrities including Prince Rainier of

Monaco, Ingrid Bergman, John F. Kennedy, Joe DiMaggio, Elizabeth Taylor, Katharine Hepburn, and Eleanor Roosevelt. With 220 rooms, the hotel recently underwent an extensive renovation resulting in larger rooms and improved amenities, including Spanish-marble bathrooms with oversized tubs and separate showers. Room rates run from $139 to $269. Be sure to inquire about the hotel's many weekend packages.

CAMPING

Located 20 miles southwest of Wilmington, **Lums Pond State Park**, 302/368-6989, covers 1,757 acres, including a 200-acre pond. The park has 68 campsites with no hookups, along with a marina, a beach, a bathhouse, an 18-hole golf course, and hiking and equestrian trails. The park's marina is situated on the Chesapeake and Delaware Canal.

NIGHTLIFE

Depending on your interests, Wilmington offers a variety of nightlife options. To enjoy classical music, opera, ballet, jazz, and popular theatrical productions, check out what's playing at the **Grand Opera House**, 818 N. Market St., 302/658-7897 or 800/37-GRAND. The 1,100-seat, Victorian-era structure was built in 1871 and is home to the Delaware Symphony Orchestra and OperaDelaware. Broadway shows as well as local productions can be enjoyed at **The Playhouse**, 10th and Market Streets, 302/656-4401. The **Delaware Theatre Company**, 200 Water St., 302/594-1104, presents classical and contmeporary plays in a modern, intimate setting.

For music and dancing in a tropical atmosphere, check out the **Big Kahuna**, 550 S. Madison St., 302/571-8402, the city's largest nightclub. The club's restaurant, Kahunaville, serves light fare and dinner entrées. **Deep Blue**, 111 W. 11th St., 302/777-2040, features contemporary jazz on Thursday and Saturday nights; its extensive seafood menu makes it a great spot for dinner as well. For an authentic Irish pub experience, try **Kelly's Logan House**, 1701 Delaware Ave., 302/65-LOGAN. Kelly's offers a variety of music—from blues to funk to motown—Thursday through Saturday nights.

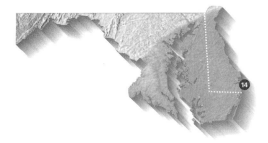

14
DELAWARE COAST

With 25 miles of coastline, southern Delaware is known for its blue waters and sandy beaches. In warm-weather months, visitors flock to the coastal communities of Rehoboth Beach, Dewey Beach, Bethany Beach, and Lewes. You can choose between a busy beach scene—with T-shirt shops galore and lively night spots—and quieter, slower-paced environments. Rehoboth Beach, known as the summer capital to migrating Washingtonians, offers a teeming boardwalk, trendy boutiques, and unique restaurants. Lewes, in contrast, attracts with historical charm and a quiet, tame atmosphere. Founded by the Dutch in 1631, Lewes was the first European settlement in Delaware and today offers visitors myriad opportunities to learn about local history. Nearby, the 3,800-acre Cape Henlopen Park has more than four miles of pristine beaches. Here you can walk, swim, play tennis, fish, or try your luck at crabbing.

Sporting opportunities abound on the Delaware Coast, from parasailing, windsurfing, and deep-sea fishing, to golf and tennis. But even if shopping is your sport of choice, you'll find plenty of unusual boutiques and bargain outlets—and none of them charges sales tax. Accommodations range from pastel-colored motels harkening to the 1970s to carefully restored Victorian bed-and-breakfasts. If you're willing to do battle with mosquitoes, you can even camp on the beach in spots and awaken to the sound of waves lapping the shore. Be forewarned that the coast operates on a strict seasonal pricing schedule; rates escalate during the peak summer months, and a number of hotels and restaurants close up shop in the off-season.

DELAWARE COAST

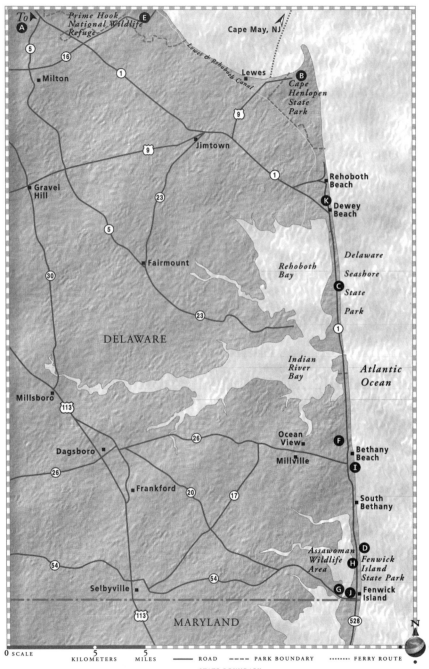

To ▶
Ⓐ

Prime Hook
National Wildlife
Refuge

Ⓔ

Cape May, NJ

⑤
⑯

■ Milton

①

Lewes & Rehoboth Canal

Lewes ■

Ⓑ Cape
Henlopen
State
Park

⑨

Jimtown ■

①

Rehoboth
Beach ■

Ⓚ Dewey
Beach ■

⑨

■ Gravel
Hill

㉓

⑤

■ Fairmount

Rehoboth
Bay

Delaware

Seashore

Ⓒ State

Park

㉚

㉓

DELAWARE

Indian
River
Bay

①

Atlantic
Ocean

■ Millsboro

⑪③

Ocean
View ■

Ⓕ

Bethany
Beach ■

■ Dagsboro

㉖

Millville ■

Ⓘ

㉖

■ Frankford

⑳

⑰

South
Bethany ■

㊵

Assawoman
Wildlife
Area

Ⓓ

Ⓗ Fenwick
Island
State Park

Selbyville ■

㊵

Ⓖ Ⓙ Fenwick
Island ■

⑪③

MARYLAND

⑤㉘

N

0 SCALE   5   5
        KILOMETERS MILES   —— ROAD   ---- PARK BOUNDARY   ········ FERRY ROUTE
                    ▬▬ STATE BOUNDARY

Sights

Ⓐ Bombay Hook National
   Wildlife Refuge

Ⓑ Cape Henlopen State Park

Ⓒ Delaware Seashore State Park

Ⓓ Fenwick Island State Park
   Complex

Ⓔ Prime Hook National Wildlife
   Refuge

Food

Ⓕ Gary's Beach Café

Ⓖ Harpoon Hanna's

Ⓗ Libby's

Food (continued)

Ⓘ Sedona

Ⓙ Shark's Cove

Lodging

Ⓚ Bay Resort

Ⓕ Bethany Arms Motel and
   Apartments

Camping

Ⓑ Cape Henlopen State Park

Ⓒ Delaware Seashore State Park

Note: Items with the same letter are located in the same town or area.

A PERFECT DAY ON THE DELAWARE COAST

Begin your day with a scenic drive up or down the coast. (Depending on which way you're headed, you may need to pursue the activities highlighted here in reverse.) Starting from Fenwick Island, drive north along coastal Route 1, stopping first at Bethany Beach for a walk around this small town and then at Rehoboth Beach to browse its many shops and boutiques. After enjoying lunch in Rehoboth, spend the bulk of your afternoon at Henlopen State Park in Lewes, where you can walk the beach and admire the 80-foot Great Dune. If history and culture are more to your liking, the Lewes Historical Complex and Zwaanendael Museum are worth visiting. End your day with a tasty dinner at one of Lewes' several fine restaurants.

SIGHTSEEING HIGHLIGHTS

★★★ **Cape Henlopen State Park**—Known for its "walking dunes," Cape Henlopen State Park is distinguished by the Great Dune—at 80 feet the highest sand dune between Cape Hatteras and Cape Cod. The 3,800-acre park, located one mile east of Lewes, has four miles of beach. Located on a sandy peninsula known as Delaware's Hook, the park is bordered on one side by the Atlantic and on the other by the Delaware Bay. A great place for hanging out or walking the beach, the park has a visitors center, nature and hiking trails, an observation tower, a quarter-mile fishing pier, golf, game courts, and ball fields.

Details: 42 Cape Henlopen Dr., Lewes; 302/645-8983. Open Memorial Day–Labor Day daily 7 a.m.–sunset, spring and fall weekends only. Entrance fee $5 out-of-state visitors, $2.50 Delaware residents. (1 hour–full day)

★★ **Bombay Hook National Wildlife Refuge**—Covering nearly 16,000 acres of wetlands, this is the largest wildlife refuge in Delaware, providing a haven for a variety of waterfowl, including migratory ducks and geese as well as herons, egrets, and the occasional bald eagle. Each year Bombay Hook hosts the greatest concentration of snow geese (over 130,000) in North America. The refuge includes a 12-mile auto loop tour, nature trails, and observation towers. The best time for viewing migratory birds in the refuge is October through November and late February through March.

Details: From Dover, take U.S. 13 north to Rt. 42 East. Turn north on Route 9 and look for signs. To reach the park office, call 302/653-9345. Open year-round during daylight hours. Visitor's center open Mon–Fri 8–4, with additional fall and early spring hours Sat–Sun 9–5. $4 per car or $2 adults on foot or bicycle; under age 16 free. (1–3 hours)

★★ **Lewes Historical Complex**—Administered by the Lewes Historical Society, the Lewes Historical Complex is made up of six buildings, including an early plank house, country store, doctor's office, blacksmith's shop, and the Burton-Ingram House (circa 1789), constructed of hand-hewn timbers and cypress shingles.

Details: Shipcarpenter and Third Sts., Lewes; 302/645-7670. Open mid-June–Labor Day Tue–Fri 10–3, Sat 10–12:30. $6 for all museums, $1–2 for individual buildings. (1 hour)

★★ **Zwaanendael Museum**—For a brief overview of the history of Lewes, visit the Zwaanendael Museum. The museum, modeled after the old town hall in Hoorn, Holland, was built in 1931 to commemorate the 300th anniversary of the first European settlement in Delaware. Small in size, it contains information and artifacts related to the

1631 Dutch settlement, the British bombardment of Lewes in 1812, and a display about the HMS *DeBraak*.
Details: *Savannah Rd. and Kings Hwy., Lewes; 302/645-1148. Open Tue–Sat 10–4:30, Sun 1:30–4:30. Free. (30 minutes)*

✻ **Delaware Seashore State Park**—Bounded by the Atlantic Ocean to the east and Rehoboth Bay to the west, Delaware Seashore State Park covers 2,018 acres of beach, grass-covered dunes, and salt marshes. Its two ocean-swimming areas feature modern bathhouses with showers and changing rooms. The park contains one of the few designated surfing areas in the state. The park also offers camping facilities, a marina, access to fishing, picnic areas, and refreshments in the summer.
Details: *Route 1 between Dewey and Bethany Beaches; 302/227-2800. Open year-round. $5 per car out-of-state visitors, $2.50 Delaware residents. (1–3 hours)*

✻ **Fenwick Island State Park**—Covering 344 acres, the park includes dunes and marshland and is home to a variety of birds, including gulls, terns, heron, ospreys, loons, plovers, ducks, and geese. In addition to three miles of beachfront, the park has fishing and boating facilities and provides rentals of watercraft including Waverunners, sailboats, pedalcraft, kayaks, and windsurfers. The park has a modern bathhouse with restrooms and showers, and it operates a concession stand. It's also a designated surfing area.
Details: *Route 1, Fenwick Island; 302/539-1055. Open daily 8 a.m.–sunset. No charge for parking in the park's small dirt lot. (1–3 hours)*

✻ **Prime Hook National Wildlife Refuge**—Located seven miles northwest of Lewes, the refuge covers 9,000 acres of marsh, piney trees, and farm fields, offering birdwatchers and hikers a variety of habitats to explore. Its two major trails include a boardwalk trail. For an optimal experience, bring a canoe to access Prime Hook Creek, which meanders for miles through the refuge.
Details: *Off Route 1, follow Route 16 east to the park. Open daily half-hour before sunrise to half-hour after sunset. Free. (1–3 hours)*

FITNESS AND RECREATION

The Delaware Coast is full of outdoor recreation opportunities, particularly for water sports at local beaches during the summer. Bird watchers

LEWES

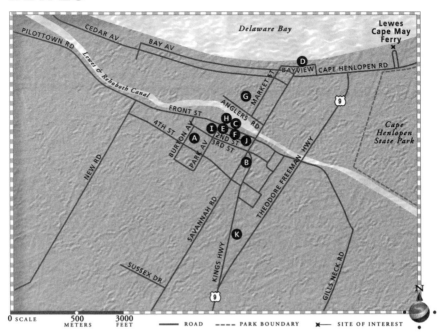

0 SCALE 500 METERS 3000 FEET — ROAD ---- PARK BOUNDARY ✕— SITE OF INTEREST

Sights

Ⓐ Lewes Historical Complex

Ⓑ Zwaanendael Museum

Food

Ⓒ Gilligans

Ⓓ Kupchick's

Ⓔ La Rosa Negra

Ⓕ Rose & Crown

Lodging

Ⓖ Angler's Motel

Ⓗ Inn at Canal Square

Ⓘ New Devon Inn

Ⓙ Sands Beach Resort Motel

Ⓚ Wild Swan

should visit the **Prime Hook National Wildlife Refuge** (see Sight-see-
ing Highlights, above) just north of Lewes. To rent bikes in Lewes, contact **Lewes Cycle Sports**, 302/645-4544. Cyclists can meander around
town or follow shoreline paths. Pontoon boats and runabouts can be
rented at **Rod 'n' Reel Boat Rentals**, 302/644-2304. To arrange half
and full-day fishing trips from Lewes, call **Fisherman's Wharf**, 302/645-
8862. Fisherman's Wharf also offers two-hour dolphin and whale-watch-
ing cruises. To sail aboard a schooner, contact **Jolly Rover**,
302/644-1501.

In Rehoboth bikes can be rented at **Bob's Bicycle Rentals**,
302/227-7966; **Wheels Bicycle Shop**, 302/227-6807; and **Rehoboth
Sport and Kite Company**, 302/227-6996. For hourly rentals of
Windsurfers, Sunfish sailboats, and jet skis, contact **Bay Sports**,
302/226-2677. Just south, in Dewey Beach, you can examine the shore
from the air while parasailing. For further information, call **Ocean
Winds Watersports**, 302/227-4359.

In Bethany the **Bethany Bike and Fitness Shop**, 302/537-9982,
rents bikes by the hour, day, or week. Sea kayaking, a great way to
experience the coast, can be arranged through **Delmarva Dennis Sea
Kayaking Adventures**, 302/537-5311. Experienced kayakers can rent
their own equipment at Bay Sports (see above). Also available are sailboats, jet skis, paddleboats, and Wave Runners.

FOOD

The majority of restaurants along the Delaware coast specialize in
fresh, creatively prepared seafood. Restaurants range from casual crab
shacks and lively bars to gourmet cuisine. Chefs at a number of the
area's best restaurants earned their stripes at more prominent urban
eateries before opting for the good life, close to the ocean. The places
listed below are grouped according to the town in which they are
located and then by price range, from moderate to expensive.

On Fenwick Island, **Libby's**, 901 Ocean Hwy., 302/539-7379, is one
of a chain of three casual, family-style restaurants in the area. Its polka-
dot exterior is distinctive. Breakfasts, extremely popular, consist of a wide
variety of pancakes, filled with such delectables as chocolate chips,
banana, ham, and bacon; waffles; egg dishes; and omelettes. Reasonably
priced salads and sandwiches are served for lunch. Dinners include crab
and fish sandwiches, and steak, chicken, and seafood specials. Weekly
dinner specials include items such as all-you-can-eat chicken and

dumplings. **Harpoon Hanna's**, Route 54, 302/539-3095, overlooks Assawoman Bay, catering to visitors coming by boat or car. This large, lively restaurant features a wide variety of fresh fish such as swordfish, mahimahi, salmon, tuna, and red snapper. Salads, sandwiches, soups, and pasta dishes are available throughout the day, along with more extensive steak, seafood, and chicken entrées. An extensive deck enables diners to eat outside overlooking the water. Nearby is **Shark's Cove**, Route 54, 302/436-5297, also overlooking the bay. Specializing in seafood, the dinner menu changes nightly and is on the expensive side. The restaurant is also open for lunch from May through September, serving a variety of salads, sandwiches, and fish dishes.

In Bethany, **Gary's Beach Café** located in the Marketplace at the Sea Colony at the intersection of Route 1 and Westway Drive, 302/539-2131, features inexpensive, healthy fare. Lunches consist of salads and grilled seafood sandwiches. Dinners include a creative mix of cajun catfish, chicken jambalaya, spinach ravioli, and other pasta dishes. People who know good food drive for miles to dine at **Sedona**, 26 Pennsylvania Ave., 302/539-1200. Specializing in Southwest cuisine, Sedona's menu includes such creative dishes as grilled loin of tuna with prickly pear puree and honey habanero swordfish. Sedona is open for dinner only from April through November.

In Rehoboth, the **Dream Café**, 26 Baltimore Ave., 302/226-CAFE, is open for breakfast, lunch, dinner, and dessert. The café features espresso drinks and a juice bar along with homemade soups, deli sandwiches, salads, bagels, and gourmet Belgian waffles with a variety of toppings. The **Dogfish Head Brewery**, 320 Rehoboth Ave., 302/226-BREW, serves its own selection of microbrews in addition to homemade soups, creative salads, sandwiches, wood-grilled pizzas with dough made from stout grains, and grilled beef, chicken, and seafood. The brewery has a casual, fun atmosphere with pool tables and video games upstairs and an outdoor deck. For Mexican food, try **Tijuana Taxi**, 207 Rehoboth Ave., 302/227-1986, offering fare such as quesadillas, salads, fajitas, burritos, and enchiladas.

The following Rehoboth restaurants cost a bit more but are worth it. **Cloud 9**, 234 Rehoboth Ave., 302/226-1999, has a decidedly contemporary feel with purple tabletops and sky-blue walls with clouds. Open for dinner only, the restaurant's a popular nightspot with a dance floor and outdoor patio. Entrées consist of a creative mix of pasta, seafood, beef, pork, and chicken dishes. Offering a colorful, lively atmosphere, the **Blue Moon**, 35 Baltimore Ave., 302/227-6515,

REHOBOTH

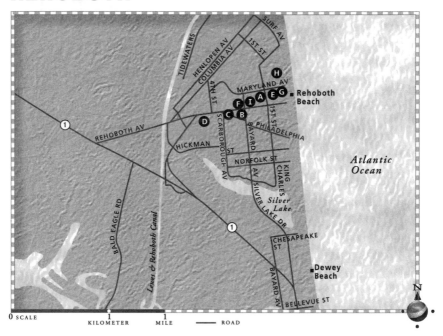

Food

- Ⓐ Blue Moon
- Ⓑ Chez La Mer
- Ⓒ Cloud 9
- Ⓓ Dogfish Head Brewery
- Ⓔ Dream Café
- Ⓕ Tijuana Taxi

Lodging

- Ⓖ Atlantic Sands
- Ⓗ Boardwalk Plaza
- Ⓘ Oceanus Motel

specializes in upscale new American cuisine. Open for dinner and Sunday brunch, the menu includes items such as Thai crusted salmon, buttermilk pecan chicken breasts, and red snapper baked in corn husks. Classic French cuisine is available at **Chez La Mer**, Second and Wilmington Sts., 302/227-6494. Open for dinner only (April through October), Chez La Mer serves up excellent bouillabaisse and delicately seasoned seafood, poultry, veal, and beef dishes.

In Lewes, the **Rose & Crown**, 108 Second St., 302/645-2373, is a British-style pub with exposed brick walls, skylights, a pressed-tin ceiling, and wooden booths. Lunches consist of a variety of salads, sandwiches, and English specialties such as fish and chips and cottage pie. Dinners feature pasta, steaks, veal, and fish dishes such as cajun pecan catfish. A wide variety of local and international beers is available. Nearby is **Gilligans**, 134 Market St., Canal Square, 302/645-7866. Housed within a former diving boat, Gilligans is named after the classic TV show. Decorated in a tropical motif, the restaurant has a bar and deck overlooking the harbor. The diverse menu features crab cakes, soft-shell crab in season, and a variety of seafood, chicken, beef, and pasta dishes.

For high-quality Italian fare, try **La Rosa Negra**, 182 Second St., 302/645-1980. The black rose adorning each table is contrasted against bright red napkins and white tablecloths. The menu includes a variety of pasta, veal, and chicken dishes, along with seafood. Of special interest are the seafood ravioli dishes. **Kupchick's**, 3 E. Bay Ave., 302/645-9420, is located right on the beach and features outdoor deck dining. Open for lunch and dinner, Kupchick's moderately priced menu includes grilled foods, sandwiches, pasta dishes, vegetarian entrées, and local seafood items such as crab cakes and flounder.

LODGING

Although lodging options abound on the Delaware coast, due to the seasonal nature of area activities most of the hotels and inns command a premium price in the late spring, summer, and early fall. Many close in the winter months. Those listed below are grouped according to the town in which they're located and then by price range, from moderate to expensive.

On Fenwick Island, the **Sands Beach Resort Motel**, Ocean Highway, 302/539-7745, is located close to the ocean and has a swimming pool. Rooms during peak season (mid-June to mid-September) run $69 to $112; they run off-season (May 22 to June 18 and mid-

September to October 1) from $29 to $75. However, a three-day minimum stay is required during peak season, and a $20 surcharge is
applied to the daily rate for stays of fewer than six nights. The motel is
closed from October 1 to May 22. Accommodations range from individual rooms to apartments with a refrigerator, stove, and sofa bed.

In Bethany, the **Bethany Arms Motel and Apartments**, P.O Box
1600, 302/539-9603, is located on the boardwalk overlooking the
ocean. Standard rooms range in price from $40 to $105 during peak
season. Apartments range in price from $50 to $145 during the summer and have sofa beds. A two-night minimum stay is required on
weekends from May 2 until October 13. The inn is closed mid-
October through February.

In Dewey, the **Bay Resort**, P.O. Box 461, 302/227-6400 or
800/922-9240, is located on Rehoboth Bay within a three-minute walk
of the ocean. All rooms, efficiencies with complete kitchenettes, overlook the bay or pool. Rooms run from $79 to $160 during the peak
summer months and from $50 to $90 in the off-season. Inquire about
weekend and mid-week packages.

Rehoboth has a wide variety of lodging options, although many of
them are large, impersonal establishments. The **Oceanus Motel**, 6
Second St., 302/227-8200, is located close to the main shopping district, within walking distance of the beach. The motel features a swimming pool, free continental breakfast, and a refrigerator in each room.
Rooms run from $99 to $120 during the peak summer months with
additional charges of $10 to $40 on weekend nights. Off-season rates
are $50 to $100. The **Atlantic Sands**, 101 N. Baltimore Ave., 302/227-
2511 or 800/422-0600, has an oceanfront swimming pool and a
rooftop sundeck. Open year-round, the Sands has rooms starting at
$129 and climbing up to $290 during the summer months, with additional charges during peak periods. In the off-season rooms run from
$60 to $220. Also located on the beach is the **Boardwalk Plaza**, Olive
Ave. at the Boardwalk, 302/227-7169 or 800/33-BEACH. The 84-
room hotel, decorated in grand Victorian style, features an indoor/out-
door pool, rooftop sundeck, and rooms ranging from standard doubles
to oceanfront suites and efficiency apartments. Rooms run from $55 to
$229 for a standard double and $90 to $385 for an oceanfront suite.

If you can afford to stay in them, Lewes has some of the most
charming accommodations in the area. On the less expensive side is the
Anglers Motel, 110 Anglers Rd., 302/645-2831. Located within walking
distance to the beach and area shops and restaurants, the motel, open

from March through November, features an outdoor pool, refrigerators in all rooms, and some kitchenettes. Rates in the summer months range from $65 to $100; off-season they're $35 to $60. Built in 1926, the **New Devon Inn**, P.O. Box 516, 302/645-6466 or 800/824-8754, is listed on the National Historic Register. The 24-room inn, open year-round, was completely restored in 1989. Rooms are furnished with antiques but have no TVs. Rates in the peak summer months range from $85 to $95 on weekdays to $120 to $130 on weekends. In the spring and winter, rates run from $50 during the week to $65 on weekends. Nearby is the **Inn at Canal Square**, 122 Market St., 302/645-8499. This waterfront B&B has spacious rooms decorated with antique reproductions. A number of the rooms feature balconies overlooking the harbor. Rates run from $135 to $165 in the peak summer months, $75 to $135 the rest of the year. The inn offers a unique houseboat accommodation featuring two bedrooms, two baths, living and dining areas, and a full kitchen.

Located a mile from the beach and within walking distance of downtown is the **Wild Swan**, 525 Kings Hwy., 302/645-8550. This quaint rose-colored Victorian bed-and-breakfast with a wraparound porch sits on a quiet street corner. Rooms during the peak season—July 4 through Labor Day—are $135. The same rooms cost $120 from mid-May to July 1 and Labor Day to mid-October. The rest of the year, rates are $85. A two-night minimum stay is required during July and August and on weekends year-round. Children and pets are not allowed.

CAMPING

There are two campgrounds on the Delaware Coast, both described in greater detail in "Sightseeing Highlights," above. **Cape Henlopen State Park** in Lewes has 159 campsites with water hookups, showers, and a dump station. Campsites are available on a first-come, first-served basis April through October. For further information, contact the park's offices, 302/645-8983. The **Delaware Seashore State Park** in Rehoboth has 145 campsites with full hookups, 133 with no hookups, and 156 overflow campsites, as well as showers and a dump station. For additional information call 302/227-2800.

NIGHTLIFE

One of the most popular nightspots in Dewey Beach is the **Rusty Rudder**, 113 Dickinson St., 302/227-3888. Live rock and reggae bands draw large weekend crowds. In Rehoboth, **Arena's**, located in the Village by the Sea Shoppes, 302/227-1272, has live music most nights. **Cloud 9** brings in a local DJ for music and dancing on weekend nights. **Sydney's Blues and Jazz Restaurant**, 25 Christian St., 302/227-1339, located in an old schoolhouse, offers live blues and jazz. While Lewes is relatively quiet at night, the **Rose & Crown**, 108 Second St., 302/645-2373, has live music on select summer nights, including rock, alternative, and top-40 tunes.

APPENDIX

Planning Map: Maryland/Delaware

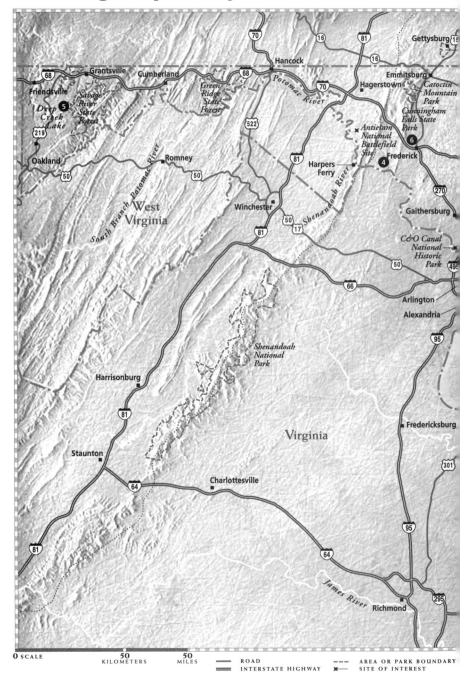

0 SCALE

50 KILOMETERS

50 MILES

ROAD

INTERSTATE HIGHWAY

AREA OR PARK BOUNDARY

SITE OF INTEREST

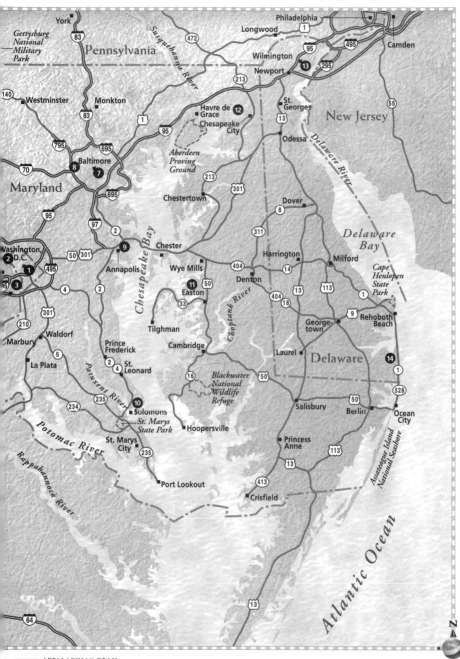

York
Gettysburg
National
Military
Park
83
Pennsylvania
Susquehanna River
472
Longwood
Philadelphia
1
Wilmington
95
95
495
Camden
Newport
13
295
140
Westminster
Monkton
83
1
95
213
Havre de
Grace
12
Chesapeake
City
St.
Georges
13
New Jersey
55
795
695
Baltimore
8
7
Aberdeen
Proving
Ground
213
Odessa
Delaware River
70
Maryland
695
Chestertown
301
Dover
8
95
97
2
Washington,
D.C.
2
50
301
Chester
Harrington
Milford
Delaware
Bay
311
404
14
Cape
Henlopen
State
Park
1
495
1
Annapolis
Wye Mills
50
Denton
113
3
4
2
11
Easton
33
404
13
18
9
Rehoboth
Beach
George-
town
301
Tilghman
Patuxent River
Cambridge
Laurel
Delaware
14
210
Waldorf
Prince
Frederick
5
2
528
Marbury
La Plata
4
St.
Leonard
16
Blackwater
National
Wildlife
Refuge
50
Salisbury
50
Berlin
Ocean
City
234
235
10
Solomons
St. Marys
State Park
Hoopersville
Princess
Anne
113
Potomac River
St. Marys
City
235
13
Rappahannock River
Port Lookout
413
Crisfield
Assateague Island
National Seashore
13
Atlantic Ocean
64

N

MARYLAND/DELAWARE MILEAGE CHART

	Aberdeen, MD	Annapolis, MD	Baltimore, MD	Cambridge, MD	Cumberland, MD	Frederick, MD	Harper's Ferry, WV	Lexington Park, MD	McHenry, MD	Ocean City, MD	Rehoboth, DE	Salisbury, MD	Washington, DC
Annapolis, MD	56												
Baltimore, MD	30	28											
Cambridge, MD	107	58	79										
Cumberland, MD	175	163	142	220									
Frederick, MD	83	71	50	125	93								
Harpers Ferry, WV	99	90	68	141	107	19							
Lexington Park, MD	113	72	85	129	206	115	132						
McHenry, MD	214	205	182	256	41	134	148	246					
Ocean City, MD	133	118	139	62	280	187	202	189	317				
Rehobeth, DE	120	90	120	68	250	158	165	163	288	26			
Salisbury, MD	119	89	110	33	251	159	179	159	294	29	52		
Washington, DC	64	28	35	85	143	51	64	67	178	145	124	116	
Wilmington, DE	40	95	69	98	214	120	137	152	251	119	97	103	103

CAPITAL REGION CLIMATE

Average daily high and low temperatures in degrees Fahrenheit, plus monthly precipitation in inches.

	Washington	Baltimore	Cumberland	Wilmington
Jan	44/30 2.7	43/29 3.1	39/20 2.4	42/25 3.0
Mar	54/36 3.2	52/36 3.6	49/30 3.1	53/32 3.4
May	76/56 3.7	74/56 4.1	72/49 3.7	75/51 3.8
July	87/69 3.8	86/70 3.7	82/61 3.8	87/65 4.2
Sept	79/61 3.3	79/61 3.5	75/55 3.1	79/57 3.4
Nov	57/39 3.1	54/40 3.6	53/32 2.8	55/36 3.3

RESOURCES

Capital Region

Alexandria Convention and Visitors Association, 221 King St., Alexandria, VA 22314; 703/838-4200 or 800/388-9119

Arlington Convention and Visitors Service, 2100 Clarendon Blvd., #318, Arlington, VA 22201; 703/358-3988 or 800/296-7996

D.C. Chamber of Commerce, 1301 Pennsylvania Ave. NW, #309, Washington, DC 20004; 202/347-7201

D.C. Committee to Promote Washington, 1212 New York Ave. NW, #200, Washington, DC 20005; 202/724-4091 or 800/422-8644

D.C. Convention and Visitors Association, 1212 New York Ave. NW, #600, Washington, DC 20005-3992; 202/789-7000; www.washington.org

Delaware

Delaware Council for International Visitors, P.O. Box 4274, Greenville, DE 19807

Delaware Division of Fish and Wildlife, 89 Kings Hwy., Dover, DE 19901; 302/739-4431

Delaware Division of Parks and Recreation, 89 Kings Hwy., Dover, DE 19901; 302/739-4702

Delaware State Travel and Tourism Office, 99 Kings Hwy., Dover, DE 19901; 302/739-4271 or 800/441-8846; www.state.de.us/tourism/intro.htm

Greater Wilmington Convention and Visitors Bureau, 100 West 10th St., Wilmington, DE 19801; 302/652-4088 or 800/422-1181

Maryland

Annapolis/Anne Arundel County Conference and Visitors Bureau, 26 West St., Annapolis, MD 21401; 410/280-0445

Baltimore Area Convention and Visitors Bureau, 100 Light St., 12th floor, Baltimore, MD 21202; 800/343-3468, 410/659-7300

Maryland Bed & Breakfast Association, P.O. Box 23324, Baltimore, MD 21203; 410/235-6222

Maryland Bicycle Affairs Coordinator, 707 N. Calvert St., Mail Stop C502, Baltimore, MD 21202; 800/252-8776

Maryland Department of Business and Economic Development, Office of Tourism Development, 217 E. Redwood St., 9th floor, Baltimore, MD 21202; 800/634-7386; www.mdisfun.org

Maryland Department of Natural Resources, Tawes State Office Building, 580 Taylor Ave., E-3, Annapolis, MD 21401; 410/9260-8186 or 800/830-3974; www.dnr.state.md.us

Other Resources
Appalachian Trail Conference, 304/535-6331
Audubon Naturalist Society for the Middle Atlantic States, 301/652-9188
Trains: Amtrak, 800/USA-RAIL; Maryland Rural Commuter System, 800/325-7245; Metrorail rapid transit system, 202/637-7000

INDEX

Map Index

**AVALON
TRAVEL**
p u b l i s h i n g

BECAUSE TRAVEL MATTERS.

AVALON TRAVEL PUBLISHING knows that travel is more than coming and going—travel is taking part in new experiences, new ideas, and a new outlook. Our goal is to bring you complete and up-to-date information to help you make informed travel decisions.

AVALON TRAVEL GUIDES feature a combination of practicality and spirit, offering a unique traveler-to-traveler perspective perfect for an afternoon hike, around-the-world journey, or anything in between.

WWW.TRAVELMATTERS.COM

Avalon Travel Publishing guides are available
at your favorite book or travel store.

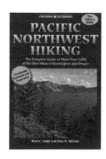

ABOUT THE AUTHOR

Sheila Kinkade's travels as a writer specializing in international development have taken her from the islands of Indonesia to the northern tip of Thailand, from Eastern Europe to South Africa. A graduate of the Columbia School of Journalism, she has contributed articles to the *Washington Post* and *Washington Times*, and has reported on local issues on the Maine coast. She has spent much of the last six years working on behalf of children's causes and is the author of two nonfiction works for young readers about life in other countries. From her current home on the outskirts of Baltimore, she takes frequent trips to explore the region's wealth of recreational, cultural, and culinary opportunities.